INDIVIDUAL PSYCHOTHERAPY TRAININGS

This *Guide* is the first publicly available source book in the field.

The world of psychotherapy may appear to be confusing, fragmented and shrouded in mystery. Why is it that one psychotherapist asks the 'client' to enact a difficulty by talking to a cushion and another psychotherapist asks a 'patient' to lie on the couch and say whatever comes to mind? By examining psychotherapy trainings in detail, questions such as this can be answered.

There are now so many types of psychotherapy in Britain that no one book could encompass them all. This volume examines the trainings of one form – individual psychotherapy for adults – and two of the most common types – analytic and humanistic. It will meet the growing need for information felt by members of the general public seeking help for themselves, potential trainees wishing to assess what is on offer, and mental health professionals seeking information about training institutions.

The *Guide* presents the training requirements of twenty-six training organizations and tries to describe the atmosphere of each one. It includes trainees' experience of their training. The *Guide* is lively, fair, thoroughly researched, and will prove to be an invaluable work of reference.

JAN ABRAM trained as a psychotherapist at the Arbours Association. She is in private practice in London and a member of the Women Therapists' Referral Service, affiliated to the Women's Therapy Centre, London. A staff member of the Squiggle Foundation, she teaches Winnicott on counselling courses and is on the editorial board of *Winnicott Studies*.

NINA COLTART is a distinguished member of the Independent Group of the British Psycho-Analytical Society. She was Director of the London Clinic of Psycho-Analysis for ten years, and has played a major role in maintaining standards in the psychotherapy field.

INDIVIDUAL PSYCHOTHERAPY TRAININGS

A GUIDE

JAN ABRAM

Foreword by Nina Coltart

'an association in which the free development of
each is the condition of the free development of all'

Free Association Books / London / 1992

Published in Great Britain in 1992 by
Free Association Books
26 Freegrove Road
London N7 9QR

The publication of this book was made possible by generous grants from
Kirsty Hall and The Human Nature Trust.

A CIP catalogue record for this book is available from the British Library

ISBN 1-85343-182-6 pb

Typeset from author's discs by Archetype.
Printed and bound in Great Britain by Billings Bookplan Ltd.

For Joan and Doug

CONTENTS

FOREWORD

Nina E. C. Coltart

This lively, readable and serious book, which covers in some detail twenty-six of the individual adult psychotherapy trainings in the UK, fills a long-felt want; not only of my own, and that of many analytical psychotherapists who carry out assessments for referral purposes; but also of potential trainees, casting about in the ever-growing jungle of different training organizations, with little to help them decide, or even tell one from another. I have known the author for many years, ever since she was going through her own selection procedure at the Arbours Association, when I was on the Training Committee; we assessed her then as an unusually able and gifted student, and her years of work after she qualified have borne out that impression.

To be a good psychotherapist is one thing, but to retain the welcome capacity for open-minded, scrupulous objectivity in one's assessment of other trainings is something else; and in Jan Abram the psychotherapy scene has encountered a creative combination of the two. Of course, she inevitably brings to it the standpoint and values of a psychoanalytically-trained psychotherapist, and sometimes her views rather engagingly, if quite subtly, emerge. This in no way influences the fairness and thoroughness of her detailed descriptions, nor colours strongly the Author's Comments which she has chosen to append to her outline of every association described. If she had no opinions at all, the whole thing could presumably have been carried out these days by a data-fed machine. What I like is that most of the hints of her own views come forth in the shape of questions; most organizations are fully described, demonstrating an admirable quantity of careful research, while the most interesting subsections appear at the ends of each – Trainees' Experience and Why this Course was Chosen, and what they think of it; the Atmosphere of the Course; and the Author's Comments, with their valuable open-ended questioning, for psychoanalytic and humanistic trainings alike.

One of the most startling features of the book is the revelation (to me) of just how many individuals are engaged in the *process* of psychotherapy at any one time, and not only in London, but all over the UK – Cambridge, Edinburgh, Bristol, Bath, Totnes, St Albans, Canterbury, to name but a few. A thriving hive of industry is revealed, using the term in its rather old-fashioned sense of hard work, and not cynically, as in 'the bereavement industry', a phrase which has recently – understandably – come to my notice. All the time, trained psychotherapists of many different orientations are sitting in their private practices, working in the National Health Service, working at the organization and administration of their own trainings; teaching, lecturing, running groups, holding workshops, reading and writing about the subject.

Or, of course, either learning to do it, or being patients, and often combining both these roles at once. It is obligatory, in all twenty-six trainings described, that the trainee, while a trainee, is in his/her own personal therapy. The training requirements vary from three times a week in the psychoanalytic organizations such as the Lincoln, Arbours and the BAP, to once a month in the earlier days of, for example, the Institute of Psychosynthesis. This tiny statistic in itself may give a glimpse of just how widely divergent are the trainings which Jan Abram has researched, and yet these belong to two main theoretical systems only, the psychoanalytical and the humanistic-integrative. The boundary had to be drawn somewhere, and these two streams were chosen because, in spite of many quite extreme points of difference, they also seem to have more in common than do disciplines involving a radically opposed mechanism of technique, such as behaviour therapy or hypno-therapy.

Also all the associations referred to were at the time of writing members of the United Kingdom Standing Conference for Psychotherapy. This body (or the Confederation which has recently seceded from it) necessarily has many other members, since what it is aiming at is a clear enough definition of the term 'psychotherapist', and the status, trainings, and ethics involved, to have these criteria, and therefore the label, ratified by legislation. At present, anyone at all can set up as 'a psychotherapist', which brings us back to one of the most useful aspects of this Guide; it defines, to a considerable extent, the professionalism, qualifications and training required of individual psychotherapists; the book acts as a series of signposts in the wilderness for hopeful, searching students and for patients.

It is particularly instructive for a member of the British Psycho-Analytical Society to study this Guide, even one with numerous contacts in the world of analytical psychotherapy, like myself, and we must hope that many do. I say this because, although the British Psycho-Analytical Society was the earliest pioneer in this country, this does not justify a certain tendency among some of its members to think and speak as if there were nothing but desert beyond our own confines. Its seniority, and the fact that many people outside it regard its exclusivity as the guardian of a grail, have contributed to the narcissistic pride which some analysts take in themselves and what they are doing, as if having admittedly illustrious forebears were somehow passed on by Lamarckian inheritance.

This book should bring us back to earth. Even the most organic of medically-trained psychiatrists, who usually have scant time for 'psychotherapy' of any description, may be given pause by the sheer weight of numbers involved, let alone the enormous quantities of scrupulous thought and care which go to the making of the various trainings, whatever their orientations. Indeed, at times I was brought up short myself by the shock of realizing just how much ground some of the teachers in the humanistic-integrative therapies are supposed to cover; one, the Psychosynthesis and Education Trust, mentions twenty authorities, ranging from Freud and Jung to Evelyn Underhill and Martin Buber as the 'theoretical models' which they hope to teach on their course.

In this connection, Jan Abram does raise the question more than once of whether such a scheme does not imply breadth rather than depth. She implies – though nowhere says, and I take full responsibility for the point myself – that it is possible, and perhaps fatally easy in this alluring field, to become a jack of all trades and master of none. The counter-arguments to this implied criticism may be first, that to be trained in multiple techniques gives one a chance of free and informed choice to go deeper into one; and second, that 'pure' psychoanalysts are rigidly conditioned into their own disciplined techniques, and that even though this may provide an incisive toolkit, the work itself is 'deep but narrow'. In this respect, it was of interest to me, in studying the whole range of therapies, to see how very many of the humanistic organizations endeavour to include theoretical and some technical teaching of a more 'traditional' (= psychoanalytic) kind, and also how many, though fewer, encourage their students to have a personal analytic therapy themselves; or, at the very least, do not raise objections if this is what the student is already having at the time of application.

This leads me to consider the rather surprising fact that at least two of the organizations are almost purely academic, and lead to an MA (i.e., postgraduate) qualification in psychotherapy. Psychoanalysis is sometimes accused to this day by the humanistic therapists – although this was more apparent in the Sixties and Seventies – of being 'all in the head', too intellectual, and therefore cold and 'inhuman'. This is partly because of the strong 'rule of abstinence', as introduced by Freud, and still strictly adhered to today, i.e., psychoanalysts use verbal interchange (the interpretation of the unconscious via the transference and countertransference) only, and do not touch their patients. In this they differ markedly from most (not all) of the humanistic-integrative therapies who use touch, massage and bodywork. However, when compared with the learning of psychotherapy as an academic subject, with – as at least one organization shows – no provision for work with patients at any point (though some degree of personal psychotherapy 'is advised'), psychoanalysis, with its reputation for high frequency of sessions, and years of devotion to a very few patients because of long treatments, comes across as positively brimming with the milk of human kindness.

I would advise a piecemeal reading of this packed book, both by interested practitioners and searching students. To read it all at once may induce a feeling of blur, as the trainings merge one with another, and an impression of having a Sorcerer's Apprentice experience may arise. But if used as a genuine book of reference – for example, to look up an organization one has heard of and wants to know more about; or as an informed guide, for students thinking of training, in conjunction with discussions with two or three different qualified therapists – it will become one of the most valuable source books to have appeared in our huge and varied field. Everyone reading it, or dipping into it, will enjoy a lightening of the darkness that most of us are still in. It can only be of maximum interest to learn something about our numerous colleagues, who, however divergent their paths, are, after all, striving for the same end – namely, the relief, by skilful, unexploitative means, of human psychic and emotional suffering.

ACKNOWLEDGEMENTS

The idea for this book was conceived in conversation with Jenny Sprince, whom I must first of all thank for all her contributions to the book's development. Thanks to Selina O'Grady, then Editor at Free Association Books, whose interest in the idea helped transform it into a synopsis. I am grateful to Robert Young who, in response to the synopsis, commissioned the book, and to Ann Scott for all her advice and support during the latter, complicated stages of preparing the manuscript for publication.

The book would not have been possible without the generous co-operation of the twenty-six training organizations, who gave up their time to meet me as well as go over all the written texts. This applies to all the trainees I met, who answered all my questions honestly and thoughtfully, and gave me much encouragement as to the value of a book like this. I must also thank those who contributed towards Part One: Bryan Boswood of the Institute of Group Analysis; Robert Hinshelwood of St Bernard's Hospital, Ealing; Stan Ruszczynski of the Tavistock Institute of Marital Studies; and Michael Pokorny, Chair of the United Kingdom Standing Conference for Psychotherapy. Every effort has been made to ensure the accuracy of information in the book and to represent fairly the views of those to whom I talked; my apologies for any errors that may remain.

Special thanks to Nina Farhi and Musa Farhi for their helpful advice and encouragement, and Laurie Spurling who commented on parts of the manuscript. My thanks to all members of the Squiggle Resource Group whose enthusiasm and support for the book were very encouraging.

I have many friends and colleagues to thank for their sustaining interest and support throughout. My warmest thanks to those whose practical help was much appreciated: Kirsty Hall, Chris Hall, Gillian Isaacs Hemmings, Marie-Christine Réguis, Viqui Rosenberg and Carlos Sapochnik. I also have to thank Carlos Sapochnik for a superb cover design.

Teachers and supervisors over the years have all contributed in one way or another to the development of my thinking about the training of a psychotherapist, and so I would like to thank each member of the Training Committee of the Arbours Association, especially Michael Kelly. I am also indebted to Christopher Bollas, whose sensitive advice and insights have been invaluable.

I am honoured that Nina Coltart agreed to write the Foreword. Dr Coltart's contribution to the psychotherapy world has benefited generations of psychotherapists, of whom I am very grateful to be one.

My very special thanks and gratitude go to Rosalie Joffe.

Last but certainly not least, I must thank my family, who had to tolerate my preoccupation with this project, and in particular John van Rooyen whose unconditional support, sound advice, patience and love made it all worth while.

PUBLISHER'S AND AUTHOR'S NOTE

When this book was written all twenty-six trainings covered were members of the United Kingdom Standing Conference for Psychotherapy. In March 1992 five members of the UKSCP officially left the organization, with the intention of forming the British Confederation for Psychotherapy. The Lincoln Centre and Institute for Psychotherapy and the Scottish Association of Psychoanalytical Psychotherapists (the learned society for graduates of the Scottish Institute of Human Relations training) are amongst those members. The British Psycho-Analytical Society indicated that they were also leaving, but when this book went to press in May there was some uncertainty about this.

Meanwhile the UKSCP continues to pursue 'with vigour', in the words of its Chair, Michael Pokorny, the task of creating a register of psychotherapists. This will appear early in 1993.

May 1992

PREFACE

The world of psychotherapy may appear to be confusing, fragmented and shrouded in mystery. It is full of different and often conflicting theories of what psychotherapy is or should be. A rapidly growing literature of the diversity of therapies aims to inform the public, but may sometimes lead to more confusion when an individual in emotional distress is looking for help.

Meanwhile, who practises psychotherapy? Psychiatrists, psychologists, counsellors? Presumably psychotherapists practise psychotherapy. But who are psychotherapists and what does their title indicate? Why is it that one psychotherapist asks the 'client' to enact a difficulty by talking to a cushion and another psychotherapist asks a 'patient' to lie on the couch and say whatever comes to mind? What is the difference between psychotherapy practised privately and psychotherapy offered through the National Health Service?

At the moment the psychotherapy profession has no legislation and although there are many people practising as psychotherapists who have had a rigorous training, it means that anybody can use the title 'psychotherapist', in the NHS or in private practice. This guide addresses the need for more detailed information, for the general public who may be seeking help, for people wishing to train as psychotherapists and for professionals who often know very little about each other's training organizations. It is one attempt to bring some of the fragments together and thus demystify the label 'psychotherapist'.

Currently there are many courses on different forms and types of psychotherapy and new ones are continually emerging, so it was not possible to encompass them all. This book examines only the trainings which lead to the qualification 'psychotherapist'. My decision to limit the book to one form of psychotherapy – individual psychotherapy for adults – and two of the most common types – analytic and humanistic – came about for several reasons.

My personal training background started off in humanistic therapy, and I worked within the National Health Service. Through courses I followed in humanistic therapy I was introduced to the work of Freud, and my excitement in discovering psychoanalysis led me into personal therapy and subsequently a psychoanalytic psychotherapy training. During these years I experienced my own confusion regarding the world of psychotherapy and, never being afraid to ask too many questions from fellow trainees, I found I was not alone in my confusion. Choosing a training, for instance, seemed to be serendipitous more than anything else. Then, like joining any profession, there was the theory and practice to learn as well as the hierarchies of trainings, myths about certain trainings, the gossip, the good, the bad and the ugly. It felt like being in strange territory without a map to orientate oneself. It is true to say that much of this was to do with the struggle for an identity – a natural process in any kind of training, but because of the fragmentation and newness of the psychotherapy profession it really takes a very long time to tune in to the political side of becoming a therapist. Wholesale demystification of the label 'psychotherapist' cannot be done through a book, as reading about something can never be a substitute for experiencing. However, the setting out of information in as dispassionate a way as possible will make a significant contribution.

Some time after my psychotherapy training, I became a member of the Women Therapists' Referral Service. We are a group of analytic psychotherapists affiliated to the Women's Therapy Centre, and offer consultations to people seeking therapy. My experience to date is that the majority of people seeking psychotherapy are very unclear as to what exactly psychotherapy is and which type would be best for them. The conflicts are so often centred on the differences between analytic and humanistic therapy, and sometimes worry about the therapist's qualifications. Although this confusion and concern as to the credentials of a therapist is linked with the internal world of the individual seeking therapy and it is the therapist's task to explore the meaning of the patient's confusion, I nevertheless believe that it is every patient's right to know what therapy is being practised and what the qualifications of the therapist are. People seeking therapy need a source of reference to assure themselves of their therapist's qualification, particularly at a time in the history of the profession of psychotherapy when anybody can use the title 'psychotherapist'. Not only that, there are so many of us using this title it is crucial that a distinction be made between psychotherapists – for instance the training of an analytic therapist is different from the training of a humanistic therapist, not only in terms of theory and practice, but also in training intensity, as will be demonstrated.

1989 saw the inauguration of the United Kingdom Standing Conference for Psychotherapy. This conference is rapidly becoming the voice for psychotherapists in this country and is committed to creating a register of psychotherapists as well as preparing for future legislation. Like all professional bodies, amongst its aims are the maintenance of standards and protection of the public (see p. 14). Amongst the member organizations of the UKSCP are the most established and longest standing trainings and each member belongs to its relevant section. The two largest sections are ANALYTICAL and HUMANISTIC and as the trainings in these two sections are already members of the UKSCP, I decided to confine the book to these trainings. Three points must be added here:

1. Membership in itself of the UKSCP does not at present indicate that a training is 'good' or 'bad'.

2. This book has been independently initiated and is not an official guide of the UKSCP, although I have maintained a dialogue with the External Relations Committee of the UKSCP during its preparation. Information has been written up in close consultation with all the member organizations included.

3. Although I have attempted to be as non-partisan as possible in presenting a picture of the psychotherapy world as it exists in Britain today, it has to be emphasized that it is one person's picture which is inevitably coloured by her own opinions and biases.

Psychotherapy trainings can be broadly separated into two different kinds: Independent – these are privately run and often have a charitable status; and Regional Diploma Courses – usually attached to a university and/or teaching hospital. Twenty-four out of the twenty-six organizations covered in this book come into the first category and the other two are MAs. This reflects the membership of the UKSCP and the division that has evolved between the independent trainings and the regional trainings. Very few of the latter are represented at the UKSCP and they are a more recent phenomenon emerging over the last twelve years or more. They cover different levels of psychotherapy and counselling for professionals already working in the NHS – nurses, psychiatrists, psychologists, etc. The Royal College of Psychiatrists would have more information on these trainings.

Part One of this book sets out to provide a basic outline of the background to the trainings looked at in Part Two: the origins of psychotherapy in this country, its practice in the NHS and privately, the relevant debates and controversies and the present political situation concerning registration and legislation of a psychotherapy profession. It is intended as a series of signposts to a more in-depth study.

Part Two presents the training requirements of 26 psychotherapy training organizations (15 Analytical and 11 Humanistic), all of which have emerged over the past forty years; the majority in the past twenty years. The same format is used for every training, to make the details of each course as accessible as possible, for easy comparison of similarities and differences.

A word on language. The terms 'analytic' and 'analytical' – when used on their own or in the phrases 'analytic psychotherapy' and 'analytical psychotherapy' – are used interchangeably throughout this book and do not signify any difference of meaning. 'Analytical psychology' is a specifically Jungian term. The use of 'analytic' and 'psychoanalytic' is clarified on p. 26.

PART ONE:
BACKGROUND TO THE TRAININGS

PSYCHOTHERAPY AND PSYCHOTHERAPISTS

One of the reasons why the world of psychotherapy may appear so confusing is that the name psychotherapy encompasses a diversity of approaches, all claiming to help the individual in emotional distress. In *The Language of Psycho-Analysis* (an authoritative dictionary on psychoanalytic terms) there are three definitions of psychotherapy, representing different levels. Most psychotherapists would probably agree on the first of these as a very basic definition of psychotherapy:

> In a broad sense [psychotherapy is] any method of treating psychic or somatic disorders which utilises psychological means – or more specifically, the therapist–patient relationship: hypnosis, suggestion, psychological re-education, persuasion.' (Laplanche and Pontalis, 1983)

The treatment of the individual by 'psychological means' is achieved through talking: hence the by now famous term 'talking cure' that psychotherapy came to be known by, at the turn of the century (Breuer and Freud, 1893–95). This method of helping individuals was considered revolutionary, even though the tradition of healing the distressed mind through talking goes back much earlier (Ellenberger, 1970).

Actually it is not talking in itself that helps but rather what is talked about and how it is heard. In other words, listening is a crucial component of psychotherapy and it is the talking and listening by both patient and therapist which develops the therapeutic relationship at the heart of the treatment. The setting in which the talking and listening takes place is in addition a crucial component in creating a sense of trust and security.

FORMS OF PSYCHOTHERAPY

The growth of psychotherapy in this century started from one-to-one therapy, generally known as individual psychotherapy. This is one form of psychotherapy from which other forms have developed, for people in small groups, large groups, couples and families (see Fig. 1). In addition, individual psychotherapy which began as a treatment for adults has been developed specifically for children and adolescents (Freud, S., 1905; Klein, 1932; Freud, A., 1955).

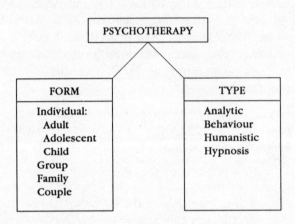

Fig. 1 Basic structure of psychotherapy

Individual psychotherapy sessions for adults, adolescents and children usually last fifty or sixty minutes, whilst other forms may last from one to two hours. Family and couple therapy is usually planned for a set number of sessions, whereas group and individual psychotherapy is open-ended unless specified as focal or brief therapy (Brown and Pedder, 1979). Focal or brief therapy will be carried out in an agreed number of sessions or months.

TYPES OF PSYCHOTHERAPY

Each form of psychotherapy is typified by a method, which will reflect something of the underpinning theory, which will vary. The type of therapy offered is used to qualify the title psychotherapist. For example, 'Behaviour Psychotherapist' will indicate the therapist's method and theoretical orientation (Behaviour Therapy).

Very broadly there are four types of psychotherapy practised in Britain today: ANALYTIC, BEHAVIOUR, HUMANISTIC and HYPNO-SIS. For the reasons stated in the Preface, this book examines the trainings of one form of psychotherapy, Individual Psychotherapy for Adults, and two of the most common types of psychotherapy, Analytic and Humanistic. The therapists graduating from these trainings mostly use the titles PSYCHO/ANALYTIC PSYCHO/THERAPIST or HUMANISTIC PSYCHO/THERAPIST (the dropping of 'psycho' is usually an abbreviation). It is important to remember that within each psychotherapy type there are many variations on shared themes, which will become apparent in the following pages.

THE PRACTICE OF PSYCHOTHERAPY

PSYCHOTHERAPY LEVELS

Another reason why psychotherapy can be a confusing label is not only because there are different forms and types as demonstrated above, but also because of the different levels on which psychotherapy can be seen to operate.

For example, there are many social workers, psychiatric nurses, occupational therapists, psychiatrists and GPs who have some knowledge of psychotherapy concepts and would see a large component of their work as being psychotherapeutic. It is a level of human interaction between professional and patient which has not been formalized and structured into a series of meetings. For example, the psychiatric nurse on the ward may be very helpful to her patients psychotherapeutically, as is the sort of work done by Samaritans and similar organizations, but however deep the conversations, in the terms of the trainings in this book, this level would not be seen as practising psychotherapy. Meanwhile, it is true to say that this experience is counted as invaluable to anybody wishing to train as a psychotherapist.

The next level is where meetings/sessions are formalized and structured – once or more weekly in a private space. This level is often described as counselling or 'supportive psychotherapy'. It is aimed at helping the patient to cope with the present crisis without delving into past conflicts and traumas.

The third level is what would most often be referred to as psychodynamic psychotherapy, and it is at this level that the analytic trainings in this book are pitched. This level of psychotherapy is aimed at deeper analysis of the unconscious through the relationship between patient and therapist. This involves the therapist's effort to understand how the feelings being presented to her are linked with an important figure in the patient's past. This is known as the transference and it can be observed in all walks of life. However, not all forms of psychotherapy use the transference. This means that when the therapist can see the past relationship being re-experienced in the present therapeutic relationship, she will reflect this back to the patient. It is the interpretation and use of the transference which distinguishes psychodynamic psychotherapy from others.

These three levels are overlapping and dynamic and have been written about extensively. There is also ongoing debate about the theory and practice of all levels, because unfortunately issues of better and worse come into play. It is important to differentiate the levels whilst retaining the value of each (for more detail regarding levels of psychotherapy see Brown and Pedder, 1979).

PSYCHOTHERAPY IN THE NATIONAL HEALTH SERVICE
AND SOCIAL SERVICES

Within the NHS and social services there are many different forms and types as well as different levels of psychotherapy which are on offer. In one and the same hospital, different forms and types of psychotherapy may be practised, although very often hospitals will have a particular bias determined by the attitude of the psychiatric team.

Of concern to many psychotherapists is the number of professionals working in the NHS and social services who may be claiming to be practising psychotherapy without the specialized training. For example, to qualify as a psychiatrist at the moment requires no knowledge of psychotherapy, although the Psychotherapy Section of the Royal College of Psychiatrists is working towards changing that. It has to be stated that the psychiatrists who go on to train in psychotherapy are few indeed, and the majority of psychiatrists working in the NHS and privately are antipathetic to psychodynamic psychotherapy.

The DHSS (now the Department of Health) recognized psychotherapy as a speciality in 1975 when a small proportion of consultant psychiatrists changed their title to 'Consultant Psychotherapist' (Pedder, 1989). A consultant psychotherapist is a psychiatrist who has additional specialized training in psychotherapy at senior registrar level. In London the extra specialist training used by senior registrars is most often the Institute of Psycho-Analysis or the Society of Analytical Psychology. Out of London the trainings for senior registrars tend to be more eclectic (see Introduction to Part Two concerning eclecticism).

The bulk of consultant psychotherapists' work is the assessment of patients for whom they will retain clinical responsibility, and the supervision (including teaching) of staff. They may also offer therapy to patients and very often run a small private practice from home.

Apart from consultant psychotherapists the only psychotherapists recognized by the Department of Health are the child psychotherapists. There are presently four trainings in child psychotherapy: the Anna Freud Centre, the British Association of Psychotherapists, the Society of Analytical Psychology and the Tavistock Clinic. The Association of Child Psychotherapists (ACP), formed in 1949, is the regulating body for these trainings, all of which are analytic, and the trainings compare with the most rigorous of the analytic trainings presented here, in terms of time commitment, depth of work, personal analysis and theoretical learning. There are no humanistic child psychotherapy trainings and unlikely to be any in the future, because the ACP's criteria only acknowledge an analytic orientation.

To date there are about 200 qualified child psychotherapists in Great Britain. The ACP has already achieved many things for child psychotherapists that have not yet been achieved for adult psychotherapists: non-medical posts, recognition by the DOH, union membership, pay scales. The trainings in child psychotherapy do entail working with adults and many child psychotherapists work privately with young adults.

Because the understanding of child development is seen to be an important component of understanding adult psychopathology, most of the analytic trainings will include some seminars on child development and Infant Observation (see Introduction to Part Two for a description of Infant Observation).

PSYCHOTHERAPY IN THE PRIVATE SECTOR

Outside the NHS there are the private psychotherapists who usually work from home or in a hired consulting room. They include some of the professionals mentioned above, who may work during the day in the NHS as well as having a small private practice. There are also psychotherapists working full-time in private practice (providing a total of 30–40 sessions a week). They will have a varied background and training and are more often than not offering individual psychotherapy. Of course there are some private practitioners working with couples, groups, families, etc., but there is a much longer tradition in the private sector of individual psychotherapy.

The second and third levels of psychotherapy, as described above, also apply to the psychotherapist working privately. Depending on their training, some therapists will practise only 'supportive psychotherapy' or counselling and others will decide which is the appropriate level to work according to each patient.

WHAT IS THE DIFFERENCE BETWEEN PRIVATE PSYCHOTHERAPY AND PSYCHOTHERAPY IN THE NHS AND SOCIAL SERVICES?

In private psychotherapy the number of sessions and time span will be negotiated between the patient (what can be afforded) and the therapist (what is considered appropriate). In the NHS the consultant psychotherapist or psychiatrist assesses the patient's appropriateness for psychotherapy. Frequency of sessions and length of therapy are very much dictated by the available budget and there is more often than not a time limit to the psychotherapy offered. In addition there are generally waiting lists, which are at present lengthening.

Another important factor to be taken into account is the degree of disturbance. It may be more beneficial for some people to be offered asylum (this may be hospital or a private clinic) for an acute breakdown (short term) or a place in a therapeutic community for more chronic conditions (longer term). Seeing a psychotherapist in private practice, therefore, is not simply a question of money. Most psychotherapists recognize that psychotherapy may not be suitable for everybody.

How Can People in Need of Help Know Which Form or Type of Psychotherapy Would be Best for Them?

The simple answer to this question is that nobody can know what will help until the help is experienced. However, there are many introductory books to the various forms and types of psychotherapy, which can be a start. The majority of the twenty-six trainings here offer a referral service. It is too simplistic and misleading to say that the best form and type of therapy is the therapy that you feel you can trust. What we trust when in crisis may not be the sort of therapy that will help us really understand our emotions and 'work through' the crisis. A good psychotherapist needs to be confrontative as well as containing. Many people are under the illusion that psychotherapy should be like medication, but getting rid of feelings is *not* what psychotherapy is aimed at. Emotions, sometimes very disturbed ones, have to be experienced in therapy, and it is hard work. Through this hard work it is hoped that the overwhelming emotions will be understood and consequently become less overwhelming. It is worth remembering Freud's famous and much-quoted imaginary dialogue with a patient when he was at the beginning of his psychoanalytic discoveries at the beginning of this century:

> *Patient*: You tell me yourself that my illness is probably connected with my circumstances and the events of my life. How do you propose to help me then?

Freud: You will be able to convince yourself that much will be gained
if we succeed in transforming your hysterical misery into common
unhappiness. With a mental life that has been restored to health you will
be better armed against that unhappiness. (Breuer and Freud, 1895)

Meanwhile, it is of considerable concern at the moment that
there is no real safeguard for the general public about the
authenticity of psychotherapists working within the NHS and social
services as well as privately. Currently, as has already been stated
(and unlike the child psychotherapists), adult psychotherapists
have no charter, no register, no legislation. However, these are the
very issues that are now being discussed at the UKSCP as the
psychotherapy profession finds a way of regulating itself.

So what is being done to inform the public about adult
psychotherapists and protect people from the unqualified practitioner?

THE UNITED KINGDOM STANDING
CONFERENCE FOR PSYCHOTHERAPY

Prompted by the bad experiences some people had had with
scientology, the Foster Report on Scientology (1971) concluded
that the profession of psychotherapy should be controlled by
legislation. In 1975, following the Foster Report, a committee was
set up known as the Sieghart Committee, named after its Chairman.
The representatives on that committee were from the British
Psycho-Analytical Society, the Society of Analytical Psychology, the
Institute of Group Analysis, the British Association for Psychotherapists, the British Association of Behavioural Psychotherapists, the
Association of Child Psychotherapists, the Royal College of
Psychiatrists, the British Psychological Society and the British
Association of Social Workers. Perceiving that there was some
conflict amongst psychotherapists (essentially between the analytic
and behaviour therapists – at this stage the humanistic therapists
were not involved), the DHSS stated that legislation would not be
possible until a coherent picture of the psychotherapy profession

could be presented. The representatives of the above organizations were basically told to go and get their act together!

It was not until 1982 that interested parties, representing the whole spectrum of psychotherapy, gathered together to discuss the issue of registration and legislation. Apart from the clear need to form a regulated profession in order to protect the public, there was real concern about the forthcoming changes due in 1992 concerning the interchangeability of professions – European psychotherapists coming to work here and British psychotherapists going to work in Europe. Nobody looked forward to a European Community dictating how psychotherapists should train and practise in this country, nor what kind of qualification they should have as a prerequisite to becoming a psychotherapist (as is the case in many European countries). It was agreed that energy should first of all be directed into forming a conference for psychotherapy that would represent all forms and types of psychotherapy. The issue of registration was for the moment put on hold. This Conference, meeting annually, became known as the Rugby Psychotherapy Conference, because the first meeting was held in Rugby under the aegis of the British Association of Counselling (BAC). Seven years and an enormous amount of hard work later, the Rugby Psychotherapy Conference was ready to inaugurate the United Kingdom Standing Conference for Psychotherapy (UKSCP), in January 1989. Thus the Rugby Conference came to an end.

The UKSCP January Conference in 1992 was attended by 123 delegates representing sixty-eight organizations. All the members are either training organizations or groups of psychotherapists who have formed an association or society, and at the AGM a great deal was achieved. The Council was strengthened by giving a seat each to the Tavistock Clinic and the Association of University Teachers in Psychiatry. Agreement was made, on a formula for appointing a Registration Board which would be powerful enough to run a register and cannot be interfered with by Council or the AGM. Conference also agreed that trainings should be at a postgraduate level with content roughly equivalent to a Master's degree, and with a requirement for appropriate personal therapy. Conference asked the Council to produce documents outlining detailed structure and functions of a Registration Board, a Training Committee, an Appeals Committee and an Ethical Committee. By January 1993 the Registration Board and other Committees will be set up. With a register of psychotherapists in place, the UKSCP will then be in a position to press for legislation.

What Will the Register Indicate About the Type and Form of Psychotherapy Practised?

Much of this has yet to be decided, but so far the Conference has divided itself into eight sections. These sections are a way of qualifying and grouping the types of psychotherapy taught and practised. Each section is responsible for monitoring its member organizations to ensure they meet the standard of training required, before being placed on a register.

In addition the Conference has finalized a Master Code of Ethics which each member organization will have to include within its own ethical code. The register will therefore indicate a measure of the training the therapist has received as well as introducing a concept of a disciplinary procedure for any registered therapist who does not comply with the UKSCP's Code of Ethics. It is important to note, however, that until a register is finalized, membership of the UKSCP in itself does not indicate any standard of training or ethical conduct, although the long-term objective is that it will.

The Sections are as follows:

Psychoanalysis and Analytical Psychology

Analytical Psychotherapy

Behavioural Psychotherapy

Family, Marital and Sexual Therapy

Humanistic and Integrative Psychotherapy

Hypnotherapy

Experiential Constructivist Therapies

Psychoanalytical based Therapy with Children

The four types of psychotherapy already mentioned (Fig. 1) will be immediately identified in the above list, except the section on Family, Marital and Sexual Therapy. This section cannot be placed into one of the four types of psychotherapy outlined, because the methods used in this therapy very much depend on both analytic and behaviour theories. Therapists may use psychodynamic concepts to assess the couples and/or families (like analytic therapists), but the techniques used in the therapy tend to be more directive (like behaviour therapists).

This book covers the training organizations who are members of two of these sections: Analytical Psychotherapy and Humanistic and Integrative Psychotherapy. They are the sections containing the largest number of societies, associations and training establishments.

The Royal College of Psychiatrists, the British Psychological Society and the British Association of Social Workers have been Institutional members of the Conference from the beginning. Recently the Tavistock Clinic and the Association of University Teachers in Psychiatry have been offered that status whilst the British Association of Social Workers has left.

Mention must be made here of the Tavistock Clinic, because of its crucial role in therapy trainings and out-patient care. Its history dates back to 1920, when it was one of the first clinics to offer psychodynamic psychotherapy. Many of the practitioners at that time, and this is still the case today, were psychoanalysts (who had trained at the Institute of Psycho-Analysis). In 1948 the clinic became part of the National Health Service and the Tavistock's contribution to the history and development of psychotherapy in this country is unique. At the present day it provides out-patient psychotherapy for individuals, families and children. Approximately 800 postgraduate students attend the various training programmes on a part- or full-time basis. There are three departments – Adult, Adolescent, and the Child and Family Department. Of relevance to this book is the Adult Department which offers a training in Adult Psychoanalytic Psychotherapy.

This training has not joined the Analytical Psychotherapy Section of the UKSCP and probably reflects the attitude of this group whose graduates see themselves as Chiefs in a new psychotherapy profession trained to lead the Indians (Martindale, 1990). It is an unusual training in that it is an in-service training for psychologists, psychiatrists and social workers. The learned society for graduates of this training is known as the Society of Psychoanalytic Psychotherapists (SPP).

Modelled on the above course is a new training which has been set up by the Department of Psychotherapy at St Bernard's Hospital, Ealing, under the leadership of Dr Robert Hinshelwood. This course is aiming to train professionals to become psychoanalytic psycho-therapists to work within the NHS and, like the Tavistock's training, it is an in-service training. The requirements of training are very much on a par with the most rigorous of the analytic trainings presented in this book, with the emphasis on working part-time as a psychotherapist in the NHS, and – unlike the Tavistock Adult Psychotherapy Course – trainees are employed in non-medical adult psychotherapist posts rather than a core profession. Presently negotiations are being held with the British Association of Psychotherapists, the Lincoln Institute of Psychotherapy and the Society of Psychoanalytical Psychotherapists to approve the graduates of this new course. If the negotiations are successful graduates will be eligible to join one of these organizations as their learned society.

As this book confines itself to looking only at the trainings whose qualification leads to individual psychotherapist, there are two important trainings which are members of the Analytical Psycho-therapy Section and not covered in Part Two but need mention here: The Institute of Group Analysis (IGA), whose qualification leads to membership of the IGA, and the Tavistock Institute of Marital Studies, whose training leads to a Diploma in Marital Therapy.

The IGA's qualification enables people to practise group analytic psychotherapy, and members describe themselves as Group Analysts. The IGA's training is associated with one of the founders, S.H. Foulkes, a psychoanalyst who developed analysis through and by the group (Foulkes and Anthony, 1957). Foulkes founded the Group Analytic Society in 1952 and the Institute of Group Analysis was given a formal constitution in 1971, but its first training began in 1970. Prior to that courses had been run under the aegis of the Group Analytic Society, but did not lead to a qualification. Relevant to this book is that many of the trainings include the experience of groups as a component to the training. There are many different types of group therapy, particularly among the humanistic therapy trainings. The type of group therapy/analysis practised by graduates of the IGA is probably the most influential in Britain today, and predominant in the analytic therapy trainings where group therapy is on the curriculum (Brown and Pedder, 1979).

The Tavistock Institute of Marital Studies (TIMS) was founded in 1948 under the leadership of Enid Balint and was originally known as the Family Discussion Bureau. From its beginnings it shared the psychoanalytic orientation and attitude of the Tavistock Clinic, to which it initially turned for training and consultative support. Dr Michael Balint was the first psychoanalytic consultant, followed by Dr Jock Sutherland. The TIMS approach is to apply psychoanalytic principles to its theory and practice of couple psychotherapy.

The training offered by TIMS in marital therapy is unique. The marital therapy is seen as psychoanalytic psychotherapy for the couple. The TIMS approach is to view the relationship as the patient, focusing on what happens between the couple. The training therefore entails the crucial components of the analytic trainings presented here, personal psychoanalytic psychotherapy along with the in-service training of working with couples and theoretical learning. The latter concentrates on psychoanalytic theory and practice (particularly Object Relations) and its application to the couple relationship (for more detailed accounts of the history and practice of TIMS, see Bannister *et al.*, 1955; Dicks, 1970; Ruszczynski, 1992; and Woodhouse, 1990).

ANALYTICAL PSYCHOTHERAPY

The subsequent definitions of psychotherapy, again from *The Language of Psycho-Analysis*, read:

2. In a narrower sense, psychotherapy in its various forms is often contrasted with psychoanalysis. There is a whole set of reasons for this distinction, but the most notable one is the major part played in psychoanalysis by the interpretation of the unconscious conflict, with the analysis of the transference tending to resolve this conflict.

3. The name 'analytic psychotherapy' is given to any form of psychotherapy which is based on the theoretical and technical principles of psychoanalysis without, however, fulfilling the requirements of a psychoanalytic treatment as strictly understood. (Laplanche and Pontalis, 1983)

Each section of the UKSCP has written a 'flag statement' to define the fundamental concepts of the therapy practised. The 'flag statement' of the Analytical Psychotherapy Section reads thus:

Analytical Psychotherapy is based in psychoanalytic practice and theory. It endeavours to reach the underlying, often unconscious, causes of distress. Together with the therapist, the patient can explore free associations, memories, phantasies, feelings and dreams, relating to both past and present. In the reliable setting of the therapy (which allows for regression) and in the exploration of the interaction with the therapist, especially within the transference and countertransference, the patient may achieve a new and better resolution of long-standing conflicts.

In the context of the British analytic trainings presented here, Freud and psychoanalysis are the beginning. The trainings in analytic therapy maximize on the discoveries and developments of the training of psychoanalysts within the International Psycho-Analytical Association (1910), in this country the British Psycho-Analytical Society (1919), and its training establishment the Institute of Psycho-Analysis (1924).

The history of psychoanalysis is well documented. Its development is littered with controversy and parting of the ways, and these conflicts are part of the legacy inherited by analytic therapists today and by the analytic trainings. There are too many issues to include here, but it is worth pointing out those that are pertinent within and between the fifteen analytic trainings examined.

AREAS OF CONTROVERSY

　Freud and Jung
　The issue of 'lay analysis'
　Psychoanalysts and psychotherapists
　Psychoanalysis and homosexuality

Freud and Jung

Carl Jung was one of the first dissenters from Freud (Jones, 1957). The final dividing of the ways between Freud and Jung, not without acrimony and pain, occurred in 1914 when Jung resigned as the President of the International Psycho-Analytical Association. Their disagreement focused on the concept of the unconscious (Kovel, 1976). Freudians see Jung's development of theories from psychoanalysis as a diversion, whereas some Jungians would see it as evolving beyond psychoanalysis. Nevertheless, the separation of these two men created two separate international organizations – The International Association of Psycho-Analysis (IAP – Freud) and The International Association of Analytical Psychology (IAAP – Jung). The two major trainings in Britain today are the Institute of Psycho-Analysis (Freud) dating from 1924 and the Society of Analytical Psychology (SAP, Jung) which commenced its training in 1946.

　　The Institute of Psycho-Analysis (1924) trains individuals in psychoanalysis leading to the qualification of psychoanalyst. It remains the only training organization in Britain whose training is recognized by the International Psycho-Analytical Association.

　　Within the Society of Analytical Psychology (SAP) there have been many partings of the ways (Samuels, 1985) and the creation of two other trainings:

　The Association of Jungian Analysts

　The Independent Group of Analytical Psychologists

These three trainings are recognized by the IAAP and whereas the qualification is as an 'analytical psychologist', graduates are generally referred to as Jungian Analysts.

The four trainings above are the only members of the Psychoanalysis and Analytical Psychology Section of UKSCP.

There was very nearly a parting of the ways within the British Psycho-Analytical Society between 1941 and 1945 by what came to be referred to as 'The Controversial Discussions' (Segal, 1979; King and Steiner, 1991). The disagreement was between Anna Freud (youngest daughter of Sigmund Freud) and Melanie Klein. These discussions concluded with a 'gentlemen's agreement', so that within the training of the Institute of Psycho-Analysis there are three different groups – Contemporary Freudian, Kleinian and Independent. This means that a psychoanalyst will belong to one of these three groups and be referred to as a Freudian, Kleinian or Independent analyst (Kohon, 1986).

The British Psycho-Analytical Society (the learned society for graduates of the Institute of Psycho-Analysis) and the SAP continue to play a major role for most of the analytical psychotherapy trainings, particularly in London, and are the resource for analysts, supervisors and teachers. Evidently these two longest standing trainings contain great diversity and conflict within their separate but interrelated worlds. Some of the analytic trainings will include the study of both Freud and Jung. The word 'psychodynamic' refers to the acknowledgement of an internal world – the unconscious – but it has also come to signify, amongst some trainings, a theoretical label of the eclectic or pluralistic combination of psychoanalysis and analytical psychology (see Introduction to Part Two regarding eclecticism and pluralism).

The issue of 'lay analysis'

Psychiatry had not been very receptive to Freud's ideas in his early years, to say the least. To a varied extent, this remains the case. As stated above, the training of a psychiatrist does not involve any study of Freud and psychiatrists who choose to follow a psychotherapy training are in the minority. The suspicions and antagonism towards psychoanalysis had a profound effect on the International Psycho-Analytical Association. Psychoanalysts were very keen to have psychoanalysis accepted by the medical profession and if non-medically trained analysts were accepted as suitable people to train as psychoanalysts, there was a general fear that this would go against the crediblity of psychoanalysis. The year Freud published his paper 'The Question of Lay Analysis' (1926), which was arguing *in favour* of lay analysts, a law was passed in New York prohibiting the practice of psychoanalysis by non-medically qualified practitioners (Kohon, 1986).

Meanwhile, perhaps it is not surprising that psychotherapy is associated with the medical profession for two main reasons: (a) psychotherapy is a form of help for people who suffer – it is a profession which has evolved out of the tradition of healing; and (b) Freud, the founder of the 'talking cure', was a medical doctor. Nowadays, in Britain, it is generally accepted that a medical degree is not a necessary prerequisite to train to be a psychotherapist or psychoanalyst: indeed Freud saw it as a definite disadvantage and dissuaded his daughter Anna from pursuing a medical training.

However, the legacy of this issue can perhaps be seen to be reflected in one of the present debates within the UKSCP about whether or not a psychotherapist should have a qualification in one of the 'core professions' (Pedder, 1989; Dyne and Figlio, 1989). The core professions refer to all those professions which are commonly known as the helping professions, and recognized within the public sector – social workers, doctors, nurses, psychologists, occupational therapists, and so on. As in the 1920s the issues are complex, but very much linked with the credibility and acceptability of psychotherapy as a profession in its own right.

It is significant that there is a tradition of lay analysts within the British Psycho-Analytical Society which has greatly influenced the character of psychoanalysis in Britain today (Kohon 1986, p. 37) and that many of the seminal thinkers and contributors to the development of psychoanalysis have been or are lay analysts. Anna Freud and Melanie Klein were lay analysts, and today many of the most original thinkers in British psychoanalysis, like Marion Milner, Christopher Bollas and Juliet Mitchell, are lay analysts. This tradition has also influenced the psychotherapy trainings where applicants from artistic, literary, educational and other backgrounds are very often encouraged to train, as long as a particular aptitude to the work of psychotherapy is demonstrated.

Psychoanalysis and psychotherapists

For the first half of this century the Institute of Psycho-Analysis and the SAP were the only training organizations in London. The early 1950s saw a small group of people coming together to form a psychotherapy association. They were individuals all interested in practising psychotherapy at their places of work or in private practice (Scarlett, 1991) and they were motivated by what was experienced as the elitism and exclusiveness of the Institute and the SAP. Analysis was an expensive form of treatment – usually requiring five times weekly attendance over several years – and the competition for places in the training programme was, and still is, very high.

The first analytic psychotherapists in this country had generally undergone personal analysis and supervision with members of the British Psycho-Analytical Society or SAP. These first therapists began to provide therapy to people who could only afford once or twice weekly therapy (see History sections of BAP and Lincoln Centre) (Herman, 1989).

This brings us to another particular characteristic of British psychotherapy. The training requirements of the Institute of Psycho-Analysis have evolved out of the early years of the developments of psychoanalysis (Balint, 1953), starting with Freud. They cover three main areas: personal therapy, supervision and theory. These components are interrelated, working in dynamic relationship to each other, with self-knowledge at the very heart. They have now become the unequivocal fundamentals of every analytical psychotherapy training (see Fig. 2).

The difference between the practice of psychoanalysis and psychotherapy therefore becomes very complicated. There are some analytic therapists whose personal analysis, supervision and theoretical learning is on a par with somebody who has trained at the Institute or SAP. The same analytic therapists very often see patients four or five times a week over a period of several years. Meanwhile, there are many analysts who see people once or twice weekly for shorter periods of time. This presents the question: who practises psychoanalysis and who practises psychotherapy? Most

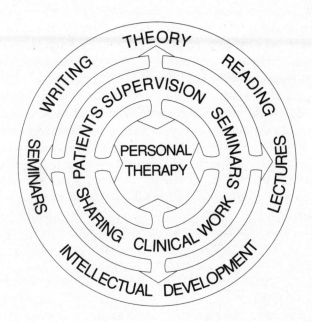

Fig. 2 Fundamentals of every analytical psychotherapy training

analysts differentiate between psychoanalysis and psychotherapy and see their training as enabling them to practise either. However, there are many analytic therapists who see their training and depth of work as equivalent to many analysts, but the majority will not call themselves psychoanalysts simply because they have not trained at the Institute of Psycho-Analysis. As with the label 'psychotherapist', there is no legislation which prevents anyone using the label 'psychoanalyst' with or without a hyphen. This issue is hotly debated between analysts and therapists (Sandler; Wolff; Obholzer; Waddell: all 1988). However, of the analytic trainings presented in this book there is one training which does not use the term psychoanalytic psychotherapy, but regards its teaching as psychoanalysis and its graduates as psychoanalysts – the Centre for

Freudian Analysis and Research (CFAR) – the first and only Lacanian training in Britain.

Jacques Lacan was a French psychoanalyst who has written extensively on his interpretation of Freud. His aim was to instigate a return to Freud's theories with an emphasis on what was difficult to accept in psychoanalytic theory. In 1953 there was a split in the International Psycho-Analytical Association, and there followed ten years of politicking which resulted in Lacan setting up L'Ecole Freudienne de Paris in 1964 (Benvenuto and Kennedy, 1986). There are now approximately 9,000 – 10,000 Lacanian analysts in the world. The work of Lacan seems to be far more accepted outside the Anglo-Saxon world of psychoanalysis and psychotherapy, which retains a mixed response to the work of Lacan and Lacanians. This is reflected in the analytic trainings, where Lacan's work is rarely studied.

The Lacanian training (CFAR) in London is very clear that its training is in psychoanalysis and its graduates will be psychoanalysts. It believes that the analytic trainings in London collude with the British Psycho-Analytical Society, by allowing them the monopoly of the title psychoanalyst and the practice of psychoanalysis. Amongst therapists and analysts there is a diversity of opinion about this issue. What must be clear by now is that although based on specific criteria of the differences between analysis and therapy, the debate becomes very blurred with the issues of hierarchy and status – the politics of the psychotherapy world, like the politics of every professional community.

There is still a lack of clarity amongst psychotherapists about the adjectives used to indicate the type of psychotherapy offered. Generally speaking, 'analytic therapist' refers to a therapist who has studied Freud and Jung or only Jung, and 'psychoanalytic therapist' refers to a therapist whose orientation is Freud (including Klein and excluding Jung).

A hyphen between 'psycho' and 'analysis' or 'analyst' denotes the qualification recognized by the International Psycho-Analytical Association. Depending on the context many analysts nowadays drop the hyphen for the words psychoanalysis and psychoanalyst, and the 'psycho' may often be dropped too. Writers and publishers use different forms, but like the label 'psychotherapist' anybody can use the label 'psychoanalyst' with or without a hyphen. These are details that may become clarified within the UKSCP and perhaps made law with future registration and legislation.

Some of these issues of hierarchy and status also apply to the differences between psychotherapy and counselling, and the different levels of psychotherapy as outlined in the section on psychotherapy levels. Many counsellors may have been in analytic therapy or analysis and their course has covered psychodynamic theory. However, they rarely see clients more than once weekly and will not use the couch. Most counsellors, like therapists and analysts, recognize the differences between counselling, psychotherapy and psychoanalysis, as well as the overlapping areas. It is the overlaps which cause the complications: if they are minimized the point of differentiation is fudged, if they are overemphasized the labels become clouded with notions of superior and inferior.

Psychoanalysis and homosexuality

Traditionally, psychoanalysis saw homosexuality as pathology. In 1910 Freud delineated different sorts of homosexuality (at that time known as inversion) (Freud, 1905). Some sorts of homosexuality were seen to be more treatable than others, but the general view of the psychoanalytic world was that a homosexual should not become a psychoanalyst or psychotherapist. This implied that homosexuality equalled pathology and as such it would interfere with the practitioner's ability to work effectively. This has meant historically that homosexuals have been precluded from psychotherapy training establishments. The issue of homosexuality is one of great controversy amongst psychoanalysts and psychotherapists, in Britain and the world. It is a topic that is not often discussed publicly, being so emotive and contentious.

The majority of trainings discussed in this book say they would not exclude an applicant solely on the grounds of homosexuality, but it is true to say that there are some analytic trainings which contain a divided opinion in their membership as to an applicant's suitability to train, consequently conveying a confused and confusing stance (Ellis, 1992). Meanwhile, the humanistic trainings would never see homosexuality as demonstrating a contra-indication to therapy training; inherent in the humanistic attitude is the rejection of viewing homosexuality as pathology.

HUMANISTIC AND INTEGRATIVE PSYCHOTHERAPY

The 'flag statement' for this section reads thus:

> Humanistic psychotherapy is an approach which tries to do justice to the whole person including mind, body and spirit and thus humanistic psychotherapists believe that psychotherapy is not a medical practice and most often speak of clients and not patients.
>
> Humanistic psychotherapists recognize the self-healing capacities of the client, and believe that the greatest expert on the client is the client. The humanistic psychotherapist works towards an authentic meeting of equals in the therapy relationship.
>
> Integrative psychotherapy does not believe that any one type of psychotherapy is necessarily adequate in all situations. Integrative psychotherapists attempt to bring together two or more approaches in a principled way. Integrative psychotherapy can be distinguished from eclecticism by its determination to show that there are real connections between different therapies, which may be unrecognized by their exclusive proponents.

The trainings listed under this section have a shorter history than the analytic trainings, as does the type of therapy practised, and there is less tension regarding a hierarchy amongst the trainings; indeed the tension seems to exist more between the humanistic therapists and the analytic therapists (Hinshelwood and Rowan, 1988).

The roots of present day humanistic therapy are associated with the Human Potential movement which rapidly grew in America during the 1960s, and became known as Humanist Psychology. The Esalen Center in California was perhaps the most famous centre for a great variety of different types of humanistic therapy on offer (Kovel, 1976). Although there are many different types of humanistic therapy with different theoretical backgrounds, like the analytic trainings, there is a common attitude which colours all of them. It contrasts sharply with the analytic attitude, so that it is not surprising that the tensions, as mentioned above, exist.

Some analytic therapists would see the key aspects of the humanistic attitude as a reaction against the analytic attitude. Historically this was the case with the therapies which were developed by psychoanalysts and based on psychoanalytic theories. It may not be the case with every training examined here, but this aspect of the history of the humanistic movement is inevitably part of the legacy inherited by humanistic therapists.

The following humanistic therapies are pertinent to the trainings examined here:

Reichian – developed from Wilhelm Reich's (one of the original dissenters from Freud) work on character analysis (emphasis on the body).

Gestalt – developed by Fritz Perls, who was an American psychoanalyst.

Transactional Analysis – developed by Eric Berne, an American psychoanalyst.

Psychosynthesis – developed by Roberto Assagioli, an Italian correspondent of Carl Jung.

Psychodrama – developed in Vienna during Freud's time and independently by Jacob Moreno, who later on emigrated to America and coined the name 'group psychotherapy'.

The use of the word 'integrative' denotes the combination of more than one humanistic therapy practised by the trainings.

WHAT IS THE HUMANISTIC ATTITUDE?

The name humanistic implies humanity and warmth in comparison to the caricature image of the cold, detached analyst. There are many humanistic therapists who are under the misperception that psychoanalytic psychotherapy is intellectual and therefore cold and inhuman. The humanistic therapist is concerned with equality, so that physical contact and friendliness between client and therapist are not regarded as irregular. In some of the therapies physical contact is an integral part of the therapy (massage). These features are linked with the main difference in attitude between the humanistic and analytic therapist – that of boundaries.

The analytic rule of abstinence (no relationship whatsoever outside of the therapeutic one) was denigrated by the Human Potential Movement, dramatically during the 1960s and 1970s, when there was a deliberate policy of breaking down the boundaries between client and therapist (Kovel, 1976). This also applied to sexual relationships between the same members of the same therapeutic group, as well as between therapists and clients.

Body work, massage and enactment are all strong features of humanistic therapy. The analytic therapist sees most forms of touch as essentially interfering with the therapeutic transference relationship. The humanistic therapist sees the use of words as a neglect of the body/feelings, and tends to take the point of view that analysis is too 'in the head'. All these arguments are still alive amongst the two different types of training set out here. But there have been some important agreements. It seems that the components of training that are fundamental to any training in analytical therapy (see Fig. 2) also apply to all of the humanistic trainings – personal therapy, supervision of clinical work and theory – although it is true to add here that the amounts of these components are far less intensive in the humanistic trainings.

The issue of boundaries seems to be changing and every humanistic training in this book now has its own detailed Code of Ethics, which would preclude any sexual relationship between therapist and client. Many of the humanistic trainings cover a small amount of psychodynamic thought in their curriculum and some humanistic trainees are in analytic therapy.

What Are the Main Differences in Technique Between Humanistic and Analytic Therapists?

The humanistic therapist tends to be more direct and directive in the consulting room, assessing the problem and directing the procedure: guided fantasies, massage, breathing, enacting a traumatic moment, and so on. The analytic therapist encourages the use of the couch and asks the patient to say whatever comes to mind – a non-directive approach.

Therapy sessions are usually no more than once weekly with the humanistic therapist, and sometimes once fortnightly. The analytic therapist will see people once weekly but encourages as many sessions as can be afforded – optimally five – but on average usually two to three a week. The humanistic therapist will often be open to changes of session times each week, whereas the analytic therapist prefers to keep to one regular time every week. Although the time span in humanistic therapy can be long term (five years or more), it is more frequently much less (up to two years). The analytic therapist is trained for long-term work and will expect a patient to stay in therapy for several years and finish by working towards an agreed finishing date.

As already stated, the factor which distinguishes analytic therapy from others is the interpretation of the transference in the therapeutic relationship. The methods of humanistic therapy traditionally do not focus on the use of the transference in the same way, although they may acknowledge its importance. Using this criterion, therefore, humanistic therapy would be seen as fitting into the level of 'supportive psychotherapy' or counselling as described in the section on psychotherapy levels (see p. 9).

There is an extensive amount of literature regarding the theory and practice of psychoanalysis and analytical psychology, spanning over a hundred years. The humanistic literature is limited, because it has a shorter history and there has been less of a tradition of developing theory and more emphasis on intuition and living in the moment (Kovel, 1976). This is an attitude which still prevails amongst the humanistic trainings examined here.

At the end of the day training organizations can be seen to be like families, all of whom have their very different ways of bringing up their children. Some therapists see the Human Potential Movement as part of an adolescent rebellion against Freud, others see it as departing from Freud in a more human way. What is clear is that humanistic therapy in this country is growing, it is less caught up with analytical politics and less London-centred. It seems that most humanistic therapists would turn to psychoanalysts and analytic psychotherapists for the understanding and treatment of more serious disturbances and often describe their therapy as being for the 'healthy neurotic'. This can be misleading because there may be many different interpretations as to the meaning of 'healthy neurotic' and it could imply that the 'healthy neurotic' may not benefit from psychodynamic psychotherapy, which of course is not the case. These issues relate to the debates and differences of opinion ongoing between the analytic and humanistic psychotherapists.

PART TWO:
THE TRAININGS

INTRODUCTION TO THE FORMAT

The twenty-six trainings examined here are members of the United Kingdom Standing Conference for Psychotherapy (UKSCP). Fifteen are listed under the UKSCP section 'Analytical Psychotherapy', and eleven under the section 'Humanistic and Integrative Psychotherapy'. All trainings may cover a wide variety of therapies in their curricula, but the principal purpose is to train students to see people on a one-to-one basis.

Of importance here is that qualification earns the title Psychotherapist. Similarities and differences between the courses and sections can be studied in detail, leading to a clearer understanding of what is meant by an 'analytic' psychotherapist and a 'humanistic' psychotherapist (see Part One).

As has already been stated the analytic therapies are different from the humanistic therapies in the methods used to help the individual in emotional distress. These differences are reflected in the method of teaching psychotherapy adopted by the organizations listed here. It is worth, therefore, mentioning the major differences in teaching methods between the two types of therapy trainings.

THE TRAINEE'S PERSONAL PROCESS

As has already been stated (see Fig. 2), the stress of every therapy training, analytic and humanistic, is on the trainee's psychological growth and personal process – reflecting the point of view that therapists must be aware of their own unconscious and their own pathology, before tackling another's. Consequently, a common requirement is that a trainee must be undergoing individual therapy throughout the training (see Part One).

In addition to this requirement the humanistic trainings believe that the trainee should also work on personal issues in the trainee group. This is what is meant by 'experiential' and in this case the teacher sometimes acts as therapist, in order to demonstrate the therapy being taught. In some cases the same teacher/therapist may also be the individual therapist of individuals in the training group. Trainees are also encouraged to practise on each other, by taking it in turns to be the therapist. This merging of the roles of teachers, and 'role play' in the trainee groups, is all in the humanistic tradition, which was aimed at breaking down analytic boundaries that the humanistic movement saw as rigid and stifling (see Part One).

Every analytic trainer is aware that the very process of training will cause different levels of disturbance in the trainee, but generally the stance taken is that the trainee's personal therapy is the place for that disturbance, not the trainee group. This does not mean that individual difficulties are forbidden in the trainee group, but rather that the trainee group's main purpose is for learning to apply theory to practice within the theoretical and clinical seminars.

Some analytic trainings do include group therapy as an experiential component, but the leader will usually be an external member of the training organization, thus avoiding the merging of roles. Some analytic trainings do have training therapists for trainees, who are also members of the training committee, whilst others follow a policy of using training therapists who are not members of the training organization.

THE FORMAT

Each training is presented in a common format which is divided into eight parts and subdivided as necessary. The format has been arranged to cover as many aspects of the training as possible, including those which are not normally covered in a prospectus or brochure. Quotation marks signify something that has been said by one of the Training Committee interviewed.

1.   History
2.   Theoretical Orientation and Curriculum
3.   Training Structure
3.1 Training Committee
3.2 Selection Procedure and Admission
3.3 Time Commitment and Length of Training
3.4 Interruptions in Training
3.5 Postgraduate Qualification and Learned Society

METHODOLOGY

The methodology used to gather the information presented in nos 1–7 of the format has been to meet for over an hour with a member (or two) of the Training Committee of each organization. For no. 8 a separate meeting was held with two to five trainees, each representing different stages of the course. Every meeting was a structured, in-depth interview, based on the common format and recorded. In some cases the historical information has been provided separately by a founder member. Draft formats were prepared after the meetings, with the aid of the recordings, relevant handbooks and prospectuses. Each format was then sent to the trainer for comment and verification that the course was accurately represented. This applied also to the Trainees' Section as well as the Author's Comments, in order to avoid misrepresentation.

The intention throughout parts 1–8 of each format is to present the information as far as possible in the language adopted by the trainers and trainees, in order to convey the prevailing atmosphere and attitude. This may mean that occasionally something may seem confusing or unclear. It has been my decision to leave this, since every organization has agreed on the entry and in a few cases completely rewritten 1–7. The difference in length of each format and its component parts also reflects the individual meetings. The reader must bear in mind that the bulk of the meetings were made between the springs of 1990 and 1991, and certain changes in courses may occur.

The trainees were in almost every case chosen by the organization and for some organizations only two trainees were met. This means that parts 8.1 and 8.2 are limited. However, it seemed that despite this limitation, the general issues raised were pertinent to that particular training as well as psychotherapy trainings in general.

The Author's Comments speaks for itself. The attempt has been to summarize reflections and questions on each particular training: to open doors rather than close them.

There are key words and expressions, controversies and debates relating to each part of the format which are explained in more detail in the following pages.

1. HISTORY

This describes how the organization came into being, its aims and objectives and how they have developed to date. Some organizations have chosen to go into more detail than others.

2. THEORETICAL ORIENTATION AND CURRICULUM

This describes the philosophy, theory and practice of the psychotherapy taught. Out of all the trainings covered there seem to be very broadly five categories of attitude to theoretical orientations. It must be stressed that these broad categories are not intended as rigid labels but rather as a way of facilitating thought and reflection about what is being offered by the different trainings.

Focal – This is the training that chooses as its theoretical orientation psychoanalysis (Freud), analytical psychology (Jung) or a single humanistic therapy. It is a more orthodox approach. It must be remembered, though, that the psychoanalysis of the British Psycho-Analytical Society is made up of three groups: Kleinian, Contemporary Freudian and the Independent Group

(Object Relations Theorists), representing the development of the three psychoanalytical schools of thought. Analytical psychology as related to the Society of Analytical Psychology (SAP) also encompasses the development of Jungian theory since Jung (including some of the Object Relations Theorists of the British Psycho-Analytical Society). The 'Freud/Jung debate' in this book is shorthand and refers not only to the separateness of trainings in psychoanalysis and analytical psychology but also to the controversy about the two theories being taught on the same course.

In a focal training the trainee is usually encouraged to see a supervisor of the same orientation as the trainee's training therapist.

Eclectic – In the analytic trainings both Freudian and Jungian theory would be on the curriculum, and the same trainee group would be in therapy with therapists of different orientation. In the humanistic trainings a combination or blend of different humanistic (and in some cases analytic) therapies would be practised.

The eclectic training claims to bring together the best of many conflicting theories, creating a harmonious balance. In fact the 'best' is usually what is seen to be the best by the teachers of the particular training organization. In other words the eclectic trainings, although claiming to provide trainees with a wider choice, have their own particular bias.

In the mid-1980s in the pages of *Free Associations* (the journal of Free Association Books) a series of exchanges were made between Deryck Dyne (psychotherapist and one of the founders of AGIP and present day teachers) and Robert Hinshelwood (member of the British Psycho-Analytical Society [Kleinian group], on the Training Committee for the London Centre for Psychotherapy and editor of the *British Journal of Psychotherapy*). They are one set of exchanges illustrating the arguments for and against psychodynamic eclecticism.

Recently, the label 'eclectic' has come to have pejorative associations, particularly in the Analytical Section of the UKSCP.

This probably reflects the ongoing debates between the training organizations as to training requirements.

Pluralistic – The trainings that will teach the diversity of therapies separately and whose teachers will represent a theoretical orientation that adheres to one school.

The pluralistic training encourages the attitude that conflict of theory is uncomfortable but is tolerable in order to enrich the therapeutic attitude. Trainings that once referred to themselves as 'eclectic' are tending now to use the term 'pluralistic', which seems to have become fashionable recently and is a more positive label than 'eclectic'.

Philosophical – This training will emphasize the study of philosophy alongside one or many theoretical orientations.

Transcendent – Although these trainings may include many different theories in their curriculum, there is a strong emphasis on meditation and/or massage in the tradition of the Eastern religions. Synthesis and harmony of conflict is the therapeutic goal. 'Spiritual' and 'transpersonal' are key words in these trainings.

Infant Observation is often part of the requirement in some of the analytic trainings. The following is a description of what constitutes an Infant Observation.

One-hour observation of an infant once a week for the first year or two of life (the Child Psychotherapy trainings observe for two years). The trainee has met the mother before the birth of her infant, and the observation takes place in the family's home. Notes are then made of every observation. In addition there is a once weekly seminar of one and a half hours, where a group of trainees discuss their observations. The leader is a trained child psychotherapist or analyst. (Graduates of the Anna Freud Centre are known as Child Analysts.)

A theoretical seminar refers to a meeting where the focus is theory, although clinical examples may often be included. A clinical seminar will usually concentrate on the presentation of a patient/client in the context of the therapeutic relationship with reference to theory. Depending on the teacher and trainees, a theoretical seminar can become more of a clinical seminar and vice versa, because of their interrelationship.

3. TRAINING STRUCTURE

3.1 *Training Committee*

The group of people responsible for the training are usually known as the Training Committee, although a few organizations use a different title.

This part describes the training and background of the teachers and how the training is organized. Decision-making about training takes place in the Training Committee. Who is responsible for choosing members of this Committee? In the longer standing and more established trainings a democratic process is in place and members of the various committees are elected by the membership. The majority of training organizations, however, are oligarchies, where the membership of the Association have no vote and no channel to contribute to the decision-making.

3.2 *Selection procedure and admission*

Each organization has a specific entry procedure. Requirements, like age limit and academic qualifications, are made clear.

The number of places a year and the average number of applicants are also mentioned, to give some idea of the competition for places, and popularity of each course.

3.3 *Time commitment and length of training*

Not all trainings can provide an exact guide to how many hours a week must be available to train, because it depends which stage of the training a trainee has reached. However, in general, an estimated 15 going up to 25 hours per week is the sort of time commitment required. In some cases this may be less and in others more. The analytic trainings tend to demand more of a time commitment because of the frequency of personal therapy sessions, as well as the frequency of training cases.

3.4 *Interruptions in training*

Some trainings would not expect a trainee to take any time out, whilst others may encourage an interruption, when more personal therapy is seen to be needed. This happens more often in the humanistic trainings. Pregnancy is accommodated in all trainings.

3.5 *Postgraduate qualification and learned society*

An essential element in the newly qualified therapist's professional life is a place to share the demands of clinical work. What can qualified trainees expect from the organization with whom they have trained? Facilities, such as a library, are also mentioned here.

4. CLINICAL AND ACADEMIC REQUIREMENTS

4.1 *Personal therapy*

Individual therapy, as mentioned above, is an essential part of the course. For most of the analytic trainings a frequency of two to three times weekly is a requirement, and sometimes before starting the training. The personal therapy of the analytic trainee will usually last for years and, more often than not, beyond qualification. In the majority of cases this will be conducted with the same therapist. In the humanistic trainings the frequency is rarely more than once weekly and sometimes once a fortnight. A change of therapist also seems to occur far more frequently amongst the humanistic trainings and is seen as positive, whereas the analytic trainings would generally see it as disruptive and ill-advised except in special circumstances.

The personal therapy a trainee undergoes whilst training is often referred to, in the analytic literature, as a training analysis or therapy and the therapist referred to as the training therapist or analyst. This is not usually the case amongst the humanistic trainings.

A training therapist is usually an experienced practitioner. Organizations will have their own set of criteria for assessing the suitability of training therapists, as well as their own system of referring trainees. Where the criteria are not spelt out, this merely reflects that criteria for this particular organization have not been stipulated. Some trainings will contact the training therapist at specified stages of the training. Other organizations may see this as an interference of the therapeutic relationship and have a policy not to contact the training therapist.

There is a difference of opinion amongst the trainings as to whether or not members of the Training Committee should also be training therapists for trainees. This issue is linked with boundaries and confidentiality.

4.2 *Clinical requirements*

Depending on the applicant's previous experience some organizations will require their trainees to complete a psychiatric placement.

In the analytic tradition, most analytic therapists refer to providing 'treatment' for a 'patient'. In the humanistic tradition, humanistic therapists refer to seeing 'clients', thus avoiding medical terms. In order to qualify for any training, the trainee will have to have seen a certain number of patients/clients, or worked a specified number of clinical hours. In the analytic trainings the general rule is that the trainee must have seen at least two training patients for a required amount of time. In the humanistic trainings, it is more general that client hours is the criterion for qualifying.

'Medical cover' is required by some trainings. This means that a medical practitioner (usually the patient's GP) has agreed to liaise with the psychotherapist about the welfare of the patient if medical intervention is necessary. Many trainings (analytic and humanistic) do not see medical cover as a necessity. However, malpractice insurance is a necessity now for every trainee and practitioner.

4.3 *Supervision*

Supervision is seen by all trainings as a crucial aspect of training (see Fig. 2). This is where the trainee can explore the therapeutic relationship with the training patient/client with an experienced practitioner. What form the supervision takes, group or individual, will depend on the attitude adopted by each organization.

4.4 *Papers and written work*

Some trainings have a minimal requirement for written work, but there may still be a lot of writing throughout the course because of clinical presentations at seminars and written reports on training patients/clients. Some humanistic trainings have written examinations.

5. REFERRALS

This is very frequently an area of much concern and anxiety for trainees, because their future qualification depends on keeping patients/clients in therapy for a certain amount of time. The range of patients/clients referred is also of some importance. Most training organizations aim to provide their trainees with training patients/clients who are not as disturbed as a borderline or psychotic patient would be. Meanwhile, experienced practitioners acknowledge that it is very difficult to assess borderline conditions in a one-interview assessment. Beyond qualification therapists need good sources of referrals, depending on how large a practice is desired.

Many trainings also have a clinic or consultation service. In the humanistic trainings qualification depends on a specific number of hours the trainee has seen the client. It is not always important how many clients are seen and over what period. In the analytic trainings, qualification will usually depend on a stipulated length of time the trainee has seen the patient.

Most humanistic trainings will make a point of telling the client that they are seeing a trainee. Most analytic trainings, although not hiding the truth, do not see it as crucial to tell the patient about the therapist's trainee status, as they would see this as an interference of the therapeutic relationship.

6. COST OF TRAINING

Training is an expensive business and it is important for the trainee to gauge the extent of the cost throughout and beyond training. Training fees do not cover individual therapy and supervision.

In the majority of organizations, trainees are expected to see training patients/clients for a low fee. The newly qualified therapist will very often continue to see patients/clients for a low fee. Some organizations will have consulting rooms available for hire.

Occasionally there are bursaries or loans; the cost of training refers to 1991 fees.

7. FUTURE EXPECTATIONS/CAREER PROSPECTS

Most trainings will include seminars and workshops on setting up in practice, although not all trainees wish to set up in full-time private practice.

Teaching and supervision are areas that many therapists will work in after several years of experience. It is worth noting what opportunities are available in each organization.

8. TRAINEES' EXPERIENCE

8.1 *Why this course was chosen*

These were amongst the questions asked of trainees.

Why did you choose psychotherapy, and how did you hear of this course? (In every case trainees had come to therapy through their own suffering.)

What were the aspects of this training that most attracted you?

What was your experience of the selection procedure?

Before the start of the course, how informed did you feel about each stage of the training?

8.2 *The atmosphere of the course*

How do you feel about the way in which information is communicated?

What do you find the most confusing aspect of the training?

How much opportunity do you have to share thoughts and feelings with fellow trainees?

What do you feel about the methods of teaching?

Has the course met your expectations?

How do you feel about your future with the organization?

Bear in mind that in every case, except one, the organization has chosen the trainees. It is worth noting how positive or negative the trainees' answers seem to be. The ability to criticize can be a sign of a healthy organization; on the other hand very negative or very positive feedback may indicate the trainees' transference towards their training organization (parents). Are they able to criticize the training or are they obliged to gloss over difficulties?

AUTHOR'S COMMENTS

The aim here is to outline the debates in order to evoke as much thought as possible about the choice of training. Each organization has had sight of this part, in order to avoid misrepresentation.

As mentioned in the Preface, the attempt throughout the book, and especially here, is to present a non-partisan point of view, but I am aware that my own opinions are bound to influence what I have written as it is not possible to be wholly objective.

Analytical Psychotherapy Section

ARBOURS ASSOCIATION

6 Church Lane, London N8; tel: 081 340 7646.

1. History

Arbours Association was set up in 1970 by Dr Joseph Berke and Dr Morton Schatzman, who had been two of the original members working with Dr R.D. Laing in Kingsley Hall between 1965 and 1968. During this time Joseph Berke worked intensively with one of the residents of Kingsley Hall – Mary Barnes. Their account of the experience of this therapeutic relationship was published originally in 1971. It was subsequently made into a play and performed at the Royal Court theatre in 1979. In 1977 Joseph Berke published a collection of papers about his work with people coming to live at the Arbours Crisis Centre, originally entitled *The Butterfly Man* (and later on entitled *I Haven't Had To Go Mad Here*). Soon to be published by Free Association Books is the most recent account of the work of Arbours Association.

In a paper entitled 'The butterfly man' Joseph Berke describes why he used the name 'Arbours'.

The temporary dwelling places where the Israelites lived in the wilderness after the exodus from Egypt were called 'Arbours' – places of shade or shelter. Arbours communities aim to provide shelter and safe anchorage for people who have been buffeted by internal turbulence or external disturbance whether in fantasy or in actuality.

The aim was to provide both in- and out-patients with psychotherapeutic help as an alternative to psychiatric hospital.

The Arbours Association is a registered charity and presently there are three long-term communities (housing between six and eight people), a Crisis Centre, a Consultation Service and a Training Programme. The development of the Training Programme was instigated by Drs Schatzman and Berke holding informal meetings for people living and working in Arbours, to share ideas and experiences. Gregorio Kohon formalized these meetings, which became more like the clinical seminars of today. Some time after he left in 1974, Andrea Sabbadini (the first Director of the Training Committee) took over as co-ordinator of the various training activities. By 1976 a Training Committee had been formed, made up of people already involved with Arbours, and one external member, Dr Nina Coltart, a training analyst with the Institute of Psycho-Analysis, and member of the British Psycho-Analytical Society in the Independent Group. Thus the training programme evolved out of work in the communities, and it is this component which is the cornerstone of the Arbours training.

2. THEORETICAL ORIENTATION AND CURRICULUM

Trainees are primarily trained to work with individuals in long-term psychoanalytic psychotherapy and the bulk of the study is the theory and practice of psychoanalysis. However, it has to be added that the training hopes to provide enough experience and theoretical background for people to develop in other areas beyond training, such as crisis intervention, group work, family and marital therapy.

The first year concentrates on Freud, Klein and the British School of Object Relations as an introduction to the development of psychoanalysis from the very beginnings: Freud and Breuer. Also covered in the first year are: Introduction to Psychopathology, Child Development and Group Dynamics. Infant Observation is optional and not a requirement of the course. However, it is encouraged.

The second and third years are a consolidation of this

introduction and study of present day developments. The second year consists of Dreams and Their Meanings, Sexuality, Introduction to Couple and Family Therapy, Introduction to C.G. Jung, Techniques of Psychotherapy, Crisis Intervention, Women and Psychotherapy, Freud Reading, Eating Problems, Comparison of Different Clinical Practices and Adolescence.

The third year consists of Transference and Countertransference, Starting To See Patients, Psychosomatic Disorders, What Might Happen In a Session, Borderline Pathology, Group Supervision, Psychoanalysts At Work.

The humanistic therapies are not part of the curriculum, but if trainees have a particular interest, the Training Committee endeavour to be as flexible as possible and do arrange special seminars. For instance recently a series of workshops was arranged on Art Therapy.

Trainees meet in their year group once a term with two members of the Training Committee. This may be used as a forum to discuss and air any difficulties that may arise during the course.

3. TRAINING STRUCTURE

3.1 *Training Committee*

The Training Programme is organized by the Director and eight senior Arbours Therapists. Their training is with Arbours, the Institute of Group Analysis and the Institute of Psycho-Analysis. There is also one external member, as already mentioned, but no student representative. However, the Training Committee at this time are in the process of setting up a meeting with a student representative once a year. The Training Committee is self-regulated but the purpose of an external member is to monitor regulation. Meetings are eight times a year to discuss admissions, student progress and curriculum.

3.2 *Selection procedure and admission*

After formal application a prospective student is interviewed by the Director, and the second interview is on rotation with members of the Training Committee. Once accepted, all trainees must complete an Associate year before entering the Full Programme. The Associate Programme is also open to people who do not want to train, but are interested in the work of Arbours. Clinical experience and academic qualifications are not a prerequisite of joining the Training Programme, although both are an advantage.

All members are assigned a personal tutor (a member of the Training Committee) and application to join the Full Programme is through the personal tutor. Trainees are assessed on personal maturity, motivation, academic competence, but Arbours has no policy on the age of an applicant. The names of two referees are required.

If a training has been started elsewhere and never completed, in some cases trainees may enter the third year straight away. This would be only where an individual can satisfactorily demonstrate their experience of working with emotionally distressed people, and has gained a substantial theoretical basis. This rarely occurs, but the Training Committee are always prepared to consider an individual case. Not more than ten students are accepted each year and there is no policy of ensuring 50 per cent male and 50 per cent female. Arbours adheres to an equal opportunities policy and actively encourages all people to apply, regardless of race, disability, religion or sexual orientation. The general background of people applying is social work, psychology and teaching as well as the Arts.

3.3 Time commitment and length of training

Associates see a personal tutor by arrangement, attend fortnightly clinical seminars, two or three termly lectures and are invited to 'network' meetings of the Arbours communities once a month. In addition to this, Full Trainees must attend two evening theoretical seminars per week.

The course is designed to accommodate people who work full-time, for the duration of the training. The placements (see 4.2) can be fitted in at the convenience of the trainee with a requirement of two house meetings a week in the therapeutic community. Consequently for two or three terms, four evenings may be taken up for a trainee on the Full Programme who is also on placement. Seminar preparation time also has to be taken into account. Trainees present their own work, usually on their experience of the placement, which has to be written up, at clinical seminars. At least one paper is expected to be read in preparation for the theoretical seminars. Qualification takes between four and six years.

3.4 *Interruptions in training*

Arbours' policy is to accommodate interruptions at any stage of a training due to any life event, such as bereavement or pregnancy. The period of interruption would very much depend on each individual trainee and their circumstances.

3.5 *Postgraduate qualification and learned society*

Qualification automatically entitles you to become a member of the Association of Arbours Psychotherapists (AAP). Membership fee is £55, which pays for *The Arbours Journal* (sharing theoretical and clinical work and issued once a year) and *The British Journal of Psychotherapy*.

The Association meets once a month to discuss clinical work (members' papers) and business. To date there are about forty members. This is a developing group in its own right and May 1990 witnessed the first conference, which will now take place annually. As a result of the 1991 Conference the following working parties were set up: Ethics and Code of Conduct, Postgraduate Training and Quarter Way House. (The latter refers to the possibility of setting up a house for people leaving the communities or Crisis Centre.) The AAP has a Code of Ethics which is currently being reviewed and developed.

Arbours owns 6 Church Lane, which houses the administration office, as well as a student room, a seminar room and consultation rooms for hire. A library is being planned.

People may apply for membership from trainings other than Arbours, although involvement in the Crisis Centre or communities is essential.

4. Clinical and Academic Requirements

4.1 *Personal therapy*

All trainees are assessed and referred by their tutor. The Training Committee have compiled a list of suitable people as training therapists and supervisors for new trainees. Associates must be in therapy at least once weekly and full trainees at least three times weekly up to qualification. Some people choose full, five times weekly analysis. Most people are expected to continue beyond qualification, but are not required to do so.

The criteria for training therapists are as follows:

(a) an analytic or psychodynamic orientation;

(b) a minimum of five years' post-qualification experience;

(c) some knowledge and understanding of the work of Arbours and the training, in terms of requirements.

It is the Training Committee's policy that trainees must be in therapy with a therapist or analyst who is not a member of the Training Committee. It is Arbours' policy not to consult the therapist of the trainee, unless there is serious cause for concern.

4.2 *Clinical requirements*

All trainees must complete the Associate year before continuing. However, placements can be started during this Associate year. Before seeing a training patient, trainees must spend a minimum of six months in one of the long-stay non-staffed communities as a student-on-placement, as well as a six-month placement in the Crisis Centre. For the community placement, it is preferred that the trainee be resident, but this placement can be completed non-residentially for people with family commitments. On satisfactory completion of these placements, a trainee is ready to see a first training patient. This would not be before the start of the third year. There is great emphasis on the placements, as they are an integral part of the training. Working with people in emotional distress under regular supervision is seen as an essential way of learning about psychotherapy.

For qualification, the first training patient must be seen a minimum of twice a week for one year, as well as a second training patient for at least six months. The second training patient can be seen two or three months after starting with the first, if all is going well and in consultation with the personal tutor.

The issue of medical cover is one still in debate within the Training Committee, but all trainees must send a letter to patients' GPs as a professional courtesy.

4.3 *Supervision*

A trainee is in supervision with one of the house co-ordinators of the community (there are three communities and six co-ordinators) for the duration of the placement.

At the Crisis Centre, each patient is known as a guest, following the principle that the resident therapists live in the house and invite guests to stay for a set period of time. Each guest will work with a team of two or three -- the Team Leader (an Arbours therapist, non-residential), the Resident Therapist and a student-on-placement. Supervision for each trainee working in a team is arranged weekly with the Team Leader throughout the placement. The trainee must choose a supervisor from the Training Committee for the first training patient, and each trainee is required to be in supervision once a week to discuss this one patient for the minimum of a year. The second supervisor can be chosen from outside the Training Committee, but with their approval. There is group supervision in the third year.

4.4 *Papers and written work*

At least three papers are to be written, of between 5,000 and 7,000 words. These papers are usually on the time spent in one of the communities and the Crisis Centre and presented at the fortnightly clinical seminars.

One paper on the case study of the first training patient is presented at the Final Case Presentation, which is the reading-in paper for qualification. The reading-in paper does not automatically entitle a trainee to qualification. The presentation of the paper has to be discussed in a Training Committee meeting before qualification is approved.

5. REFERRALS

Training patients must be referred to trainees by a Training Committee member, usually via the Arbours Consultation Service. After starting with two training patients, trainees may accept referrals from other agencies, and further referrals may come through the Consultation Service. The Consultation Service is under the impression that there is a wide range of patients seeking consultation, the majority being suitable for psychotherapy. Arbours has no policy of telling patients they will be seeing a trainee, unless asked.

6. COST OF TRAINING

Currently the Associate Programme is £175 per term, and the Full Programme £400 (1992), reviewed biannually, which covers all aspects of the training including supervision of the placements. However, on top of this expense is personal therapy and supervision for each training patient. Therapy and supervision sessions cost between £15 and £30 per session. The Full Programme takes three years and if a trainee has not qualified by then, the fees are currently reduced to £130. The most expensive year is the final year when two supervisors, as well as personal therapy, have to be paid for.

All trainees may charge training patients between £3 and £8 a session and the fee is payable to the trainee. With referrals from the Consultation Service the limit of £8 must be adhered to, until qualification. It is generally expected that newly qualified therapists see people for a low fee. Arbours has consulting rooms for trainees at £2.50 a session.

Arbours can offer two bursaries a year to cover training fees, but not personal therapy. There are no loans available.

7. FUTURE EXPECTATIONS/CAREER PROSPECTS

During the training, trainees will get practical advice on setting up in practice. However, there can never be a real forecast of the number of referrals likely. In other words, it is not always possible to guarantee a set regular income for some time after qualification. There are limited prospects of work at the Crisis Centre and teaching or supervision. Arbours as an organization is currently addressing this issue, with plans in the pipeline.

8. Trainees' Experience

8.1 *Why this course was chosen*

Some people applying had not had clinical experience and were interested in the Arbours placements, as a way of understanding other ways of treating people in emotional distress, both acute and chronic. It was also felt that the Arbours approach to people coming from an Arts or Science background with no experience in the 'helping professions' was more flexible than other trainings.

The selection procedure was experienced as really taking place during the obligatory Associate year. Trainees found this a useful way of being introduced to the work of Arbours as well as the atmosphere of the training programme.

8.2 *The atmosphere of the course*

All agreed that the experience of the placements was invaluable even though confusing and anxiety-provoking at times. With a demanding full-time job, however, placements would be difficult to fit in and one trainee felt that this had not been spelt out enough before starting the Full Programme.

There had been some cases of inconsistency in answers from different tutors, which had tended to undermine trust in the Training Committee. This seemed to link with a general feeling that there was a lack of communication between trainees and the Training Committee and a lack of policy over certain issues. However, all trainees agreed that the system of meeting with designated members of the Training Committee once a month as well as having a personal tutor meant that there were opportunities to air difficulties and make complaints. The general feeling was that changes were often made in response to trainees' difficulties. This was felt to be the biggest advantage in having a personal tutor – that conflicts and complaints could always be talked about, as well as the anxieties that go with training.

In general people were happy with the curriculum and were pleased that the Training Committee had tried to adapt certain seminars to the requests of the group. The quality of teaching was felt to be excellent and thoroughly monitored by the Training Committee. Trainees acknowledged the Training Committee's concern for teachers who were experienced and knew thoroughly the subject being taught. It was felt to be difficult to complain or make criticism of an Arbours teacher, however.

Most seminars took place at Church Lane, where there was also a student room for people to study or meet for coffee, etc., and this was welcomed. The general attitude was experienced as very much a psychoanalytic approach to working with people in the communities, Crisis Centre and consulting room, well rooted in each trainee's personal analysis and understanding of their own unconscious. It was felt to be a thorough course academically and emotionally very supportive, particularly during the placements.

In conclusion all agreed there should be a student representative on the Training Committee, which would be one way of addressing the feeling of a lack of communication. Despite the demands, in terms of time and finance, trainees felt that by the time the placements were achieved they were well prepared for the most difficult patient in their consulting room. Working with disturbed people outside the confines of psychiatric hospital was more intense and more anxiety-provoking, but invaluable in relation to personal therapy and understanding of the meaning of madness.

AUTHOR'S COMMENTS

Arbours as an organization may retain some of its anti-psychiatry image. This is inevitably linked with the pioneering work of Dr Joseph Berke, who is the Director of the Crisis Centre, an active member of the Training Committee and the Association of Arbours Psychotherapists. Dr Berke's published works may and often do attract people to working and training with Arbours. Anti-psychiatry ethos has developed and changed, and the Arbours way of working in its communities and Crisis Centre is no exception. The environment offered to residents of the communities and guests of the Crisis Centre would probably more accurately be described as an alternative to the psychiatric hospital. This training, with its built-in placements, offers the opportunity for trainees to experience an Arbours way of providing a therapeutic environment, away from the atmosphere of hospital, for acutely and chronically ill people, and it is this aspect of the training which makes it unique. Trainees clearly appreciated this.

Meanwhile, the main theoretical orientation is psychoanalysis; the majority of training therapists and some teachers are psychoanalysts and members of the British Psycho-Analytical Society. Andrea Sabbadini was the Director of the Training Committee for many years, and is a Full Member of the British Psycho-Analytical Society. From spring 1992 Alexandra Fanning is taking over as Director of the Training Committee. The theoretical stance of the Training Comittee is predominantly psychoanalytic; this has greatly influenced the orientation of the training, which does not include Jungian theory (other than introductory seminars). Most members of the Training Committee have a long-standing professional association with the Women's Therapy Centre.

Marie-Christine Réguis won the first prize for the first Student Essay Competition of the *British Journal of Psychotherapy*, with her paper 'A tale of two chairs', and she is presently Chair of the Association of Arbours Psychotherapists (Réguis, 1988).

Relevant questions and reflections about this training would be associated with historic and present day tensions between psychoanalysis, psychotherapy and psychiatry.

ASSOCIATION FOR GROUP AND
INDIVIDUAL PSYCHOTHERAPY (AGIP)

1 Fairbridge Road, London N19 3EW; tel: 071 272 7013.

1. HISTORY

The institutional roots of AGIP reach back to the Association of
Psychotherapists (founded in 1951, later to become the British
Association of Psychotherapists). More generally, however, they lie
in the ferment that was stimulated by discontent with the limited
number and form of analytic trainings and by a wave of newer –
often group – therapies arriving mainly from the United States.
Penelope Lady Balogh, a founder member and member of the
Council of the Association of Psychotherapists, became interested
in what these 'new therapies' could offer traditional models. She
withdrew from the Association and, with colleagues, worked to set
up a training envisaged as both thorough and adventurous.

So, although AGIP could be seen as an 'off-shoot' of the
Association of Psychotherapists, it actually evolved from the work
and experience of a network of psychotherapists, over several
years, on fundamental training issues. They envisaged a training that
was to be psychoanalytic but also to employ other approaches
inside the psychoanalytic framework. Underlying their philosophy
was the belief that experienced psychotherapists integrate different
orientations in their practice, as they mature, and that this implicit
notion of a personal synthesis could be developed into an explicit
principle of training. As such, it could use different approaches,
including both analytic and active groupwork, to highlight and
sharpen the nature and understanding of psychoanalytic thinking.
It could also enable students to 'become the therapists in
themselves' and help them to refine their work, both conceptually
and practically. In this way it could benefit not only the patient and
the psychotherapists, but also the field as a whole, which needed
more public, common values and means of development.

In addition to the above founding principles, there were more
specific concerns, which referred to the professional climate of the

time, but remain relevant today. These concerns included the wish to break away from the dichotomies that were the foci of so many theoretical discussions of the time, in which one school denigrated another; the decision to create a training that did not segregate different analytic orientations (when AGIP was founded it was innovative to include Freud and Jung in the same course); and the commitment to exploring the differences, similarities and complementarities between individual and group psychotherapy. A constitution was approved in 1974, establishing AGIP as part of the Penelope Lady Balogh Psychotherapy Trust.

The idea of personal synthesis, the use of groupwork in an individual training, the critical bringing together of different theoretical and clinical approaches and a non-sectarian attitude, have remained at the heart of AGIP's work. All are located within the psychoanalytic tradition, with Freud, Klein, Jung and Object Relations theorists at its core.

2. THEORETICAL ORIENTATION AND CURRICULUM

The aim of the training is to prepare students to work autonomously as individual psychotherapists. There is also an opportunity, post-qualification, to supplement the training with a postgraduate group training. The theoretical orientation is psychoanalytic and encompasses Freudian, Kleinian, Jungian and Object Relations schools.

The Training Programme comprises a three-year basic course, mandatory postgraduate modules, supervised clinical work and a final paper. Satisfactory completion of these requirements leads to Associate Membership, currently the principal membership category. The curriculum for the basic three-year course is as follows:

Year One: Introduction to Psychotherapy, Freud, Groddeck, Klein, Jung, Metaphor of the Year.

This year concentrates on a grounding in psychoanalytic theory and on the attitude of the psychotherapist towards theory and practice (see History). It includes, as do years two and three, experientially orientated workshop/group settings, as well as an analytic group (see below).

Year Two: The Fairy Tale (an exercise, based on a major essay and seminar work, in applying Freudian, Kleinian and Jungian theory – see 4.4), Object Relations, Transference and Counter-transference, Clinical Work, Symptoms and Diagnosis, Working Classically, Narcissism, Personality Types, Preparation for Working with Patients.

This year concentrates on clinical work and on developing a critical, comparative attitude towards theory. It also includes seminars on setting up in practice and on ethics of practice.

Year Three: Psyche–Soma, Metaphor, Working Situation, Synthesis, Groups and Institutions, Conceptualizing Clinical Work.

The format of this year emphasizes fundamental evaluation of theory and practice. The teaching setting includes several all-evening seminars, in which there is sufficient time to explore themes in depth, building upon the clinical experience of trainees as well as on texts. A range of specific issues is covered, such as transference, countertransference, methodology, per-version, objectivity, unconscious dynamics in peer relations, the nature of the psychotherapy setting and its boundaries, as well as a continual review of basic psychoanalytic theory. The attitude conveyed by the term 'synthesis' (see History) is strengthened through the series on 'metaphor', which explores theory ('metapsychology') as metaphor that can be found in other fields, including literature. The series 'synthesis' continues in this comparative and pluralistic mode, but stresses the 'perversions' of the psychotherapeutic attitude and of objectivity. Both series rely heavily on student input and both review and deepen basic theory. The exploration of these themes is grounded in clinical material, as well as in the experiences of trainees and in texts.

Throughout these three years, there is an ongoing closed analytic group held once weekly, as well as all-day groups held about six times a year. The all-day groups provide a place for meeting as peers in intensive, expressive situations and for supplementing theoreti-cal study with experience-based teaching. They complement the analytic group and psychoanalytic theory, thereby providing both material for the analytic group and a place from which to examine psychoanalytic thinking. Both groups provide an important experience of undercutting intellectualization. AGIP is fully aware of the value of non-participant observation, including Infant Observation, as an important element in the training of a psychotherapist, and for a time it was an obligatory part of the course. There has been much discussion about the inclusion of observation, and the present policy is to offer it as an option, post-basic course. Some applicants have already carried one out and trainees without this experience are encouraged to obtain it. Shorter periods of observation are required for parts of the course.

After successfully completing the basic course, trainees must also complete three ten-session modules within the postgraduate programme:

(a)   psychotherapy assessment;

(b)   an in-depth seminar series on Freud, Klein or Jung;

(c)   an option, approved by the Training Committee.

They must also complete their supervised clinical requirements and a major paper, which is assessed by two readers and is read in open seminar.

There are many channels for trainees to air difficulties that may arise. Each trainee has a personal tutor throughout the training. There is a Year Tutor for the first year and a Senior Tutor to co-ordinate the work of the tutors. In addition, the Director and Co-ordinator of Training offer a year-group meeting each term if so desired by the group.

3. TRAINING STRUCTURE

3.1 *Training Committee*

Council holds the ultimate authority in AGIP, and all committees, including the Training Committee, are subcommittees of Council. The minimum number of Council members is constitutionally twelve, some of whom, including the Co-ordinator of Training, are ex officio members, whilst others are elected. The Co-ordinator of

Training is elected for three years. The Training Committee are currently mostly, but not exclusively, members of AGIP. The committee may co-opt extra members who can best contribute to its running. The training background of most members of Council and the Training Committee is AGIP. Other training backgrounds include the Institute of Psycho-Analysis and the Institute of Group Analysis. Meetings of the Training Committee are held once monthly. Matters for discussion centre on the selection and monitoring of trainees, curriculum and policy.

3.2 *Selection procedure and admission*

Applicants must be at least twenty-eight years old. Previous qualifications, education, experience and training, particularly in allied fields, are taken into consideration, but AGIP looks primarily for evidence of personal and professional qualities that make for a reliable and effective psychotherapist. There is an application form to be submitted and two referees are required. If selected for interview each trainee will have two individual interviews, one with a male psychotherapist and another with a female. These are followed by a large-group and a small-group session.

The cornerstone of the selection process is the meeting of interviewers who, over the years, have shared the experience of selecting trainees and seeing them through to qualification. A procedure has therefore developed from psychotherapists evaluating qualities that are important in choosing a suitable applicant. The following guidelines are amongst the conclusions that have evolved.

The interviewer will look for qualities such as the capacity for insight, self-examination, honesty, readiness to respond and an enquiring mind. These qualities might be summarized as 'psychological mindedness', which would show the ability for affective and intellectual processing. The interviewer will also look for evidence of perseverance, discipline and the capacity for intellectual grasp. The capacity to form sound relationships, which would be apparent in the applicant's personal history, but also in the immediate capacity to relate to the interviewer, is important. The interviewer will take into account his or her own general response to the applicant with respect to anxiety, defensiveness, the capacity for warmth and indications of an inner security. A personal therapeutic history might suggest a capacity to deal with problem areas. A financial sense of reality is important: not just whether or not the trainee can pay for the course, but whether or not the reality of commitment has been grasped, both now and for his/her future professional life. Finally the interviewer will look for an intrinsic interest in self-development as opposed to a wish to become a psychotherapist as a career choice.

It is not possible to join this training from another training because of the analytic group component of the course and because of the integrated nature of the curriculum. The general background of people applying tends to be quite diverse. People come from the 'core professions', the clergy and teaching, and to a lesser extent from a variety of other backgrounds. There is an effort to balance numbers of men and women in the training groups.

3.3 *Time commitment and length of training*

The following is extracted from AGIP's brochure:

(a) seminars and analytic groups: two evenings per week, comprising 3 to 4 sessions of approximately 1 hour 20 minutes each, for three 10 week terms over three years;

(b) day groups: normally two all-day groups per term, starting in the second term of the first year, for three years;

(c) personal psychotherapy: at least two sessions per week throughout the year, until Associate Membership (at least 5 years);

(d) training patients: at least two patients at a minimum of twice weekly; thus four hours plus time writing up the sessions, plus any additional caseload;

(e) supervision: one weekly individual supervision and one weekly group supervision for at least two years, starting before the first training patient is seen;

(f) observation: some units require observation in a prescribed setting, probably about 10 hours plus writing-up during the course (observational studies are under review);

(g) private study and essays: allow about five hours' study time per week for the basic course plus time for essays.

The personal tutor is seen twice per term during the basic course, and then a minimum of twice per year until Associate Membership. It takes three years to complete the basic course. Depending on a trainee's work with training patients, the postgraduate requirements and the final essay, it could take another two to four years to qualify.

3.4 Interruptions in training

Interruptions are difficult to accommodate because of the analytic group. However, there are exceptions and each case is dealt with individually.

3.5 Postgraduate qualification and learned society

The following is a list of the categories of AGIP membership:

Student Member – students on the basic course

Training Member – students who have successfully completed the basic course and are working towards qualification (fee of £60 per annum)

Associate Member – psychotherapists qualified as independent psychotherapists through AGIP's training (fee of £100 per annum)

Full Member – psychotherapists qualified through AGIP who have substantial clinical experience and have successfully read in a major clinical or theoretical paper (fee of £120)

There are also special categories of membership (Affiliate, Honorary) not based on the AGIP training. People from other trainings may apply to become Affiliate Members of AGIP. Honorary Members must be invited. There are weekly professional meetings open to all postgraduate members. In addition, there is a variety of seminars, conferences and study days which can be internal or open to the public.

AGIP has its headquarters in a large house which contains a library, seminar and group rooms, and consulting rooms. There is a regular newsletter.

AGIP has a Code of Ethics, including a complaints and disciplinary procedure.

4. Clinical and Academic Requirements

4.1 *Personal therapy*

Trainees must be in psychoanalytic psychotherapy for a year before starting the course. Referrals can be made through AGIP's Clinical Committee if so desired. AGIP holds that the training therapy is a personal issue, and wishes to give trainees and their psychotherapists maximum clinical freedom. The guidelines are that a trainee must not drop below twice weekly and it is expected that trainees will work at a greater frequency during much of their training.

The Training Committee consult the training therapists only to seek agreement on a trainee's taking the first training patient. If there is serious cause for concern a further consultation may be made, after informing the trainee. The criteria for training therapists are that they have trained at a training establishment recognized by AGIP, and that they have been established as independent (qualified) psychotherapists for at least five years.

4.2 *Clinical requirements*

Training patients cannot be seen before the second year of the basic course. The minimum requirement is that the first training patient be seen for two years and continuing, and the second eighteen months, both at a minimum of twice weekly. AGIP stresses, however, that training members must also demonstrate that they have a varied caseload before applying for qualification.

Medical cover should be assured in appropriate cases. It is part of an essential ethical attitude towards patients that AGIP encourages trainees to build a network of medical back-up for

patients who may need that provision. If a patient has a psychiatric
history or is under medication or regular medical care it is suggested
that the psychotherapist write to the GP.

4.3 *Supervision*

There must be individual supervision for the first training patient
and group supervision for the second training patient. The
individual supervisor also acts as an adviser to the trainee and to
AGIP on matters such as caseload and the suitability of a referral.

4.4 *Papers and written work*

There are three major essays. The first, submitted at the beginning
of the second year, compares Freud, Klein and Jung through their
application to a fairy tale, myth, legend, or other material of
sufficient depth for such an analysis. The second, submitted at the
beginning of the third year, examines in depth a theoretical concept
from the second year's work. The third, submitted as part of the
qualification for Associate Membership, treats a topic, agreed with
the student's tutor, in depth, as a final paper. In addition, students
are asked to write essays on particular topics from the course, for
example, essays on Freud and on Object Relations; to present
overviews of themes to seminar groups, and to report reflectively
to these groups on their work, both to sharpen their own
understanding of topics discussed and to aid the group's sense of
what it has accomplished.

5. REFERRALS

AGIP comprises, in addition to the basic training course and
postgraduate programme, an active Clinical Centre, which has
access to a large referral network of both AGIP and outside
psychotherapists. Most training patients are referred through this
Centre, and all trainee referrals are screened by the Clinical
Committee for general suitability as training patients before the
individual supervisor's advice is sought on the appropriateness of
the particular referral in question. In the case of referrals from the

Clinical Centre assessments are done by an experienced psycho-therapist who is also a member of the Clinical Committee. Occasionally, for trainees living outside London, a training patient may be referred from their place of work. In these cases the Clinical Committee must agree to the proposal of an assessor and screen the referral. Qualities that would not be appropriate for a first training patient are: psychotic tendencies, extreme acting out, marked perversion, too negative an attitude.

Training patients are not told they are seeing a trainee. As with all referrals, arrangements are made privately between the psychotherapist and the prospective patient.

6. Cost of Training

The fee of £850 for the first year (rising for the second and third years) covers all aspects of the training except therapy and supervision. The most expensive period of the training would be the third year when two sets of supervision fees are being paid. Fees from training patients go directly to the trainee. There is no set charge, although trainees often see training patients for a low fee. Consulting rooms are available at AGIP at a reduced fee for trainees.

There is a small fund to help trainees if they were to find themselves in financial difficulties.

7. Future Expectations/Career Prospects

There is a series of seminars on the practicalities of setting up in practice. There are also seminars on the issues concerning ethics. There are prospects of teaching and seminar leading, though these opportunities would normally be offered after gaining Associate Membership.

AGIP psychotherapists are employed in a variety of public-sector positions, as well as in private practice. Additionally, experienced psychotherapists may become training therapists or supervisors to trainees in AGIP and in other organizations.

8. TRAINEES' EXPERIENCE

8.1 *Why this course was chosen*

There were many aspects of AGIP's training which attracted
trainees:

1. the inclusion of Freudian, Kleinian, Jungian and Object
   Relations theory;

2. the provision of an analytic training group and experiential
   day groups, which were both supportive and teaching, for
   the duration of the basic course;

3. emphasis on and time spent in bringing different models
   together for comparison, contrast and synthesis;

4. the concern for trainees from different backgrounds shown
   in the 'value for money' level of fees.

Trainees experienced the selection procedure as thorough. This
began with a written application form on which applicants were
asked to answer various questions concerned with their wish to
train as psychotherapists. There were mixed responses to the two
individual interviews; some were experienced as helpful and
supportive and others as quite difficult and demanding. The group
interview was experienced as quite a pressure, with the sense of
being watched throughout. All agreed it was tense and demanding,
but nobody could see how else it could have been conducted.
Trainees realized the group interview was an essential part of the
selection procedure because of the group component of the course.

Most trainees felt they were as informed as they could be before
starting the training. There was some discussion about the amount
and timing of information during the course, and an awareness that
AGIP tried to achieve a balance between providing sufficient
information for clarity, but not overwhelming or confusing trainees.

8.2 *The atmosphere of the course*

Trainees expected this training to be hard work and so were not
surprised by the sheer density of the theory covered in the first
year – Freud, Klein and Jung – and how heavy going it was. Both the

first and second years were intense learning years. The third year allowed much more time for discussion of theoretical ideas, and clinical and personal experience to facilitate reaching a sufficient depth of analysis, comparison and synthesis.

Some teachers were seen to be more inspiring than others, but mostly trainees felt happy about the level, quality and different styles of teaching from AGIP staff and visiting tutors. The day group and analytic group settings were places where very intense feelings were aroused. However, trainees felt little doubt that the experience of these different sorts of groups aided each individual's process – that they were useful in really addressing the whole person. These groups also served to bridge the gap between the dense theoretical material and the emotional processing of it. The trainees felt that the groups had an added advantage of allowing the issues that arose between students on a training course to be addressed and processed. People felt that they got to know each other – the group context was a place where the struggle of integrating personal process was shared by every member. As far as was possible in a training, trainees felt that AGIP did not infantilize trainees, but expected and allowed them to take responsibility for a wide range of matters. In general, trainees felt that AGIP's course more than met their expectations and there was a very positive sense that the training was enriching. Trainees particularly valued the forum for discussion of a range of theories, and the opportunity to explore the unfolding of thoughts and feelings in a creative way.

Concern was expressed by trainees at the importance of locating AGIP squarely in the psychoanalytic psychotherapy community. Trainees felt that there were many very inspiring members of AGIP who were involved in research, publication and issues relating to the future of the profession. Because of the controversy in the field about more theoretically uniform orientations, students were concerned that AGIP's rightful place in the work of psychoanalytic psychotherapy be publicly sustained.

AUTHOR'S COMMENTS

AGIP's historical roots derive from the Assocation of Psychotherapists (see Scarlett, 1991). The analytic core of AGIP's theoretical orientation (Freud, Klein, Object Relations and Jung) relates to the debate concerning the compatibility of these schools of thought, and the difference between eclectic and pluralistic psychotherapy training (see Part One and the Introduction to Part Two). Recently, tensions in the analytic psychotherapy world have arisen, regarding the meaning of the label eclectic (see Dyne, 1985; Hinshelwood, 1985, 1986). This training does not define itself as eclectic, although the debate concerning the issues of eclecticism and pluralism in training psychotherapists is relevant to it.

AGIP is the only analytic training that puts such an emphasis on the group process, with the inclusion of an analytic group as well as the all-day groups, ongoing throughout the basic course. The function of the groups is aimed at the trainees' self-development. AGIP's stance is that the groups are 'part of, or essential to, training in individual psychotherapy', whilst being clear that they are not a training in group therapy. There are many trainings which do not see that self-development in the group setting, humanistic or analytic, is a necessary component of an individual psychotherapy training. Meanwhile, there are other trainings (all the humanistic trainings presented in this book) that see the trainee's emotional growth in the group setting as an essential complement to individual therapy. Trainees had a mixed response to the all-day groups (which AGIP makes clear are not humanistic therapy groups, but experiential non-analytic groups 'for meeting peers in intensive, expressive situations'). Some found them useful because 'unresolved stirred up emotions spilled over into the analytic group': others did not find them so useful and had chosen AGIP for its analytic core. AGIP has been and continues to be very active in its participation at the UKSCP.

BRITISH ASSOCIATION OF PSYCHOTHERAPISTS (BAP)

37 Mapesbury Road, London NW2; tel: 081 452 9823.

1. HISTORY

The Freudian and Jungian trainings

The following account is a brief summary of a history of the BAP written by one of the long-standing members, Elspeth Morley, in 1988. Quotation marks signify paragraphs taken directly from that account and it must be stated that this is one member's point of view.

'In 1951 a small group of Freudian and Jungian psychotherapists met together to form the Association of Psychotherapists [see Part One]. At that time the only trainings in existence were The British Psycho-Analytical Society and The Society of Analytical Psychology. Founder members of the Association of Psychotherapists were not members of the two main trainings and many had trained abroad.'

Meetings would take place in the homes of the members, with the aims and hopes of 'providing mutual support with the additional stimulation that would come from a dialogue between Freudians and Jungians. A small library, of members' own books, was started and a clinic for referrals particularly for patients who could not afford large fees.'

By 1963 two separate streams (later called sections) of training had emerged: Freudian and Jungian. In 1972 the 'British' was added to the name of the organization, giving birth to the BAP. By 1977 the BAP became a limited company with a new constitution, followed by charitable status two years later.

Training fees were kept to a minimum since no one was paid except for expenses. Any student in difficulty could apply to the Kathryn Cohen Scholarship Fund which gave interest-free loans, to be repaid after qualifying.

'The principles and format of the training (always the same rules for both Freudian and Jungian, although in separate sections) have remained substantially unaltered throughout the Association's history. In 1978, small group discussions were organized by Nathan Field for the membership to consider the question "Can the sections merge?" A majority wished that they should remain equal but separate.'

From the late 1950s analysts from the British Psycho-Analytical Society and the Society of Analytical Psychology have been involved at all levels of the trainings. In 1982 a training in child psychotherapy was included, accredited in 1988 by the Association of Child Psychotherapists. In 1989 the Jungian Section was accepted for full membership of the International Association of

Analytical Psychology. In 1990 the British Psychological Society awarded the BAP provisional accreditation.

Between 1972 and 1973 significant founder members decided to leave the Association and form their own trainings independently – they became known as the Association for Group and Individual Psychotherapy (AGIP) and the London Centre for Psychotherapy (LCP).

The objects for which the Association is established are to promote, provide and increase for the benefit of the public the knowledge and skills which comprise psychotherapy and the educational training and competence of psychotherapists and to advance psychotherapy as a profession in all or any of its aspects and thereby to relieve mental distress.

2. THEORETICAL ORIENTATION AND CURRICULUM

Freudian Section

The two fundamental aspects of the training are to teach trainees to work independently and psychoanalytically.

First Year – Basic Freudian Theory: Dreams and Libido Theory, Freud's Model of the Mind, Freud's Clinical and Technical Papers; Infant Observation for one year is obligatory.

Second Year – This year basically covers a combination of the work of Melanie Klein and the Independent Group of the British Psycho-Analytical Society. There are seminars on: Transference and Countertransference, Klein, Fairbairn, Winnicott, Balint and Ego Psychology.

Third Year – During this year trainees study the application of the first two years to psychopathology. The seminars will cover: Neurotic Disorders, Character Disorders, Depression, Perversions, Psychosis, Borderline and Narcissistic Disorders and Psychosomatic Disorders. At the end of the third year there are four seminars on Bion and two seminars on the overview of the theories. The humanistic therapies are not studied and neither is Jung.

Jungian Section

The main theoretical orientation is analytical psychology, and the theoretical seminars are as follows:

First Year – Internal and External Family, Introduction to Jungian Theory, Jungian Concepts, Infancy to Depressive Position, The Toddler and Pre-school Child, Latency and Adolescence, First and Second Half of Life, Interpretation and the Analytic Attitude, Ethics and Practical Planning, Starting Training Patients.

Second Year – Reconstruction, Transference and Countertransference, Early Defence Mechanisms, Use of Dreams, The Body as Messenger, An Overview of Defence Mechanisms, Depression and Depressive Personality, Borderline Personality Disorder, Psychotic Disorders.

Third Year – History of Psychoanalytic Thought, Bion and Jung, Winnicott and Jung, Object Relations and Archetypal Theory, The Coniunctio and its Vicissitudes in the Schizoid Compromise and the Core Complex, Archetypes and Other Sub-personalities, Enactments and Acting Out, Sexuality in Analysis, Jung and the Post-Jungians, Writing the Reading-in Paper, Assessment.

Infant Observation is part of the course for two years. The humanistic therapies are not part of the course; however, a broad map of the world of psychotherapy is discussed throughout the course.

For both trainings a training adviser is assigned to a training year who is responsible for meeting trainees once a term and individually when required. There is also a students' association, meeting more than once a year, consisting of the whole student body.

3. TRAINING STRUCTURE

3.1 Training Committee

There are at least twelve people in the Freudian Training Committee, including the Chair of training, a student adviser for each year (generally up to five representatives) and the Honorary Secretary. Other members are responsible for the following aspects of the training: theoretical seminars, clinical seminars, finance, the reduced fee scheme (where trainees obtain training patients) and clinical tutors who meet with trainees to talk about their reports on patients and their final reading-in papers. Subcommittees of the Freudian Training Committee include the Selection Subcommittee, which is responsible for the selection of new students, and the Curriculum Subcommittee, which is responsible for the organization of the theoretical seminars. All members of the above Training Committee have trained with the BAP.

The Jungian Training Committee are members of the BAP and SAP. Meetings are held once monthly and there are various subcommittees. These have been formed to deal with (1) courses offered to non-members of the BAP, (2) academic training matters, (3) selection and (4) monitoring of trainees' progress. The Chairs of Training are elected by Council of the BAP for five years. The Council is the Executive Body responsible for the three trainings of the BAP, Freudian, Jungian and Child Psychotherapy. Council is made up of twelve people and elected by members of the BAP.

The Training Committees are regulated by Council, who receive all the minutes of all committee meetings, including the Training Committee. There are some members of the Training Committees who are also members of Council. The members of Council are amongst the most senior psychotherapists in the BAP and they have ultimate responsibility for each training. There is liaison between trainees and the Training Committees through a student representative.

3.2 *Selection procedure and admission*

There is an application form followed by two interviews with either a member of Council or a member of the relevant Training Committee.

There is no obligatory introductory year. Both Freudian and Jungian Sections of the BAP run Introductory Courses for non-members, but this is not a prerequisite for the professional training. Clinical experience is not essential before applying, but it is preferred. There is an age limit of forty-five for the Freudian training and fifty for the Jungian training, which may be waived in exceptional circumstances. Two referees are required.

Academic qualifications are essential for the Freudian and Jungian trainings. A degree in Medicine, Psychology or Social Science, or an equivalent professional qualification, is required. The suitability of applicants depends on a combination of the following: life circumstances – the ability of the individual to commit themselves to the training in terms of time, finance and accessibility to London; personality – the ability of the individual to think and work analytically.

There is no accommodation for people joining the course midway, although there are external courses offered by the BAP. There are also postgraduate courses offered to BAP graduates to apply for Full Membership and Training Therapist status.

There is an upper limit of twelve places per year. In the Jungian Section most training groups tend to be fewer than twelve. There is an average of thirty-six people applying for each year. There is no policy of having an equal number of men and women in each group, although there is a wish to strike a balance. The general background of people applying, and in training, tends in the main to be the 'core professions'.

3.3 *Time commitment and length of training*

The student adviser meets the year group once a term, as well as each individual once a year and more if required.

In the first year theoretical seminars are given on a Tuesday evening and this continues into the second and third years. Clinical seminars are held once a fortnight, from the second year of training, which a trainee is expected to continue to attend until qualification. Infant Observation seminars take place one evening a week throughout the first year for the Freudian training and two years for the Jungian.

The courses are designed to accommodate people in full-time work and indeed the majority of trainees are working full-time; it should be remembered that time must be set aside for reading papers in preparation for the theoretical seminars, as well as journals, books, etc., and often trainees have to arrange for their own photocopying of papers, etc.

Each trainee is recommended to be prepared for fifteen hours a week for following the course. This would include personal therapy, supervision and training patients. It generally takes five years to qualify and may take less.

3.4 *Interruptions in training*

In the BAP's experience it is unusual for people to want to take time off. However, there have been unusual circumstances where people have done so. The limitation would be a year.

3.5 *Postgraduate qualification and learned society*

There is automatic Associate Membership when a trainee qualifies. Subscriptions for Full and Associate members resident in London are £143.00 per year (1990–91). There is one AGM in December of each year, three members' meetings a year (including trainees), three scientific meetings a term where someone presents a paper, and a Freud and Jung forum (an informal clinical meeting), which is held three times a term. There are conferences held on a yearly basis on particular topics. For example, the conference in 1990 was on 'Language and Psychotherapy'.

A graduate may apply (to the Post Graduate Committee) to become a Full Member, three years after qualification. A document on a graduate's practice is required – stating how many patients have been treated, for how long and what sort of patient. There must be two referees who report on work since qualification, or have been present at postgraduate workshops. There is a minimum requirement of having treated two patients three times a week, for two years, other than training patients. The BAP has recently acquired its own building in Mapesbury Road, where there will eventually be seminar rooms, consulting rooms, administrators' office and a library. People trained in analytic psychotherapy may apply to become members of the BAP. These applicants come mainly from the British Psycho-Analytical Society, the Society of Analytical Psychology and the Tavistock.

There is an informal BAP newsletter, for members only and circulated three times a year. A journal is published twice a year and is open to members inside and outside the BAP. All members of the Association subscribe to a Code of Ethics.

4. CLINICAL AND ACADEMIC REQUIREMENTS

4.1 *Personal therapy*

There is no procedure for a trainee to be referred to a therapist or analyst. The majority of people who apply are already in therapy. Members and non-members of the BAP may apply to become training therapists. They must have been qualified for at least five years, and their application will be considered by the Post Graduate Committee.

Each trainee must be in therapy for a minimum of three times a week. The training therapist or analyst of a trainee is consulted with by the Training Committee, four times during the course of the trainee's training. To begin with, to verify the suitability of the applicant; secondly, to check the trainee's readiness to take on the first training patient; thirdly, readiness to take on the second training patient and fourthly, to ensure the trainee's readiness to practise independently. It is often the case that the training therapist or analyst will not want to discuss the patient/trainee in any detail and will simply give a 'no objection' to each stage, which is the minimum requirement.

4.2 *Clinical requirements*

After the first year of seminars a trainee may start seeing their first training patient, as long as the therapist agrees and an approved supervisor is available. Before qualification a trainee must have seen two training patients, one for two years and one for eighteen months, each for the minimum of three times a week. Medical cover and malpractice insurance are required.

4.3 *Supervision*

Criteria for approved supervisors are the same as for approved training therapists. A trainee must see a different supervisor for each training patient, in once weekly individual supervision. There is no formal group supervision, although the clinical seminars provide a forum for discussion and sharing of clinical work.

4.4 *Papers and written work*

One paper has to be written at the end of the Infant Observation. There must be a six-monthly report on each training patient up to qualification, aimed at conveying the clinical essence of the work with the training patient. The reading-in paper should be of about 6,000–7,000 words, on one of the training patients. This is read to the group of fellow trainees as well as two assessors as nominated by the Training Committee.

5. REFERRALS

There are two separate low cost therapy clinics where suitable training patients are referred on to trainees of the relevant trainings. There is at present no policy of letting the patient know routinely that they will be in treatment with a trainee as it is felt that this is more appropriately addressed in the patient's therapy. Assessment of the appropriateness of a training patient is made, amongst other criteria, in terms of their ability to commit themselves to three times weekly psychotherapy on a long-term basis, as well as how much the trainee could learn from the patient.

6. COST OF TRAINING

There is a subscription of £65 a year to be a student member of the Association. Fees are £676 per annum for years 1, 2 and 3. Years 4+ are £391 per annum. Supervision and therapy is in addition and is currently between £25 and £30 per session. Training patients are usually charged between £7 and £12. The most expensive period would clearly be for the time a trainee is seeing two supervisors as well as being in therapy.

The Victor Kanter fund provides trainees an interest-free loan of up to £500 in exceptional circumstances.

Consulting rooms will be available at some time in the future.

7. FUTURE EXPECTATIONS/CAREER PROSPECTS

Prior to the second year trainees are given seminars on setting up in practice, but many people may only want a small private practice – a full-time psychotherapy practice may take many years to establish.

For qualified trainees, there are opportunities, in time, to teach within the BAP. Supervision opportunities would have to be five years after qualification, once the requirements have been met for becoming a Full Member of the BAP. This also applies for therapists wishing to become training therapists.

8. TRAINEES' EXPERIENCE: FREUDIAN TRAINEES

8.1 *Why this course was chosen*

Trainees had been attracted to the Freudian BAP course for the following reasons:

1. Trainees were interested in the theory and practice of psychoanalysis, and it was considered important that many of the teachers, supervisors and analysts at the BAP were also members of the British Psycho-Analytical Society.

2. The BAP's prestigious reputation. Trainees were looking for the best training they could find.

3. The focused training. Most people were already in therapy or analysis and so understood, from a patient's point of view, something of the psychoanalytic therapeutic relationship. Trainees were aware that the Freudian BAP course would be a concentrated specialized training in psychoanalytic technique and practice.

The selection procedure was experienced as being thorough and necessarily anxiety-provoking.

It was agreed that all the relevant information about the different stages of the course was available on starting. However, trainees were struck that it was only the experience of training which informed their understanding of the relevant information on the different stages of the course; and that as the course progressed so unforeseen details arose, like the usual requirement that a student have a patient and supervisor of the opposite sex.

8.2 *The atmosphere of the course*

Trainees felt that the student adviser system worked well and had experienced advisers available for any difficulties.

There was a common experience that it had taken a long time to feel comfortable in the year groups, mainly because there was very little opportunity to meet and chat to fellow trainees outside the theoretical seminars. After some discussion it was felt that the BAP should attend to the dynamics within the group, as some trainees felt that the feelings of discomfort had interfered with their learning process. It is not that people were expecting to learn group dynamics or group therapy, but that since all the theoretical and clinical seminars and the bulk of the training took place in a group, some awareness of this could have been helpful and perhaps facilitating. It was also felt that this problem had much to do with the lack of a building where trainees could meet informally and a more friendly atmosphere could perhaps be generated. (Since September 1991, the BAP has been using its newly acquired house.)

There was a sense that not enough 'thought had been given to the process of teaching psychotherapy', although there was some agreement that this was probably true of every training organiza- tion. This linked with the way in which theoretical seminars were taught. In the main the teachers were usually experts on a particular topic and had often published papers or books. They are not always members of the BAP and trainees experienced pluses and minuses of this system. Disadvantages were seen as the sense that very often the teacher was not aware of the group's stage of training, so that trainees felt that however good the teacher was there could sometimes be a disparity between what was being taught and what could be understood by the trainee group. Advantages enjoyed were to do with meeting and working with some very special and experienced clinicians, where being a trainee in such a group was seen as a real privilege and intellectually very exciting. There was general agreement that it was not so important for the teacher to be a member of the BAP.

The curriculum had been satisfactory, although most trainees agreed they would have preferred more seminars on Klein. Age, homosexuality and racism were also areas where it was felt more in-depth discussion could have taken place, although it was agreed that these were topics which needed to be ongoing debates within the BAP as a whole and post-qualification. Trainees felt that it was curious that no Jung whatsoever was taught on the Freudian course and that apart from informal contact with Jungian trainees, it was not known what their training consisted of. In general people felt that this should be addressed.

Most trainees felt that they had been tremendously supported during difficult stages of the course such as taking on the first training patient. Trainees had experienced enormous changes from the organizational side of the BAP, since the beginning of the course. The students' organization was very active and there had been discussions about student representatives on Council. Previously, it was felt, this would not have been possible, but trainees were pleased with the changes and felt that there were now genuine moves from Council and other committees towards accommodating and listening to students. This meant that communication was vastly improved, which was experienced as a benefit to the whole organization.

There was a sense that the BAP was in the shadow of the Institute of Psycho-Analysis and some concern over the issues of status of training between the two organizations. People felt it was changing but needed to be addressed and discussed more.

8. TRAINEES' EXPERIENCE: JUNGIAN TRAINEES

8.1 *Why this course was chosen*

Trainees were attracted to the BAP because of the Jungian training within a long-established organization which would ensure a sound clinical training. Trainees felt they did not want to be part of the elitism of the SAP and Institute, whereas the BAP seemed to be the umbrella organization bringing Freud, Jung and Child Psychotherapy together; therefore the BAP would facilitate more flexibility. Another reason given was that analytic therapy of four/five times weekly was thought unlikely to be the common need for the majority of people and trainees were looking for a training where their way of working would meet the requirements of the majority rather than minority of the patient group.

Trainees felt they had been sufficiently informed about each stage of the course, although difficulties had arisen as the course had progressed. One such difficulty had been about acquiring an approved supervisor and there was a feeling that the BAP should provide trainees with a list of supervisors. There was much agreement that the commitment in terms of time and money was not something that was fully appreciated until starting.

The selection procedure was experienced as very fair and thorough in terms of the interviews, but some people had been very unhappy about the length of time they had had to wait to hear whether or not they had been accepted – it was felt that not enough time was allowed to change one's life in the way which a training requires.

8.2 *The atmosphere of the course*

At the end of the first year there are seminars in setting up in practice. Trainees felt there was a great deal of advice and support concerning taking on training patients and all the practicalities of setting up in practice.

People agreed that the student adviser system worked well and there were plenty of opportunities to feed back to trainers the experience of the theoretical seminar leaders/teachers. Most of the latter are SAP members and a few are BAP members. Confusion was expected regarding certain theoretical areas and their application in the clinical setting. This was felt to be all par for the course. The work of Klein was found to be particularly confusing and people felt this was more to do with the lack of dialogue between Jungians and Kleinians than with an incompatibility of ideas. One of the course's recent changes in curriculum was linking Winnicott and Klein contributions with Jungian thought. This was made directly at the request of the trainee group. It had been appreciated by trainees, as it not only provided them with a theoretical area they felt was missing but had also shown evidence of the Training Committee's flexibility and ability to listen.

There was a feeling that relationships with teachers, trainers and fellow trainees were very good, although there was a general consensus that some experiences in the training groups, at the beginning, were very difficult. People did not feel necessarily that this needed to be addressed by having a course on group dynamics, but that some attention needed to be paid to the group process.

Trainees experienced a hint of tension regarding the Freudian and the Jungian Sections, which was difficult to locate since in large meetings where all members met everybody seemed to get on very well. It was agreed that there was not enough interaction between the two sections. Trainees were aware that their training overlapped to quite an extent with the Freudian training, whereas Jungian thought is not covered at all on the Freudian training. There was a general feeling that this issue had not been addressed with enough thought by the whole membership body of the BAP. The training had surpassed trainees' expectations in terms of curriculum as well as support.

AUTHOR'S COMMENTS

The BAP is the longest standing psychotherapy organization and training dating back to the early 1950s (see Scarlett, 1991). The Freudian Section has gained a reputation of being a Middle Group Training, although members of the three psychoanalytic groups (Contemporary Freudian, Kleinian and Independent: see Part One) are equally represented in the functions of training therapists, supervisors and teachers. Meanwhile, the Jungian Section align themselves to the Jungians of the Society of Analytical Psychology whose theories differ from the Zurich school and the other Jungian trainings (see Part One). The British Psycho-Analytical Society and the Society of Analytical Psychology tend to be be seen as the parent bodies of all the analytic trainings where Freud and Jung are taught, and this is particularly accentuated in the BAP because many of the members of the parent societies also become members of the BAP.

It is striking to note that BAP Freudian trainees felt not enough Klein was studied, and this seems to reflect and confirm that the BAP training's emphasis is that of the Independent Tradition of the British Psycho-Analytical Society (see Kohon, 1986). It is significant that both sets of trainees felt that more attention needed to be paid to the group process. Is this a sign of a lack in the trainings or simply a difficulty at the beginning of any new experience which has to be endured?

Trainees felt enthusiastic about the positive signs that the BAP was listening to trainees' complaints and subsequently adapting. The need to give trainees a voice on the relevant committees is being addressed.

A more recent development in the BAP is the inclusion of a training in Child Psychotherapy, which was set up in 1982. The BAP is the only psychotherapy organization which offers this specialized training, which is accredited by the Association of Child Psychotherapists (ACP).

CAMBRIDGE SOCIETY FOR PSYCHOTHERAPY

41 Beaulands Close, Cambridge CB4 1JA.

1. HISTORY

The following quotes have been taken from a paper published in *Free Associations* 20 (1990) by Peter Lomas in discussion with the Cambridge Society for Psychotherapy (formerly the Cambridge Psychotherapy Training Group).

> The group began in 1980 when a small number of people came together in Cambridge with the aim of providing a learning environment for those who wished to become psychotherapists. Some of this group were trained therapists, some potential students. Our aim was not to organize a training course in psychotherapy similar to those existing elsewhere but to explore the possibilities of learning therapy according to a certain

ideology. We centred on the belief that the most profitable way to learn psychotherapy is in a setting in which students have as much autonomy as can be managed and can develop their own approach in their own way and their own time rather than having a structured course imposed on them. The training we offer can therefore be seen to mirror the experience of being in a therapy which emphasizes mutuality; and it is supported by our belief that only in a free, open dialogue can genuine learning and creative exploration take place. The group, therefore, is not organized in a conventionally hierarchical way. It has no explicit power structure. There is no chairman or training committee. [There is now a Constitution and a Code of Ethics.] Decisions are made by the group as a whole. There are no rules as such. Although one of the students acts as secretary and there is a small administrative group, there is no formal committee or written regulation. It is, however, expected that students will have personal therapy and supervision and that before they finish training they will have had an appropriate variety and depth of practical experience as therapists. But we do not specify lengths of time for these undertakings.

None the less we seek to be informal, to be worthy of (self-) respect without compromising our integrity in the pursuit of conventional respectability (an enterprise hardly foreign to psychoanalysis). Our dilemmas over this are exemplified by the naming of the group. We have a formal, name-on-notepaper: The Cambridge Society for Psychotherapy. More commonly we are known as the Outfit. Originally coined, somewhat jokingly, as an in-house anti-name, this has now escaped into more general usage.

One of the changes over the years has been that, although the training is student directed, the responsibility for training has shifted more to the collective student group rather than the individual student. At present there is a process of formalizing the training in a way which may go against the grain of some of the aspects of the original philosophy of the group. This process may be to some degree inevitable as the group increases in size; and the Society's application for membership of the Analytic Section of the UKSCP also increases pressure to codify procedures. The Society intends, however, not to become overly rigid in its requirements and will continue to preserve its fundamental raison d'être, particularly its responsiveness to individual needs.

2. THEORETICAL ORIENTATION AND CURRICULUM

All of the therapists who have joined the group have a particular, albeit broad, theoretical orientation. Although not adherents to any specific school of thought (e.g. Freudian, Jungian) their approach could be called, for want of a better term, that of psychoanalytically orientated psychotherapy – provided that this does not imply a watered down version of psychoanalysis and allows for the fact that we aim to explore the boundaries of contemporary theory and practice. Students are not only introduced to analytical concepts (transference, counter-transference, and so on) but offered the means to make a critique of these concepts.

There is no set curriculum. Trainees plan their weekly meetings for about ten weeks in advance. These meetings are focused on a specific theme such as transference. Meetings are held in each other's houses. There is a monthly meeting of the whole group and three meetings a month for trainees, who will discuss a book or paper they have chosen to study pertaining to the theme that term. Occasionally therapists will be invited to these meetings. Trainees also meet in twos on a regular basis for six months at a time, to talk about anything that is relevant to the process of becoming a psychotherapist.

3. TRAINING STRUCTURE

3.1 *Training Committee*

There is no Training Committee. The administration, selection and all the work that a Training Committee normally carries out is organized by the group as a whole, most of this responsibility being taken on by the student group.

3.2 *Selection procedure and admission*

The applicant first of all meets one of the trainees for an informal preliminary meeting. Following this a written application is submitted. This is followed by a meeting with one of the therapists as well as a meeting with a therapist and trainee together.

The interviews are structured, as far as possible, on the basis of equality, that is to say, the applicants are encouraged to scrutinize us as thoroughly as we scrutinize them. There are no formal criteria for acceptance by us. We are looking for people whose commitment to becoming a therapist is strong, who appear to have the necessary sensitivity for the work, and who, by virtue of their world-view, are likely to feel at home in a group of this kind.

It is the last of these criteria which has made selection an arduous and time-consuming task. In particular, the fact that students need to be able to teach each other means we must try to select those applicants who will be receptive to the needs of the group and its individual members.

3.3 *Time commitment and length of training*

There are weekly evening meetings as well as individual therapy, supervision, meetings in twos and reading groups. It has been taking between three and six years for trainees to feel they are ready to qualify.

3.4 *Interruptions in training*

Because of the nature of this training, interruptions would be accommodated.

3.5 *Postgraduate qualification and learned society*

Graduation:

One of our aims is to provide the kind of setting that will best enable a student to gain realistic evidence of her or his progress during the course of training. When, however, we come to the final evaluation of the student's overall capability, problems arise. In our view the conventional methods of assessment at the end of training are unsatisfactory, and the results of such measures are unimpressive. The correlation between successful qualification and actual therapeutic ability is, to put it mildly, not as close as one might hope for. Moreover, the disadvantages of such methods are many: the criteria are selective and stifle creativity of thought; the values tend to be based on respectability and prestige; the criteria used are often quantitative (how many patients seen, etc.) and are a poor substitute for really knowing the students and their work. Most of all, we wish to avoid having a group in which evaluation is emphasized at the expense of creative and lively interchange.

With these thoughts in mind we place emphasis on self-responsibility and openness in personal communication in the hope that it will thereby be unlikely for a totally unsuitable student to stay with us for a period of years and that in most cases student and group will be able to gauge a time when enough training has been accomplished.

If the group is prepared to say with integrity that a certain student has been accepted as a trained member we would, of course, need to reserve the right to refuse such an endorsement. However, from our experience hitherto, we believe that to do so would be a drastic and exceptional move. A custom has emerged whereby students present themselves to the group when they feel ready to do so. There is no formula for this presentation and students have their individual ways of conveying their attitudes, beliefs and the nature of their practice. A further custom is that students who become accepted as trained therapists mark the occasion by a ritual or celebration of their choice.

There are at present fourteen therapists and seven trainees; therapists meet at irregular intervals to discuss clinical matters. Therapists may also apply for membership of the Cambridge Group. Their application is less formal than that of a trainee, and the decision for accepting a therapist would be taken by the whole group.

4. CLINICAL AND ACADEMIC REQUIREMENTS

4.1 *Personal therapy*

This is considered to be the cornerstone of the training. Since the students are normally in training for a substantial number of years and may wish to have experience of different frequencies of attendance, the number of sessions per week is not stipulated but is left for the student and therapist to decide. Prospective students may be given guidance in their selection of a suitable therapist, who may come from within or from outside the Society. It is expected that students be in therapy for at least six months before joining the training group.

4.2 *Clinical requirements*

The relevant experience for the training is of analytic psychotherapy with individuals, seen at least once weekly, and more often if it is appropriate. Students have usually been members of the training group for at least a year before beginning work with their first patient. Students are expected to have a variety of experience during their training. Of the students who have graduated thus far, the therapy hours worked are in the region of four hundred to six hundred hours before graduating, a proportion being devoted to patients who have attended therapy more than once a week, and to therapies lasting up to four years.

4.3 *Supervision*

Supervision always takes place individually and some students join a small group as well. The student's goal is to acquire some variety of supervisory experience, and at the same time to establish a continued relationship with one particular supervisor. Supervisors are very often trained therapists within the Society, although students do sometimes approach experienced analytical therapists from outside to be their supervisors. In no cases do students undertake clinical work without supervision.

4.4 *Papers and written work*

Though it is not a requirement of the training programme, written work of various kinds is likely to be undertaken by students at relevant times. They may, for instance, produce written material as part of seminar work, or in order to present a case study. Students and members are involved in writing the application for the UK Standing Conference, and on documents concerning Core Philosophy, Code of Ethics and Graduation.

5. REFERRALS

Trainees are responsible for finding their own clients with the help of the trained members and in consultation with their supervisors.

6. COST OF TRAINING

There is a fund to which trainees contribute for the costs of outside teachers, membership of Therip (The Higher Education Network for Research and Information in Psychoanalysis), etc. The present fee of £60 p.a. is under review. Trainees will charge training clients a low fee of approximately £15, and the usual fees for therapy and supervision are between £20 and £25. Trainees provide their own consulting rooms.

7. FUTURE EXPECTATIONS/CAREER PROSPECTS

Most graduates of the Society are working in private practice. Some have taken jobs in organizations offering psychodynamic counselling (university and college counselling services, university research project). Some combine the two. Many members living in the area continue to attend group meetings on a regular basis, and contribute to the life and work of the Society.

8. TRAINEES' EXPERIENCE

8.1 *Why this course was chosen*

Trainees chose this course for the following reasons:

(a) the freedom to draw from a number of psychotherapy theories;

(b) responsibility for formulating their own training curriculum rather than fitting into a structured course.

One of the consequences of being part of a training like this is that occasionally trainees experienced an amount of uncertainty about whether or not they were doing the 'right' thing. However, this uncertainty presented a challenge for trainees then to question what the 'right' thing means in psychotherapy. Trainees' concerns may always be shared with therapists of the Cambridge Society.

The experience of the selection procedure was very positive. Trainees felt they really had to examine their reasons for wishing to become psychotherapists whilst writing the first application. The subsequent meetings with trainees as well as a therapist and finally the whole group were experienced as an excellent way of finding out whether or not the Cambridge Society was the sort of training looked for. Experiences differed slightly regarding the information on how to find supervisors, personal therapists, etc., at the beginning of the course.

8.2 *The atmosphere of the course*

The structure of the regular evening meetings was appreciated. Trainees organize their meetings around a theme, like transference, for a term in advance. The whole group meet once a month. However, trainees do not feel they are restricted in these meetings and if issues unexpectedly arise, these may be discussed rather than the planned topic. The six months of meetings in twos is also experienced as very valuable since trainees felt they really get to know each other and appreciate the support these meetings facilitate.

There were some debates within the whole group where there were differences of opinion. One such debate recently was about the issue of how much trainees should charge their clients. Some members of the group felt these charges should be low whilst others felt that trainees should not downgrade themselves. Over many meetings of in-depth discussion there was eventually a general consensus that trainees should decide themselves. This was experienced as an example of the advantages of following a student-led training, where the arguments of different sides are thoroughly aired by therapists and trainees together, rather than by a training committee which makes the decision which is then imposed on the trainees whether they agree or not.

The intake is relatively small and there was some anxiety experienced by trainees as they began, regarding how they compared their knowledge to that of others further on in the course. However, this seemed to be part and parcel of joining a training of this nature, and anxiety was gradually overcome. The graduation procedure was something which was experienced as very positive. Trainees are encouraged to choose their own way of graduating which will demonstrate their work with clients and their understanding of the therapeutic relationship. There is complete flexibility in how this procedure should take place and it is entirely up to the trainee, in consultation with the whole group.

There was some concern about the sources of referrals for

building up a viable practice as most trainees were aiming to become full-time psychotherapists. Another present concern was the implications of being members of the UKSCP. Trainees felt it was an important body to join, but were unhappy about the possibility of having to compromise on the Outfit's overall philosophy and ethos, which was not something they were prepared to do.

AUTHOR'S COMMENTS

The philosophy of creating a facilitating environment where individuals (trainees) will discover and grow in their own way is something which all training organizations talk about and aim for. This training is the only organization which operates this philosophy by allowing trainees to create their own training programme. 'Empowering' is a word often used by humanistic therapists and yet it seems this is the only training which empowers its trainees to function as their own training committee. There may be many criticisms from all quarters (humanistic and analytic) that inexperienced, unanalysed trainees should not, cannot, teach themselves. But the selection procedure is thorough and affords plenty of opportunity for the group and applicant to get to know each other in order to ensure there is sufficient ability and motivation of the prospective trainee to utilize such a structure.

There may also be much criticism about trainees functioning as a training committee. However, it seems very clear that in reality it is the entire group which functions as a training committee, and the therapists are always available for consultation on any issue concerning the trainees' process. Nevertheless, an enormous amount of responsibility is entrusted to the trainee, which may be one of the reasons that the trainee group has developed towards functioning as a collective, out of the need to share the anxieties of training with a peer group (common to all groups of trainees). Some people may argue that the infantilizing process of undergoing a training is all 'grist to the mill'. The Cambridge Society's attitude is that it makes no sense to treat professional people over thirty as people who don't know. On the contrary, the questions of the less experienced are valued as a challenge to the comfortable assumptions easily made by the more experienced therapists.

This training seems to be the product of the development of the thinking and attitude of Peter Lomas, who was trained as a psychoanalyst in the 1960s. He was a member of the Independent Group within the British Psycho-Analytical Society, before resigning. In 1973 he published *True and False Experience* and it was his philosophy and inspiration, at about the same time, which were largely responsible for setting up the Guild of Psychotherapists. This training is breaking new ground in a way that no other training attempts, and for that reason it is probably the most controversial of all the trainings presented here.

CENTRE FOR FREUDIAN ANALYSIS AND RESEARCH (CFAR)

23 Primrose Gardens, London NW3; tel: 071 586 0992.

1. HISTORY

CFAR was set up by a group of Lacanian psychoanalysts (Bice Benvenuto, Bernard Burgoyne, Richard Klein and Darian Leader) in 1985 for the purpose of addressing the absence of any systematic study of Jacques Lacan's work in the Anglo-Saxon world of psychoanalysis and psychotherapy. Cartels (study groups) were initiated to study Freudian theory within Lacan's perspectives. By 1987, in response to a growing interest from members of the cartels, clinical practice became an important addition to discussions in the cartels and a training programme began. The training programme aimed at combining the traditional model of trainings in the UK with a Lacanian approach. The latter is much more focused on creating a psychoanalytic environment which trainees can use in their own way rather than having to comply with the structure of a linear course.

A cartel is a group of four people plus one further member who functions as the analytic absent presence and is invited to a cartel meeting when it is felt necessary, in order to facilitate its work. The fifth member is usually a member of CFAR. Cartels are dissolved after two years when members form new cartels.

> The training was born out of the activity of the cartels which are at the core of the training.

2. THEORETICAL ORIENTATION AND CURRICULUM

The main theoretical orientation is psychoanalysis with the emphasis on Lacan's interpretation of Freud. To this end CFAR is the only training in Britain in Lacanian psychoanalysis (see Part One). It is accepted that trainees develop in their own way and at their own pace and as far as is possible the training programme takes account of this. However, for some stages a time element has to be imposed.

The Preliminary Year (two terms) is a way of introducing Lacanian thought and for trainees to decide if they wish to join the Full Programme. In this Preliminary Year a trainee is not obliged to join a cartel. Following the Preliminary Year trainees must join a cartel to proceed with the next three-year Full Training Programme.

The first year of the training studies the structure of the neuroses: Hysteria, Obsessional Neurosis, and the closely related structures of Phobia and Perversion. The second year studies the Differential Structure of Psychosis, together with the themes of Transference and Identification. The third year studies Interpretation, the Relation of Phantasy to Symptom, and the differentiation of the beginning, the middle and the end phases of the analytical work. Throughout this, there will be a study and critique of the whole of the international psychoanalytic development since Freud. This would not include Jung, since Lacanians would see Jungian theory as departing from Freud. One of the optional, though recommended, seminars within the programme is the child analysis study group, which works in association with the Centre for Research in Child Analysis (CEREDA) in Paris.

There are no Infant Observation seminars, mainly because from a Lacanian viewpoint it is not possible to see the unconscious process in an infant. So Lacanians do not believe in Infant

Observation. There are many reasons for this and it is an important difference between Lacanians and others, too complex to outline here, but it is linked with the Lacanians' attitude that there is no truth that can be observed merely empirically, and that the psychoanalyst does not have a knowledge to impart through an interpretation. The interpretation is aimed at possibly touching the unconscious, or instigating a train of thought in the analysand's mind.

Humanistic therapies are acknowledged as overlapping with psychoanalytic theory but are essentially seen as too major a departure from Freud for them to be a part of this training. Group therapy is not within the Lacanian tradition, although there are some Lacanians in France who do work in groups.

3. TRAINING STRUCTURE

3.1 *Training Committee*

There are six committees of CFAR which report to the Executive Committee: the Translations Committee, the Library Committee, the Newsletter Committee, the Cartels Committee, the Finance Committee and the Events Committee. In addition to this, there is the Members' Committee, the Training Committee and a Trainers' Committee.

At present the Training Committee consists of the four founder members plus one further member, and their training is in Lacanian analysis in Europe or South America. As the membership of CFAR grows, so places on the Training Committee will become open to the membership as they qualify through the training programme. The Training Committee meet once a month to discuss all the matters to do with the training, and once a term the Training Committee meet with the complete student body.

3.2 *Selection procedure and admission*

After an application form is submitted, there is one interview with two members of the Training Committee. The preliminary year can be used by the trainee and the Training Committee to assess suitability for continuing on the full course. It is possible for someone with previous experience to enter the Full Training Programme directly, without doing the Preliminary Year.

There is no age limit, and academic qualifications are not seen as essential. Qualities that are looked for in a suitable applicant are: an ability to listen, the desire to be in analysis and the interest in relieving suffering along with the ability to tolerate another's suffering.

3.3 *Time commitment and length of training*

A personal tutor is seen on a regular basis, and in addition to this there are cartels, theoretical and clinical seminars and personal therapy.

Trainees following this course should expect to commit a total of 500–600 hours over a period of three to four years to seminar and cartel work. Seminars are generally on Saturday afternoons; the time of cartel meetings is negotiated by cartel members. It can take three years to qualify if an advanced trainee has joined post-preliminary, but it will probably take around four years to qualify for people without previous experience.

3.4 *Interruptions in training*

Each case would be individually assessed.

3.5 *Postgraduate qualification and learned society*

CFAR is quite a new organization and at present has five full members. Trainees automatically become members as soon as they qualify. Further to this, CFAR has two Associate Members, three Research Associates in British universities and arranges numerous visiting seminars given by members of associated Lacanian organizations in Europe. Categories of membership are still in the process of being worked out.

Psychotherapists or psychoanalysts who have trained elsewhere may join the training programme for a minimum of one year – during which time they are in supervision – and thereby acquire Associate Membership status of CFAR. CFAR works in conjunction with the Psychoanalysis Unit at Middlesex Polytechnic, and has close ties with the Ecole de la Cause Freudienne in Paris, the international Lacanian organization the Fondation du Champ Freudien, and the European School of Psychoanalysis. All these agencies function as learned societies.

A suite of rooms is permanently used by CFAR for all the diverse activities of the training, and a library is in the process of being formed. There is a Code of Ethics.

4. CLINICAL AND ACADEMIC REQUIREMENTS

4.1 *Personal therapy*

If necessary trainees will be referred to analysts by members of the Training Committee. In the Lacanian tradition the quality of an analysis is not proven by its quantity and for this reason frequency is left up to each trainee. However, it is seen that twice weekly would be the minimum frequency.

Lacanians do not use the term 'training analysis' or 'training analyst', in the same way as they prefer the term 'analysand' instead of 'patient'. This is because they see the analysis a trainee goes through during training as being at the heart of the training in its own right. The analyst of a trainee must be a psychoanalyst (including analytic therapists), although for a trainee not already in analysis at the time of application the Training Committee would recommend that this be a Lacanian analyst. Sometimes trainees will be in analysis with a member of the Training Committee. During the training there is no consultation between the Training Committee and the trainee's analyst.

4.2 *Clinical requirements*

The timing of starting to see analysands is discussed with the tutor, who will give recommendations and advice on the details of setting up in practice. Trainees are expected to see their analysands at the same frequency as their personal analysis. Two analysands should be seen under supervision for at least one year.

Medical cover is not a requirement: an arrangement for automatic CFAR indemnity insurance is pending.

4.3 *Supervision*

Supervisors must be Lacanian analysts, and the same supervisor can be used for both analysands the trainees are seeing. Supervision sessions must be once weekly.

4.4 *Papers and written work*

Four papers must be written throughout the training, two of which must be clinical papers. The final paper must be an in-depth clinical paper demonstrating the trainee's work.

5. REFERRALS

At the moment referrals for trainees come through various channels. A referral service is being developed by the Trainees' Committee.

According to Lacanians there are two personality structures: the neurotic and the psychotic. Trainees could see analysands with both or either structure as long as they were carefully supervised. It is generally advised not to let analysands know they are seeing a trainee since this is felt to interfere with the analytic relationship.

6. COST OF TRAINING

Fees are £760 per year excluding analysis and supervision. Fees for analysis and supervision sessions range between £20 and £30. Trainees decide which fee to charge their analysands, and there are consulting rooms available for hire.

There are at present no bursaries or loans.

7. FUTURE EXPECTATIONS/CAREER PROSPECTS

Throughout training there is ongoing advice on setting up in practice for trainees who so wish to do. Because CFAR is a new and growing organization and the first Lacanian training in Britain, there are many prospects for supervision and teaching once a trainee has qualified.

8. TRAINEES' EXPERIENCE

8.1 *Why this course was chosen*

Trainees were attracted to this course because it is based on Lacan's work and philosophy. The aspects of Lacan's work that trainees were interested in are the following:

(a) the in-depth debate on the philosophical and socio-cultural context within which analytic practice takes place;

(b) Lacan never moves his developments from Freud;

(c) the incorporation of linguistic ideas with philosophy enriching what was already there in Freud;

(d) the interest in what defines subjectivity;

(e) the cartels creating an analytic environment;

(f) the dimensions of symbolic, imaginary and real;

(g) logical as opposed to clock timing.

The selection procedure was experienced as searching, intensive and quite difficult, but trainees felt very clear about the different stages of the course and the commitment required.

8.2 *The atmosphere of the course*

Trainees appreciated the meeting once a term of the whole group to discuss all the issues pertaining to the training. In this meeting they had the opportunity of going through the minutes of the Training Committee and the developments of the UKSCP. It was found to be productive and useful and trainees did not get the impression that information was withheld.

Trainees found the reading of Lacan's work sometimes necessarily confusing, which resisted access. His writing was experienced as circular with cross-references to all his writings. It provoked hard intellectual questioning, resisted simplification and reduction.

Trainees felt they were having to learn to deepen and question, forming a practice in relation to Lacan's body of knowledge. Lacan calls into question what happens in a session – that nothing can be solved in a knowing position – that the analyst is not there to reinforce the ego.

There was a general feeling that it was not ideal to have teachers who were also the analysts, but that it was unavoidable at the moment since the group was so young, and there were no problems since analysis was kept very separate. Some trainees are in analysis with approved analysts from the British Psycho-Analytical Society, but although there is a requirement of twice weekly the Lacanian attitude is that the practice of psychoanalysis should not be defined by quantity but by quality.

A criticism was that not enough of Lacan's work is translated into English so that the study of Lacan is limited, and this was an issue that CFAR needed to address. There was a general feeling that the trainee group was particularly stimulating because people from philosophy and education were attracted to Lacan, rather than only the core professions.

As was expected, occasional hiccups occurred as with all new organizations, but in general trainees felt very positive about being part of CFAR and looked forward to contributing in the future, in Britain and internationally.

AUTHOR'S COMMENTS

That this training is the first Lacanian training in London confirms the view that the work of Jacques Lacan has been far less accepted in the Anglo-Saxon community than anywhere else in the world.

Within the analytical psychotherapy training establishments the use of the word psychoanalysis and the label 'psychoanalyst' are reserved only for members of the British Psycho-Analytical Society, even though every analytic therapist is aware of the many overlaps between psychoanalysis and psychotherapy (see Part One). CFAR refuses to comply with this and does not accept the criterion of frequency of sessions as something to differentiate psychoanalysis from psychotherapy. This is just one of its disagreements with psychoanalysis as developed by the British Psycho-Analytical

Society and the International Association of Psycho-Analysis. Consequently CFAR's attitude challenges a long-standing tradition of the analytic psychotherapists in Britain since the 1950s (see Part One). Simultaneously CFAR challenges the long-standing tradition of the Institute of Psycho-Analysis. The question is: how will the challenge be received by British therapists and analysts?

CENTRE FOR PSYCHOANALYTICAL PSYCHOTHERAPY (CAP)*

6 Upper Harley Street, London NW1 4PS; tel: 071 935 3070.

1. HISTORY

The CAP was set up in 1979 by a group of psychotherapists and psychoanalysts in consultation with the Institute of Psycho-Analysis. It was felt that more trainings needed to be available in psychoanalytic psychotherapy in order to draw on a wider group of applicants for entry. The aim was to provide as wide a theoretical input as possible but most definitely psychoanalytic in orientation.

> In recent years the training has become much more precise in the emphasis it gives to observation and understanding infantile transference in the context of psychotherapy.

2. THEORETICAL ORIENTATION AND CURRICULUM

> The main aim and hope (and it's interesting that it takes years to achieve) is to help people to translate whatever they learn about psychoanalytic theory into quite simple sentences within the context of work with patients.

The main theoretical orientation is psychoanalysis and the schools represented in the British Psycho-Analytical Society.

The Introductory Course is aimed at enabling trainees to observe and think about their own experiences before theoretical considerations. To this end trainees participate in an analytic group where they are encouraged to observe the group process, and their own

---

* For change of name, see Author's Comments, p. 106.

contribution to its process. An Infant Observation is also followed for one year as well as discussion and study of the pioneering work of the Robertsons and their observation of children in hospitals, so that, although the Introductory Course will include introductions to psychoanalytic theory, the emphasis will be on the individual trainee's development.

There are three years which follow the Introductory Course where the work of the major theorists will be studied: Freud, Klein and Winnicott. Among the topics covered will be Dreams and Symbolism, Defence Mechanisms, Understanding and Not Understanding, Perversions, Containment and Acting Out, Silence, Eating Disorders, Termination and Addiction. Although it is felt that there are sometimes overlaps between behavioural therapy, humanistic therapy and analytic therapy, the former two are not studied since it is felt that for this training the focus has to be on the study of psychoanalytic theory in the context of psychotherapy.

Each trainee is assigned a personal tutor for meetings twice a term.

3. Training Structure

3.1 Training Committee

There is a Director of Studies, a Council and five members of the Training Committee. The Chair of the Training Committee is appointed by Council for a three-year term of office. The Training Committee meet once a fortnight to discuss: issues to do with training therapists, selection, details for contacting external teachers, and so on. The monitoring of trainees takes place in separate meetings with the Senior Tutor.

3.2 Selection procedure and admission

An application form, with two referees, is submitted before two separate interviews by members of the Training Committee. The age of applicants tends to be between twenty-five and fifty, but there is no stipulated age limit. Academic and/or professional qualifications are a requirement.

During the assessment interview attention is first of all paid to the applicant's self-description of personal and family background and subsequent work experience and qualifications that have been achieved. The interviewer would be noting why the applicant wants to do this sort of training and whether or not it fits into their abilities and life experience. The interviewer is looking for an aptitude to learn and an ability to listen. An awareness of the financial commitment as well as a stable life situation have also been found to be important attributes of the suitable applicant. The majority of applicants are from the core professions and are generally working in the NHS.

3.3 Time commitment and length of training

The personal tutor is seen twice a term during the Introductory Year and the subsequent three years, and once a term whilst trainees are completing their training cases. There are two seminars a week which take place on one evening a week. In the Introductory Year this would include the seminars on Infant Observation and the analytic group. Personal analysis, supervision, reading and training cases also have to be taken into account in terms of time commitment, so that the amount of time will be cumulative as the training progresses.

3.4 Interruptions in training

Each case would have to be negotiated individually and the Training Committee try to be as flexible as possible.

3.5 Postgraduate qualification and learned society

Qualification enables trainees to become Associate Members of the CAP and after four years of psychotherapy practice, graduates may apply for Full Membership with the presentation of a clinical paper. This part of CAP is presently being developed.

CAP does not have its own building or library and seminars take place at College Hall in Malet Street. There is a Code of Ethics.

4. Clinical and Academic Requirements

4.1 *Personal therapy*

Trainees are referred to training therapists/analysts by the personal tutor. Criteria for training therapist/analyst are by personal reputation as an experienced and practising clinician. This generally means that trainees will be referred to psychoanalysts, but experienced psychoanalytic psychotherapists and Jungian analysts may also be training therapists/analysts. Minimum frequency is three times weekly.

The training therapist/analyst is not consulted during the training.

4.2 *Clinical requirements*

Trainees are expected to be in therapy for at least one year before starting to see their first training patient. Trainees must see two patients: one for two years and the second for one year in three times weekly therapy. Medical cover and professional indemnity insurance are required.

4.3 *Supervision*

Two supervisors are required for each training patient who must be seen once weekly: criteria for supervisors are the same as those for training therapists/analysts.

The clinical seminars are seen as a sort of group supervision where trainees will share their work with each other.

4.4 *Papers and written work*

In the Introductory Year a brief paper on observation must be presented. This will be part of the assessment as to whether the trainee is ready to go on to the Full Programme. There are a number of essays to be presented to the tutor which will not go to the Training Committee but will contribute to the tutor's termly report to the Training Committee. A paper must also be presented on the Infant Observation seminars.

Tutors would be looking for evidence of psychotherapeutic work and the ability to release the patient, using psychoanalytic technique and understanding.

5. REFERRALS

Some training patients may come from trainees' work situation or from CAP. Borderline and psychotic patients would not be seen as suitable training patients, but CAP recognizes the difficulties of assessing how people will respond to treatment.

It is felt to be more helpful to the trainee if patients do not know they are working with a trainee. Some training patients may be seen in the NHS and therefore would be seen for no charge.

6. COST OF TRAINING

Fees are £230 a term including everything except personal therapy and supervision. Supervision and therapy tends to be in the region of £25 per session.

Trainees are expected to arrange for their own settings to see patients, and charges for training patients will depend on affordability. CAP is not able to offer bursaries or loans.

7. FUTURE EXPECTATIONS/CAREER PROSPECTS

Setting up in private practice is not something that is so relevant to CAP's training as it stands at the moment, but this may be something that will need addressing in the future.

CAP would like to encourage qualified graduates eventually to supervise and teach on the training and one graduate is already a member of the Training Committee.

8. TRAINEES' EXPERIENCE

8.1 *Why this course was chosen*

The aspects of this course which attracted trainees were:

(a) it was [mistakenly] thought to be an Independent Group training;

(b) it was thought to be an eclectic training;

(c) personal recommendation;

(d) possible to follow if living outside London.

The selection interviews were not experienced as intimidating, and it was felt that there was a genuine desire to assess suitability whilst also putting trainees at ease.

8.2 *The atmosphere of the course*

Just recently the CAP's training had undergone major changes and this inevitably had a disruptive effect on all trainees. The tutor system was experienced as a helpful aspect, because anxieties could be aired in addition to receiving academic help. The personal tutors were available by telephone when necessary.

The theoretical orientation is that of the British Psycho-Analytical Society, although the emphasis is Kleinian as most of the seminar leaders are psychoanalysts of the Kleinian Group, and trainees missed the input of Fairbairn and Guntrip. To this extent one trainee felt she had been misled into thinking that the training was eclectic. The seminars were experienced as excellent, as well as the clinical workshops which were felt to outweigh the negative aspects of the training.

Criticisms were to do with three main areas: the distribution of papers before a theoretical seminar – it was felt that trainees were left to organize this and sometimes without enough notice; the allocation of training patients – again trainees had to wait a long time, which delayed their training as CAP does not have its own clinic; and all aspects of administration. However, there was a general feeling that these difficulties were being addressed.

AUTHOR'S COMMENTS

The CAP has recently changed the middle part of its name from analytical to psychoanalytical, and this was largely to do with applicants thinking that the training was Jungian. The theoretical orientation is firmly that of the British Psycho-Analytical Society. Some trainees saw it as having a Kleinian bias. With the recent changes in management of the course it is difficult to assess the popularity of the organization. It seems that trainees were all impressed with the level of teaching of the seminars. There was some feeling, however, that criticisms of the training could sometimes be 'analysed away' rather than responded to on a practical level.

It is striking that private practice is not something that CAP is intending to prepare trainees for, although there are trainees who have that intention. If this is a training aimed at developing psychotherapy skills of the person already involved in the NHS in one of the core professions, how is the trainee wishing to develop a private practice accommodated? Tensions in this course, as in many others, may arise concerning the issue of the graduate's identity as a psychotherapist (see Part One). Training therapists and teachers tend to be exclusively analysts (graduates of the Institute of Psycho-Analysis or the SAP), and there is no established association within the CAP for graduates to share their work, post-graduation. It remains to be seen if these areas will be addressed by the recent changes.

GUILD OF PSYCHOTHERAPISTS

Marion Holt (General Secretary), 19b Thornton Hill, London SW19 4HU; tel: 081 947 0730.

1. HISTORY

The idea central to the Guild's formation came from Peter Lomas and a group of psychotherapists who were agreed on the central importance of the relationship between therapist and patient beyond what might be called detached technique. Peter Lomas felt that techniques inhibited the trainee from the beginning and he sought to promote the idea that psychotherapy training should concentrate on enabling ordinary people to develop and extend their skills in helping people in distress. Problematic in setting up the training was the fact that this philosophy did not lend itself to the traditional idea of being taught.

It was founded in 1974 by an eclectic group of people – Dr Peter Barham, Ben Churchill, Dr Camilla Bosanquet (Training Analyst at the SAP), Dr John Heaton (linked with the Philadelphia Association), Dr John Payne (former Director of Student Health at LSE) and Dr Joseph Redfearn. The philosophical inspiration behind this group was the work of Ivan Illich and his ideas of 'deschooling'. The above were a group of Freudians, Jungians and Existentialists who wanted to teach what they and their students felt to be important, rather than being confined to teaching in the linear traditional way. They also felt that psychotherapy was an ordinary activity which could be practised by ordinary people – that psychotherapy was a craft deriving from the human experience and something to which you could be apprenticed, hence the name Guild.

However, the theory put into practice caused tension between trainees and trainers who were endeavouring to implement an anti-structural bias with no formal teaching. Peter Lomas left the Guild in 1976 and his views on psychotherapy can be read about in his book *True and False Experience* (published in 1973 when the Guild was conceived). By this time the rest of the group were beginning to create a more formal structure to the training. However, 'it's still very much influenced by the idea that what is taught is taught by the very nature of the people on the training committees who have an inherent bias to resist dogmatism and doing the same thing over and over again.' The eclecticism was within the framework of psychoanalysis and analytical psychology but 'there was an agreement that the conflicts between the different schools did not have to be resolved – that you could live and thrive with systems that didn't necessarily share identical theoretical bases.'

2. THEORETICAL ORIENTATION AND CURRICULUM

The training is very much aimed at offering a pluralistic analytic orientation. In the first term of the first year, each member of the Training Committee will present, at a clinical seminar, a vignette from their own practice. This is a way for the trainee to get to know the Training Committee, as well as experiencing the differences in orientation. The commonality between these presentations is the emphasis on the clinical work. These presentations make up the first half of the one evening meeting per week.

The first part of the evening session is taken up with an experiential group where the tensions, the considerations, the experience of being in training – what it means to be in training – are looked at over the year with a group facilitator. There is no reporting back of these meetings to the Training Committee, unless there is significant cause for concern. The group facilitator is either a member of the Training Committee or an external group analyst.

In the second term of the first year the second half of the evening looks at Freud: the early case histories, present day Freudian thinking. depending on the teacher. Then in the third term the second part is taken up with the work of Jung.

An experiential group is held over the first year to explore the experience of training. There are plans to extend the experiential group through the full length of the training. Infant Observation is not compulsory but students are encouraged to seek their own Infant Observation seminars.

In the second year during the first part of the evening trainees present their own work, usually on their training patients. These groups are led by the year tutor or a senior member of the Guild or a member of the Training Committee. The second part of the evening is taken up with Freud 2. Klein is taught in the spring term and then in the third term Object Relations, Fairbairn, Balint and Winnicott.

The third year departs from the earlier years by taking a thematic approach to major theoretical concepts such as transference and countertransference. These seminars are led by people of different orientations, for it is assumed that by this year trainees have grasped enough theory to be able to cope with such differences. Psychosis, borderline disorders and narcissism are some of the themes of the spring term. The summer term is influenced by the theoretical and clinical preoccupations of the trainees. Most recently the themes covered have been dreams, psychosexuality and phenomenology.

There is now a compulsory fourth year where case discussions continue, as well as themes relevant to the theory and practice of psychotherapy. Humanistic therapy is not part of the curriculum.

Each trainee has a personal tutor throughout the training, with whom they must meet at least once a term.

3. TRAINING STRUCTURE

3.1 *Training Committee*

The Training Committee is a permanent subcommittee of the Management Committee who are responsible for the general control and administration of the Guild. They deal with the election of members, the admission of trainees and the assessment of progress of trainees but are not answerable to the Management Committee in those areas. People may be co-opted on to the Training Committee for up to one year without election because of their contribution to the life of the Guild as well as their teaching skills.

There are twelve people on the Training Committee. More than half of the Committee are now Guild-trained psychotherapists. Others have been trained at the Society of Analytical Psychology, the Philadelphia Association and the Tavistock Clinic. There is no student representative on the Training Committee but there is one student for each year of the training, who are part of the Management Committee. The trainees have a vote and are elected at the AGM. The Chair of the Training Committee is rotated every three years.

The Training Committee meet once a month to discuss all the issues concerned with the training: admission and student progress, the future curriculum, teaching, approaches from other bodies, etc. A detailed review is held each term on individual student development. A biannual brainstorming day is held without an agenda to explore issues that are not necessarily overtly evident.

3.2 *Selection procedure and admission*

There is an application form, and referees are required. Each applicant has two separate interviews by two people from the

Training Committee. Without some clinical experience acceptance for training is unlikely.

There is no age limit, but because of the pressure for places age may have to be taken into consideration. Academic qualifications are not necessary, but the ability to conceptualize and prove intellectual ability is essential. It is not possible to join the course from another training establishment. There are twelve places for each year, and there is a hope that there will be a balance of men and women. There is a subgroup working on intercultural issues.

The general background of people applying tends to be social work, teaching, clinical psychology, medicine, and so on. Although people from an Arts background are often accepted, they are in the minority. There is an increasing number of applicants for each year and last year there were more than seventy applicants for the twelve places.

3.3 Time commitment and length of training

The personal tutor must be seen at least once a term. There is one evening a week, 6.30–9.15, for two seminars, to accommodate trainees living outside London.

The amount of time to read is optional; acquisition and photocopying of papers is expected to be carried out by trainees.

Each trainee is required to fill a psychiatric placement in a psychiatric setting, and personal therapy, supervision and training patients are other time factors. In general it takes a minimum of four years to qualify, but depending on the trainee's readiness can take much longer.

3.4 Interruptions in training

Interruptions in training are accommodated. There is no limit, although trainees would be expected to keep in touch with their tutors and, depending on the length of interruption, may have to reapply.

3.5 Postgraduate qualification and learned society

There is automatic membership of the postgraduate scientific meetings and to date there are over 100 members of the Guild. A member takes responsibility for presenting a theme for the year such as The Impact of the Image, Adolescence, Mythology. There are meetings once a month and these are also open to trainees.

There is a residential conference once a year and a winter conference, which are for members and trainees. There are Study Days which are open to members of the public; the Guild operates from the LSE, where there is a library.

There is a Graduate Training Scheme for people who may never have had a formal training or who have had a training elsewhere. They must be seen in consultation once a month or be in regular supervision, with a member of the Training Committee, as well as attend all the Guild's members' meetings and present a 7,000-word clinical paper at the end of the year.

There is an in-house journal, and there is a Code of Ethics and an Ethics working party to deal with any complaints.

4. CLINICAL AND ACADEMIC REQUIREMENTS

4.1 *Personal therapy*

Before application a trainee is obliged to be in therapy for at least one year before the closing date of application and the Guild has its own referral service. The trainee is required to be in the minimum of twice weekly therapy, and is strongly recommended to increase the frequency at some point in the training.

Criteria for training therapists or supervisors are determined by the Training Committee. They must have been qualified for at least five years and be able to demonstrate their supervision and teaching experience. Confidentiality is respected and the analyst or therapist is never consulted during the training.

4.2 *Clinical requirements*

Before taking on a training patient the trainee will have discussed this with the personal tutor and supervisor. This would not generally be before the end of the first year. A trainee must have seen at least two training patients for at least one year, each in the minimum of twice weekly therapy. The trainee must be in supervision until qualification. Appropriate medical cover is recommended.

4.3 *Supervision*

Trainees must be in supervision with a member of the Training Committee but the other supervisor may be from another recognized analytic training. Group supervision takes place in clinical seminars.

4.4 *Papers and written work*

Clinical and theoretical presentations are made by each trainee over each term. Six-monthly reports on training patients are presented to tutors. By the beginning of the third year a theoretical paper of 3,000 words must be presented to the personal tutor. There is also a reading-in paper and this is the stage at which a trainee is ready to submit the final qualifying paper. The criteria for assessing qualification are dependent on all aspects of training as well as the presentation paper.

5. REFERRALS

A training patient is generally assessed by a member of the Training Committee, before being referred to a trainee. In the tradition of the Guild, experience working with a full range of patients is required.

6. COST OF TRAINING

The fees are £600 a year for seminars and tutorials. Supervision and therapy are an extra and vary within the normal rate. The trainee must not charge the training patient more than £8 a session, but may charge other patients whatever is appropriate. Consulting rooms have to be found or provided by each trainee.

There is a Studentship Trust for students in financial difficulties.

7. Future Expectations/Career Prospects

Practical advice on setting up in practice is something that is discussed in the tutorials and it seems that most people have a viable practice two years after qualifying.

There are prospects to supervise and teach, and be involved as much as one would like in the life of the Guild.

8. Trainees' Experience

8.1 *Why this course was chosen*

The aspects of the Guild training which most appealed were the following:

1. The Guild offered a less orthodox and 'rigid' course.

2. There was a larger breadth of theory offered within the analytic spectrum, without being too broad (humanistic therapy not being covered).

3. No consultation with trainees' therapists was felt to be a very important non-interfering policy.

4. The Guild was experienced by trainees in the interview procedure as very open and positive to people in their forties who wanted a career change or who were openly homosexual. This was seen as a positive difference from the more traditional trainings.

5. There was an emphasis on the trainee's personal development. This was seen as the training fitting in with the trainees' requirement rather than the trainee fitting in with the trainers' requirement.

6. Time commitment was less demanding than for other courses: one evening a week.

7. Because of the above factors trainees expected a greater sense of freedom in the Guild's training than others they had heard

of or looked at. The Guild was seen as 'anti-authoritarian' and
tolerant of self-expression.

The selection procedure was experienced as thorough and in
some cases a third interview was required. People felt that the
trainers interviewing were open and clarified many aspects of the
course. Trainees felt they had been as informed as they could be
about the different stages of the course. Recently changes had been
made and a fourth year is now compulsory. However, trainees who
were already training did not have to meet this requirement,
although they are encouraged to. The fact that these sorts of
changes were not imposed on trainees who did not know about
them before starting the course was experienced as very fair.

8.2 *The atmosphere of the course*

There is a student handbook with all the necessary information on
all the stages of the training. Trainees felt that information on all
aspects of the course was very accessible, through their personal
tutors and the student representative on the Management Committee.

Difficulties were experienced in obtaining training patients. This
was not seen as the fault of the Training Committee but rather as a
dearth of patients who were prepared to commit themselves to a
period of therapy more than once a week. Trainees sometimes
found their own training patients through work contacts.

In one year a trainee had been asked to take a year off. This had
been experienced as confusing for the rest of the group, who
realized something was wrong and felt they were not being kept in
the picture. Inevitable anxiety had been aroused and this took some
weeks to resolve. However, the rest of the group felt ultimately
reassured that this was evidence of how seriously the Training
Committee thought about the quality of trainees.

In the experiential group trainees were not sure how much the
leader was going to report back to the Training Committee, if at all.
This issue of confidentiality as well as the sheer volume of theory

that was covered throughout training were other confusing and anxiety-provoking aspects of training.

People felt they were getting the kind of training they had hoped for. The issues of psychotherapy and psychoanalysis were live debates throughout the training, and a tolerance and respect of differences was experienced. The Guild was experienced very much as as an organization in its own right and not second best to other organizations. The emphasis on psychotherapy as a craft and the deliberate rejection of hierarchical competition with other trainings, whilst still setting a high standard, was both enjoyed and appreciated by trainees, as a philosophy which they espoused.

AUTHOR'S COMMENTS

The Guild's training has become one of the most popular psychotherapy trainings in recent years. Although attempting to break away from the more traditional way of teaching and encouraging a system based on apprenticeship, the course over the years has become more rigorous. Nevertheless, trainees still experienced a sense of freedom in the encouragement of having to find their own individual way of working, within the analytic framework.

The theoretical orientation of this training, like many others in this section, brings up the debate concerning eclecticism and pluralism. The Guild makes a very conscious attempt to create a pluralistic environment and trainees will meet diverse teachers who may or may not align themselves to one school of thought. Meanwhile, graduates of this course may continue to choose not to align themselves with one school and refer to themselves as eclectic therapists.

Questions that arise would be linked with long-standing debates and controversies concerning eclecticism (see Part One), such as: Is psychotherapy an ordinary activity? Is it possible to maintain the depth of learning required when presenting new trainees with the breadth of differences between schools?

INSTITUTE OF PSYCHOTHERAPY AND SOCIAL STUDIES (IPSS)

5 Lake House, South Hill Park, London NW3 2SH; tel: 071 794 4147.

1. HISTORY

The two founder members of the IPSS came from different therapeutic backgrounds: Dr Giora Doron, a psychoanalyst, who came from Hungary, and John Rowan, an English humanistic psychotherapist. They came together to create a training because they felt the social and political dimensions of the trainings in existence were seriously lacking. They also felt that trainings had become too expensive and wanted to make their training more accessible. In January 1991, they were both designated 'emeritus'. The first intake of trainees with IPSS was 1978.

2. THEORETICAL ORIENTATION AND CURRICULUM

The course aims to put the theory and practice of psychotherapy firmly into the social and political context. So the interface of the inner and outer worlds is paid particular attention, as well as the philosophical underpinnings to psychoanalysis and critical theory. The student body formed the St Pancras Group to develop this further. Fundamental to the training is that trainees will become competent practitioners in individual psychotherapy.

The theoretical orientation is psychoanalytic and humanistic, and the theoretical seminars form the backbone of the training. For the first year the analytic and humanistic teaching run in parallel. Then in the second year trainees can opt to do a humanistic seminar. The analytic seminar is compulsory and again in the third year they have the humanistic option. The analytic seminars are mandatory throughout the three training years and in October 1991 the weekly two-hour analytic seminar was increased by half an hour to two seminars of an hour and a quarter.

First Year: The week is divided up as follows – for the first day there are three theoretical seminars of two hours each. The first is analytic, the second humanistic and the third sociological. For the second day there is a clinical seminar followed by an Advanced seminar which is shared with the other training years. The last session of that day is taken up with group therapy.

Second Year: Since 1990 trainees can choose whether to continue with a humanistic seminar or whether to have only the analytic. The sociological seminar is replaced with analytic supervision in groups.

Third Year: The format is the same as the second year. Amongst the analytic theorists studied are: Freud, Jung, Fromm, Sullivan, Winnicott, Searles, Guntrip, Lacan, Kohut, Ferenczi, Klein, Bion and Kernberg. Humanistic theorists studied are: Rogers, Perls, Schutz, Assagioli, Moreno, Lowen, Lake, Grof, Swartley, Mahrer and Wilber.

Any difficulties throughout the course are aired with the individual tutor, each student being assigned a tutor at the beginning of the first year for the duration of the course.

3. TRAINING STRUCTURE

3.1 *Training Committee*

There is a General Council of nine members, who are the staff members. There are six members of the Training Committee, each of whom is a psychotherapist in private practice: five whose training background is analytic and one who is humanistic. There is a Chair of the Training Committee who is elected at full council meetings; he or she must be an analytic orientated therapist. The IPSS is still in the process of forming a constitution and gaining charitable status.

Council meet five times a year and the Training Committee meet just before these meetings to discuss issues concerning the training programme. At least two extra meetings are convened in the summer term. There are members of Council who are involved with other trainings such as CAP, AGIP and WPF.

3.2 *Selection procedure and admission*

An application form is first of all submitted, with two referees. This is followed by two separate interviews with members of Council. Related experience is more important than clinical experience, but a degree or equivalent is required because the training is pitched at a postgraduate level. The 'equivalent' needs to be a demonstration of academic ability.

There is no age limit, although there would be a caution to very young or very old applicants. It is not possible to join the training at any point other than the beginning.

There are a maximum of twelve places for the three-year training programme and a maximum of twenty places for the Introductory Year. The number of applicants varies from year to year, and there is a wish to make the groups as balanced as possible. The general background of applicants tends to be the core professions.

3.3 *Time commitment and length of training*

The personal tutor is seen as often as required. The seminars take place from 3 p.m. to 9.30 p.m. two days of the week. The minimum time to qualify is three years and some may take up to five years.

3.4 *Interruptions in training*

Each case is assessed individually.

3.5 *Postgraduate qualification and learned society*

Graduates automatically join the IPSS and the fee is £20. Meetings are on the first Sunday afternoon of the month: there are nine meetings a year and four or five outside speakers are invited. The meetings are open. A small library is being developed and there is a permanent office with three seminar rooms.

4. CLINICAL AND ACADEMIC REQUIREMENTS

4.1 *Personal therapy*

There is a combination of ways of referring trainees to therapists which will depend on each trainee's situation. The trainee is required to be in twice weekly analytic therapy throughout training. Trainees opting to do the humanistic seminars in the second and third years are in therapy with an analytic therapist. Training therapists must have a psychotherapy qualification.

4.2 *Clinical requirements*

Training patients are not seen before the second year, and a minimum of two training patients must be seen for two years and eighteen months respectively. Medical consultation can be made with the psychiatrist who is consultant of the IPSS, for patients who may need medical care.

4.3 *Supervision*

Supervision takes place in groups of four and extends six weeks into vacation time.

4.4 *Papers and written work*

Three papers are required.

5. REFERRALS

Training patients are generally referred through the network, but can also come through a trainee's place of work. A patient who has had a very difficult early history would not be seen as an appropriate training patient. Patients may know they are seeing a trainee because of the low fee.

6. COST OF TRAINING

The cost of the training is £1,500 per year. This includes all training and supervision, but individual therapy would be an extra.

Training patients are seen for a low fee which goes directly to the trainee; consulting rooms are expected to be arranged by each trainee.

There are no bursaries or loans but on occasion the three-year cost can be spread over five years.

7. FUTURE EXPECTATIONS/CAREER PROSPECTS

Setting up in practice is discussed throughout the course. The IPSS is still developing and there would be prospects for graduates to teach and supervise; this has already happened.

8. TRAINEES' EXPERIENCE

8.1 *Why this course was chosen*

Trainees chose this course because, with reasonable fees, it offered an analytic training in conjunction with a humanistic component and experiential group work, which took into account the socio-cultural dimension. But since the analytic and humanistic elements could not be satisfactorily integrated, the latter will now be available as a separate option.

To rectify what was felt to be lack of adequate administrative consultation and coherent planning of courses, staff–student committees have now been set up.

8.2 *The atmosphere of the course*

The lively and stimulating case discussions and theoretical seminars attended weekly by the whole student body engendered a strong community feeling, and supervision of work with patients was consistently helpful and instructive. However, some of the theoretical teaching was felt to be poorly prepared and relied too heavily on student-led discussion, while students would have welcomed clearer guidelines. Fortunately, though, this resulted in a rich coverage of theory and practice as well as the fostering of independent thought.

Trainees were concerned that the IPSS lacked a good referral network, and steps have been taken to improve this. There was acknowledgement that while, so far, the IPSS is less well established than some of the better known trainings, for the patients in their care this would not count as much as the quality of the individual trainees' actual experience, supervision and personal analysis.

AUTHOR'S COMMENTS

The IPSS has had very specific aims in creating two very different sorts of trainings in parallel, as well as including a sociological aspect which some feel is a neglected area of a psychotherapy training. It is clear that there is no attempt to combine the different approaches of analytic and humanistic therapies, but to offer the two approaches in order that trainees will make an informed choice of what kind of therapist they want to be. It seems that this training is going through many changes and developments, and the humanistic strand has become secondary. This will inevitably mean a process of change of identity for the organization as well as trainees.

Criticism may come from both analytic and humanistic practitioners that the training is not focused enough on one attitude and that this can lead to too much confusion for a trainee. The direction of the IPSS seems to becoming predominantly analytic, but that will need to be clarified in the future.

LINCOLN CENTRE AND INSTITUTE FOR PSYCHOTHERAPY

19 Abbeville Mews, 88 Clapham Park Road, London SW4 7BX; tel: 071 978 1545; Referrals: 071 978 1543.

1. HISTORY

A brief history of the Lincoln Centre can be read in a booklet entitled *Twenty Years of the Lincoln Clinic – A Personal Account of its*

Origins, History and Structure (it can be obtained on request from the above address). The account was written by Lionel Monteith who was the inspiration and founding member of the Lincoln. The following is an edited version.

Lionel Monteith started thinking of forming a psychotherapy clinic in the early 1950s: 'primarily because of the help and effectiveness of a personal analysis I became aware of the benefits of the effective use of psychoanalysis and its derivative psychotherapies.' Along with recognizing a need for a psychotherapy clinic came the recognition of a need for more psychotherapists and a training programme. At this time the only significant trainings available were the Institute of Psycho-Analysis and the Society of Analytical Psychology. (Two other organizations were attempting to set up a training in the early 1950s – Open Door and the Association of Psychotherapists. The former folded and the latter became the British Association of Psychotherapists.)

Meanwhile Lionel Monteith was combining his duties as a Congregational minister with a growing interest in psychoanalytic psychotherapy, and gradually, after six years' personal analysis, clinical work under supervision and directed studies, set up in practice as a psychotherapist. Originally, he felt the best way to start a psychotherapy clinic and training was via the Church, but it was Harry Guntrip (an eminent member of the British School of Object Relations) who dissuaded Lionel Monteith: ' . . . He offered me the discouraging (but as I found, quite justified) opinion that the Church – at least at that time – was far too obsessed with its own anxieties and guilt to give effective support to psychotherapy work within its own structure.'

In 1966 Mrs Monteith suggested using two of the rooms in the abandoned Lincoln Tower to start a psychotherapy clinic. By 1967 the Lincoln had been founded. A legally non-profit-making company (later a Registered Charity) was formed, which would henceforward regulate the affairs of the clinic and its work, as well as giving it independence from the Church. Dr Margaret Stern was the first Lincoln Clinic Trainee, and assigned a room in the tower to see patients attending the clinic. So that although training was certainly a feature of the Lincoln Clinic, and indeed an informal training was in existence from the earliest days, it really began as a treatment organization.

Lionel Monteith increasingly felt that psychoanalysis should be at the core of the Lincoln's work and teaching: ' . . . This is why it is written into the rules of the Clinic that the Chairman of the Professional Committee shall be a person who holds, or has held, the post of Consultant Psychiatrist in the National Health Service and is also a Member of The British Psycho-Analytical Society.' It is the Professional Committee who are responsible for the overall functions of the Lincoln Centre and who delegate the responsibility of the training programme to the Training Committee.

In the last paragraph Lionel Monteith writes: 'Far from diminishing, the need for the skills of psychodynamic therapies in the community has greatly increased. And with this increase there remains the need for such therapies to be provided and upheld by centres of training and practice that can reach out to the community – while remaining firmly grounded in analytical psychotherapy of the highest standards. The future of the Lincoln Clinic will lie in its response to this need.'

2. THEORETICAL ORIENTATION AND CURRICULUM

The training is seen as a specialist postgraduate training that enables and qualifies therapists to work independently. The skills gained may be used in private practice, in the Health Service or in allied fields.

The main theoretical orientation is that of the British Psycho-Analytical Society, that is to say the work of all three schools: Klein, Independent and Contemporary Freudian. (Jung and humanistic therapy are not part of the curriculum.)

First Year
Infant Observation: This is a requirement for the first year and lasts for one year.
  Theory: Thirty seminars on Freud readings, dreams, the human life cycle and an introduction to the psychotherapeutic setting and technique. Infant Observation and child development

seminars are conducted by psychoanalysts or child psychotherapists.

Work Discussion: In addition 15 work discussion seminars are arranged for students in order to begin looking at work experiences in a psychodynamic way. These lead on to the clinical seminars in subsequent years.

Second and Third Years

Depending on their level of experience, some students may take two years before entering the clinical phase of training, but most will be expected to commence their first training case at some time in the second year.

Thirty theory seminars a year on: Development of psychoanalyic theories from Freud, Abraham, Klein, Fairbairn, Winnicott, Anna Freud and Bion to current writings.

Basic psychoanalytic concepts and components of technique including Orientation, Basic Framework and Boundaries, Formulation of Timing, Interpretation, Transference and Countertransference, Resistance and Defences, Acting Out and so on.

The following areas are given special focus during the course of training: Psychotic States of Mind, Psychopathology, Sexual Development and Disorders, Perversions, Suicide and Psychopathy, Narcissism, Projective Identification, Depression, Pregnancy, Sexuality, the Oedipus Complex and so on.

Thirty clinical seminars a year are also given for the group supervision and discussion of training cases. These are offered by psychoanalysts from all three groups in the British Psycho-Analytical Society.

Post-third Year(s)

Thirty clinical seminars (once weekly) with a focus which may not have been previously covered and for which relevant papers are read.

Throughout each course variations and changes are made to be flexible to the needs of different groups and individuals.

Tutors: each trainee has a tutor throughout training. The tutor is available for discussion with the trainees about their progress or difficulties and to liaise between trainees and Training Committee. Although group tutorials may sometimes be held, the tutor is always available for individual meetings.

3. TRAINING STRUCTURE

3.1 *Training Committee*

The governing body of the Lincoln Centre is the Board of Trustees. The Professional Committee is the highest authority in the Lincoln Centre on professional matters. The Chair must hold an appointment as consultant psychiatrist or psychotherapist in the NHS and be a Member or Associate Member of the British Psycho-Analytical Society. All other members are psychiatrists/psychoanalysts or senior psychotherapists. The Professional Committee appoint the Dean of Studies.

The Training Committee is chaired by the Dean of Studies and comprises a further four or five members. At present three are psychoanalysts, two senior psychotherapists. The work of the Committee, who meet two or three times a term, comprises a number of tasks among which are organizing and reviewing both the curriculum and teaching, monitoring the progress of all students at every stage of training, approving choice of supervisors and timing of taking patients, approving and recommending qualification. The Dean, in discussion with the Committee, appoints seminar leaders. Regular feedback from students about the teaching is fully considered. The continuous monitoring of students' progress allows difficulties to be foreseen. The Training Committee have a subcommittee for the purpose of considering new admissions. At present there is no policy to include a student representative on the Training Committee; students have access to the Committee through their tutors.

3.2 *Selection procedure and admission*

Candidates complete an application form on which they detail their academic attainments, employment, relevant experience and reasons for wanting to train as a psychoanalytic psychotherapist.

The postgraduate nature of the training means that a degree or equivalent is necessary. Clinical experience is usually required; personal suitability is essential.

Two interviews are undertaken by senior members of the Lincoln Centre or other psychoanalysts known to the Training Committee. Written reports as well as submitted information by candidates, references and therapists' reports (when available) are considered by the admissions subcommittee before a final decision is taken by the Training Committee. In some cases a third interview may be arranged.

When interviewing and in the selection procedures, the Lincoln seeks candidates with the potential for analysability, a healthy motivation for training and the integrity which will allow them to achieve a basic safe competence in becoming independent psychoanalytic psychotherapists.

While the Lincoln is willing to receive an application to train from students already involved in another training, such application would be dealt with in the same way as any other; however, the previous training experience would be taken into account.

Course Affiliates: in order to help people who for a variety of reasons may not wish or be able to do the full training but who wish to further their knowledge and experience, the Lincoln is willing to arrange for them to participate in relevant parts of the course. Infant Observation is a case in point. The acceptance of Course Affiliates depends on there being space in the relevant group.

There are between five and ten trainees in each year group, and usually more women than men apply so this is reflected in year groups: the ratio changes from year to year. People who apply are usually from backgrounds in health and social service, clinical psychology and education. Nevertheless the training is open to applicants from non-clinical backgrounds; if accepted they would be required to take up a psychiatric placement. There are approximately fifty to sixty applying a year for the maximum of ten places.

3.3 *Time commitment and length of training*

The course is designed for people in full-time work although it is acknowledged that in such a case it is very hard work. Throughout the course time is needed for therapy, two evening seminars per week (with a fortnightly third in the first year), reducing to one seminar after the third year. Additionally, in the first year: one hour to observe an infant and time for writing up observations and to write a paper; subsequent years: time for two three times weekly patients and two weekly supervisions and for writing reports.

Trainees have to read approximately two to three papers each week during term time and the Training Administrator may be able to help trainees in obtaining papers. It usually takes between four and five years to qualify.

3.4 *Interruptions in training*

Interruptions are accommodated for serious reasons and trainees can come back with the agreement of the Training Committee when they wish as long as they have remained in therapy.

3.5 *Postgraduate qualification and learned society*

Once a trainee has qualified, he or she is elected to Associate Membership of the Lincoln Centre by the Professional Committee. The subscription is £40 per year (December 1990).

Membership: there is a two-year post-qualification course leading to graduation as a Full Member. This comprises:

(a) the fortnightly supervision by two different psychoanalysts of two three times weekly patients of different sexes over two years;

(b) full participation in 60 group clinical seminars conducted by psychoanalysts. The focus of seminars includes: timing and formulation of interpretation (by psychoanalysts from the three groups of the British Psycho-Analytical Society), projective identification, transference and countertransference, perverse states of mind, trauma and anxiety, defensive structures, acting out, dreams, female sexuality, psychic change and termination.

Assessment for qualification is primarily based on detailed written reports from supervisors and from seminar leaders.

This course is also open to psychotherapists who have trained with other training institutions where they have undergone a personal therapy comparable with that required by the Lincoln's own training. Applicants must submit a detailed relevant curriculum vitae and have up to two interviews with members of the Professional Committee. Final selection of applicants and assessment on completion of the course is by the course tutors. Course participants proceed to Full Membership if they complete the course to the satisfaction of the tutors and, finally, the Professional Committee.

The course fee is £350 per annum and the membership subscription is £57 per annum.

Meetings: there are regular meetings for Associate and Full Members, as well as trainees, where papers are presented by Lincoln people or invited guests.

There is a building: the Lincoln began in the Lincoln Tower in Lambeth which Lionel Monteith writes about in his history of the Lincoln Centre. The Centre moved to its present building in Clapham in 1988. There is an in-house newsletter and a small library.

Code of Ethics: the Lincoln follows a code similar to that covering medical practice. The Professional Committee (see 3.1) oversees policy and the maintenance of standards and ethics in relation to training and treatment. Through its own activities and through the Training Committee it ensures that psychotherapists and students under clinical supervision adhere strictly to a code of ethics similar to that of medical practice.

4. CLINICAL AND ACADEMIC REQUIREMENTS

4.1 *Personal therapy*

Most people are already in therapy when they apply, but help is given to refer people if this is needed. Before final acceptance the trainee must be established in a minimum of three times weekly personal psychoanalytic psychotherapy with – with only rare exceptions – a Member or Associate Member of the British Psycho-Analytical Society. The Lincoln Centre encourages trainees to be in four or five times weekly analysis when possible. The training analyst is consulted at three stages: once during the selection procedure, before taking training cases and lastly just before qualifying.

4.2 *Clinical requirements*

Most trainees will take a first training case during their second year. It must be very clear to the Training Committee that the trainee is ready for this step. The minimum amount of supervised work students are required to undertake is two training cases of different sexes three times weekly, one for at least two years and one for eighteen months dependent on quality of work. The first case must be in treatment for at least six months before a second is considered. The total amount of work required for qualification is at the discretion of the Dean and Training Committee. Medical cover must be held by the patient's general practitioner or by the referring consultant psychiatrist/psychotherapist.

Additional clinical work is required for those students who have little clinical experience, particularly before taking training cases. This work is evaluated in the fortnightly work discussion group in the first year. Students with little or no experience of psychotic patients are usually required to take a placement in a psychiatric unit.

4.3 *Supervision*

The training cases are supervised by different supervisors, psychoanalysts, one of each sex, on a weekly basis for the duration of treatment until, and sometimes beyond, qualification. The first supervisor should be of the same orientation as the trainee's own training therapist.

4.4 *Papers and written work*

There are three types of paper to be written: the Infant Observation paper, six-monthly reports on training cases (a short report on each case summarizing treatment over the previous six months and read by supervisor, tutor and Dean) and the qualifying paper. The latter is a paper of between 7,000 and 10,000 words on one of the trainee's training cases and should demonstrate understanding of the concepts of psychoanalytic psychotherapy and the meaning of the transference. The paper goes anonymously to a senior external psychoanalyst, independent of the training, for assessment. When the Training Committee, therapist, supervisors and examiner are agreed that the trainee is ready to work independently, his or her election to Associate Membership is recommended to the Professional Committee.

5. REFERRALS

Training patients are referred through the Lincoln Centre, GPs, consultant psychiatrists and psychotherapists and allied professionals. Training cases are strictly assessed by psychoanalysts or psychotherapists competent in the assessment of patients. While the Lincoln endeavours to find training cases for all students, geographical factors cannot always be met. Students should be aware of referral sources in their area and prepared to take some responsibility for finding their cases. What is looked for in the training patient is that they are 'motivated enough to look at their problems and to stand some psychic pain; that they can tolerate frustration and dependency and a reasonable degree of intelligence where they need help in thinking about their life, rather than managing it.'

It is preferred that training patients do not know that they are seeing a trainee, as it could be something that is used to denigrate the therapy in a way that would not be useful to either trainee or patient.

6. COST OF TRAINING

The fee for one year is £816. The Lincoln, as a registered charity and in endeavouring to prevent the cost of training becoming prohibitive, does all it can to keep the cost to a minimum, while covering its costs. As with most courses, personal therapy is extra, and arranged between therapist and trainee, as is supervision, though it is expected that the fees paid by the training patient will cover the supervision fee.

Trainees are encouraged to be involved in as much clinical work as possible during their training years, preferably in an appropriate place of work (child guidance clinics, hospitals, social services, etc.).

The Lincoln is well aware that until registration of psychotherapists a trainee may legally call him/herself a 'psychotherapist', but until qualification trainees are not encouraged to do so.

7. FUTURE EXPECTATIONS/CAREER PROSPECTS

Practical advice on setting up in practice is part of the course. The time taken to set up a viable private practice will inevitably vary according to the individual, but many trainees have the foundations of their practice established while they are still training. Qualified Lincoln psychotherapists also take up posts in institutions such as hospitals and clinics, in the community, in independent helping agencies, and recently in general practitioner surgeries.

There would be opportunities to teach on the training programme for Full Members of the Lincoln after considerable experience and evidence of an ability to teach on a particular subject. It is expected that the special skill of supervising someone in training will remain for the foreseeable future with psychoanalysts.

8. TRAINEES' EXPERIENCE

8.1 *Why this course was chosen*

The rigorous and professional presentation of the Lincoln's training programme was one of the main factors attracting trainees. Dr Anton Obholzer F.R.C.Psych., who is Chair of the Professional Committee as well as Chair of the Tavistock Clinic, contributed to the already developing credibility of the Lincoln.

Trainees felt they were well informed as to the commitment of undertaking such a course on the financial and practical level, but agreed that any amount of information can never inform in the same way as experience of the course. At the initial stages trainees felt helped, encouraged and held, through the advice and support they felt they received from the trainers concerned. The selection procedure was found to be very thorough, in-depth and very stringent.

8.2 *The atmosphere of the course*

The Dean of Studies had changed recently and this had brought about further professional development, in a rigorous fashion, which was appreciated by all. The seminar leaders and teachers were excellent. However, one of the changes meant that all teachers and supervisors had to be psychoanalysts, and there was the strong message that only psychoanalysts were good enough to teach and supervise. One trainee said she wouldn't want to see rigidity take the place of sensibility, and there was some concern that the rigour could turn into an inflexibility.

Trainees felt that the Dean of Studies influenced the programme profoundly and the fact that Judith Jackson is a psychoanalyst of the Kleinian school, as well as having also trained as a child psychotherapist with the Tavistock, has inevitably affected certain aspects of the course. People felt, for instance, that there was a larger input from the Kleinian than from the Independent Group of the British Psycho-Analytical Society.

Communication at the general level was felt to be clear and defined, although there was some criticism that when there was a change in rule or expectation, it took some time to come down through the hierarchy to the trainees. The library facilities were a problem and trainees had had difficulty in finding some of the papers they needed, despite the great trouble taken by the training administrator. The most confusing and challenging part of the course was felt to be grappling with the different schools within the British Psycho-Analytical Society; for instance being in analysis with an analyst from the Independent Group whilst studying the difference in techniques of the Kleinian school.

Trainees felt that the training had more than met their expectations and they were satisfied with the curriculum and the support they felt was available for them. Support did not seem so available for trainees whose training patients may have left just before the required time limit. Perhaps this is a situation where the flexibility of a particular training is tested. Lincoln trainees, however, felt it important to comply with the requirements of the Training Committee with regard to each individual student's perceived needs.

AUTHOR'S COMMENTS

The Lincoln is one of the longest standing psychotherapy trainings, with its roots going back to the early 1950s (see History; Scarlett, 1991). In addition to the psychotherapy course, the Lincoln offers courses in Counselling and Group Dynamics. The Inner City Centre was set up in 1982 by Gil Parker and Prophecy Coles, as a non-sectarian, non-profit-making venture, offering help to people in the local community. Some Associate Members of the Lincoln Centre are involved with offering amenity places for therapy.

There is much talk, amongst people in the psychotherapy world, that since the appointment of Judith Jackson as Dean of Studies, the Lincoln's training has become more Kleinian. This was confirmed by the trainees. Judith Jackson made it very clear that she felt that the work of Melanie Klein and the post-Kleinians was the most exciting contribution to psychoanalysis. It is inevitable, therefore, that there will be an emphasis on Klein. The criticism from some quarters (mainly non-Kleinians) would inevitably link with the Controversial Discussions of the 1940s in the British Psycho-Analytical Society. This is the legacy which has been inherited by psychoanalytic psychotherapists. The debate is ongoing in the British Psycho-Analytical Society, and almost all the analytical psychotherapy trainings (referred to in Part One).

This would also apply to the conflicts and eventual parting of the ways between Freud and Jung. The latter is also not studied and a Jungian training therapy is not acceptable whilst undergoing this training. Some trainings may criticize this, and they would be the trainings that include Jung or are Jungian. The Lincoln is clear that Jung and the Jungian school is not compatible with their training.

The issue of trainees feeling second best seems to reflect the perennial debate on the differences between psychoanalysis and psychotherapy. Judith Jackson was very clear that she saw a training in psychotherapy as different from a training in psychoanalysis, and not inferior. Meanwhile, in the area of supervision, the Lincoln's attitude is that only psychoanalysts may supervise for the 'foreseeable future'. Why?

Some of the ongoing debates within the world of analytic psychotherapy are alive in this training as they are in every analytic training. Are they being debated in a lively way? How do trainees resolve their confusion when finding themselves in the midst of a historical disagreement (Controversial Discussions) that some therapists feel is irresolvable?

LONDON CENTRE FOR PSYCHOTHERAPY (LCP)

19 Fitzjohn's Avenue, Swiss Cottage, London NW3 5JY; tel: 071 435 0873; 071 435 5512.

1. HISTORY

'The London Centre for Psychotherapy has its origins in the 1950's, becoming a registered charity in 1974. The aims have been two-fold: to provide analytical psychotherapy through its Clinic, and to integrate various schools of analytical thought and practice in its training. Over the last few years the Centre has expanded considerably and currently provides an association for about 180 practising psychotherapists.' (Quotation marks denote passages taken from the LCP brochures.)

2. THEORETICAL ORIENTATION AND CURRICULUM

The main theoretical orientations are psychoanalysis and analytical psychology.

First Year: Theoretical seminars on: Freud, Pathological States of Mind, Practical Techniques of Psychotherapy and Contemporary Case Studies.

Second Year: Theoretical seminars on: Klein, Object Relations, Freud, Jung and the post-Jungians and further Contemporary Case Studies.

Third Year: 'Studies in Depth' – Seminars in the third year focus on a particular idea or theoretical concept. These are taken by senior members of the LCP and other recognized organizations: Freud – 10 seminars; Jung and the post-Jungians – 10 seminars; Klein and the post-Kleinians – 20 seminars; The Independent Group – 20 seminars.

Other seminars cover the following topics: Diagnostic Formulations, Integration and Dialogue (looking at the different schools of thought relating to psychotherapy) and Management and Practice.

In addition to the theoretical seminars there is an Infant Observation seminar for two years as well as an ongoing experiential group 'designed to give trainees experience of group dynamics and of their own behaviour in a group setting'.

3. TRAINING STRUCTURE

3.1 *Training Committee*

Council of the LCP carries the ultimate responsibility for all aspects of the Centre's work and policy. It is made up of fifteen elected, experienced and senior psychotherapists. There are then four sections responsible for specific areas, one being the Training Section. For each year in training there is a subcommittee of four members. Each member of the subcommittee serves as a tutor to assigned trainees.

The committees meet once a month; monitoring of the trainees and the running of the Training Programme is discussed.

3.2 *Selection procedure and admission*

An application form and one reference are required for the Introductory Year which is obligatory for trainees wishing to continue on to the full programme. People who do not want to become psychotherapists but are interested in psychotherapy are eligible for the one-year Introductory Course.

The Introductory Year is also used as a way of assessing people to be interviewed for the full training programme. People wishing to apply for the full programme will have two separate interviews which will take place at some time during their introductory year. The therapist or analyst interviewing is not given a previous written report of the applicant, so as not to influence the meeting, but after the interview they will write a detailed account for the Training Committee. Suitable trainees are assessed on both their intellectual ability and an emotional capacity to deal with the work of psychotherapy.

There is no upper or lower age limit. Academic qualifications are important but not essential as long as the applicant can demonstrate an ability to cope intellectually with the academic side of training, and in some cases the Introductory Year can be waived. Between ten and fourteen people are accepted for each year out of on average 25–35 applicants and there is no policy of an equal number of males and females for each group. The majority of applicants are from the 'core professions', but there are some applicants from other backgrounds.

3.3 *Time commitment and length of training*

Most people work full-time whilst following the three-year course. At least twenty hours per week would be required to follow the full programme. Personal tutors are seen at least once a term and more often if required. Seminars are held on two evenings a week. Additional time is needed for personal therapy, supervision, reading and training patients, and in general it takes four to six years to qualify.

3.4 *Interruptions in training*

Each individual request for a sabbatical is considered separately and the length of interruption would depend on the individual circumstances.

3.5 *Postgraduate qualification and learned society*

Qualified graduates may apply for Associate Membership, three months after qualification. Full Membership may be applied for three years post-qualification. There are monthly meetings for presentations and discussion of papers.

The LCP is planning to introduce a group course for qualified analytical psychotherapists and also a postgraduate course dedicated to further learning and to improving skills.

There is a building where seminars and so on take place, but there is no library; there is an in-house journal and a newsletter. Members of other recognized psychotherapy organizations may apply to become members.

There is a Code of Ethics.

4. CLINICAL AND ACADEMIC REQUIREMENTS

4.1 *Personal therapy*

On the Introductory Year there is no requirement for personal psychotherapy but a trainee will discuss with the personal tutor the requirement, if planning to apply for the three-year training. The personal tutor is then responsible for helping the trainee find the appropriate therapist, but only in terms of vacancy situation and orientation.

A trainee must have been in twice weekly therapy for a year before the full training programme and then three times weekly up to qualification. The training therapist or analyst is consulted twice, once on the trainee's application to train and a second time when the trainee feels ready to start seeing a training patient. The criterion for training therapists and analysts is that they have trained at one of the following training institutions:

The British Psycho-Analytical Society

The Society of Analytical Psychology

The London Centre for Psychotherapy

The British Association of Psychotherapists

The Tavistock Clinic Four-year Full-time training in Adult Psychotherapy

Applications from other analytical training institutions will be considered.

The therapist or analyst must have had at least five years' post-qualification experience of intensive psychotherapy cases and be working a minimum of twenty-five hours per week.

4.2 *Clinical requirements*

Trainees are assessed on their readiness to start seeing a patient during the Infant Observation seminars, the experiential group and the ordinary theoretical seminars. The first training patient must be seen three times weekly for two years and the second training patient a minimum of twice weekly for eighteen months. The Clinic takes medical responsibility for Clinic patients. The trainee is expected to inform the patient's GP.

4.3 *Supervision*

Each trainee has an individual supervisor for the first training patient and is in group supervision for the second training patient.

4.4 *Papers and written work*

Four papers must be written during the course: one on the Infant Observation, one theoretical paper and two clinical theoretical papers based on work with patients; these should be from 2,000 to 3,000 words. There is no formal reading-in paper.

5. REFERRALS

There are diagnostic reports from the therapists assessing people in the LCP Clinic. Statements will be made in these reports as to patient suitability for trainees. The most appropriate training patient is seen as someone with no extreme 'acting out' like anorexia, bulimia, suicidal tendencies, alcoholism and addiction, but with a capacity to work psychodynamically. It is left entirely up to the trainee and supervisor as to whether or not a patient will know the trainee status of the therapist.

6. Cost of Training

Training fees are £1,200 per year which does not include supervision (individual) or personal therapy. Training patients pay trainees directly and fees from the first training patient are retained by the trainee to pay for individual supervision. Fees from the second training patient go to the LCP to cover group supervision for that patient. The LCP recommends trainees charge a minimum of £10 per session. There is no upper limit and again it is left to the trainee and supervisor on the patient's ability to pay. Consulting rooms are available, but mainly during the day.

There are no bursaries or loans at present.

7. Future Expectations/Career Prospects

There are special seminars on the practicalities of setting up in practice, and application can be made to supervise or teach.

8. Trainees' Experience

8.1 *Why this course was chosen*

Trainees had heard about the LCP training through people they knew who had followed the training and who worked within the NHS. People also felt that the LCP would be more open to older applicants and flexible about qualifications.

The Introductory Year was experienced as a very real way of learning about the realities involved with training to become a psychotherapist. Trainees were grateful for the opportunity to assess themselves and the LCP during this year, as a way of deciding if the full programme was what they wanted to move on to. There had also been some pain involved during the year as it became clear that there were some people in the Introductory Year who would continue and others who would not or might not.

Some trainees found the selection procedure for the full course very difficult and anxiety-provoking, but on reflection could see that it was related to their own anxiety about being acceptable or not. Meanwhile, it was felt that it was a very long process between deciding to follow the full course and knowing a place was available. This was not the case for every applicant.

Trainees did not feel as informed as they could have been about every stage of the course as they set out on the full programme. However, it was acknowledged there was a difference between knowing about a requirement and realizing the full experience of that requirement.

8.2 *The atmosphere of the course*

Contradictory information was experienced on occasion which was linked with some teachers and supervisors not being members of the LCP. Trainees, however, felt that people tried very hard and worked very conscientiously and that problems of communication probably occurred because committee work was voluntary.

Generally trainees felt that the teaching had been superb and the academic part of the course was well organized, and people were very happy with the curriculum. Trainees had on occasions experienced difficulties when a particular subject had been taught in a highly complex way, leading to more confusion than understanding. However, complaints had been listened to and trainees were impressed that changes had been made in response to criticisms and complaints. Trainees were agreed that having a representative on the Training Committee was a very effective channel for their communications, positive and negative, and this engendered a sense of trust.

A party is held once a year for all the training years. People felt enthusiastic about this as a way of trainees sharing the experience of training.

The LCP owns its own building where there is a notice-board for relevant communications. Everybody felt this was an extremely helpful system, although all agreed a bonus would be a room just for trainees; it was understood that this was not possible and not the fault of the LCP. There had been some difficulty in finding training patients, although the system had improved recently.

Overall trainees were pleased about their choice of the LCP's training. There was some agreement that having to study the three main theorists (and the developments), Freud, Klein and Jung, caused some difficulties but that they were glad to have had the breadth of theoretical input that some other trainings do not offer.

AUTHOR'S COMMENTS

The LCP is one of the longest standing therapy training organizations with its roots in the Association of Psychotherapists (see Part One and Scarlett, 1991). Many of the teachers and members are also members of the British Psycho-Analytical Society and the Society of Analytical Psychology. Melanie Hart won the Student Essay Prize of the *British Journal of Psychotherapy* in 1989 with her paper, 'The arrival of the bee box: poetry and mental mechanism' (Hart, 1989).

The curriculum includes all the schools of the British Psycho-Analytical Society and the Society of Analytical Psychology. Relevant to this training, therefore, would be the differences in theory between these two Societies representing the original parting of the ways between Freud and Jung (see Part One and Introduction to Part Two). The breadth of theory is sometimes experienced as confusing by trainees, yet they all felt it was preferable to having followed a training that adhered to only one school.

Perhaps what needs to be asked is how the different theories are incorporated into the training. For instance, which theoretical orientation would influence the Infant Observation, and would a trainee's supervisor be of the same orientation as the training therapy? These questions would be linked with the issues related to eclecticism and pluralism (see Introduction to Part Two).

PHILADELPHIA ASSOCIATION (PA)

4 Marty's Yard, 17 Hampstead High Street, London NW3 1PX; tel: 071 794 2652.

1. HISTORY

The Philadelphia Association was founded in 1965 as a registered charity. The founder members were a group of psychiatrists, psychoanalysts and social workers who developed a philosophical critique of psychoanalysis grounded in phenomenology, and an 'anti-psychiatry' critique of the institutional treatment of the mentally ill. They set up therapeutic community households of which the best known was Kingsley Hall in London.

The celebrity and notoriety of R.D. Laing, one of the PA founder members who became famous in the 1960s and 1970s for the publication of his work, and radical ideas (notably *The Divided Self*), made it part of the counter-culture of the time – it staged, for example, the famous Dialectics of Liberation Congress at London's Round House in 1967.

The PA's unorthodox contribution to the development of psychoanalysis drew people from Britain and all over the world to its communities and study programmes. These had consolidated by 1970 into a formal training in psychoanalytic psychotherapy. A more detailed history can be read in the PA's book *Thresholds Between Philosophy and Psychoanalysis: Papers from the Philadelphia Association* by Robin Cooper and others (Free Association Books, 1989).

2. THEORETICAL ORIENTATION AND CURRICULUM

The main theoretical orientation is psychoanalysis. Trainees are trained to be psychoanalytic psychotherapists. However, unlike any other analytical psychotherapy training, philosophy is a part of the curriculum. 'We feel that psychoanalysis has neglected the philosophical enquiry to its own basic presuppositions . . . no one

teaches the basic philosophy that psychoanalysis came out of . . .
we feel that it's absolutely crucial to any training in psychoanalytic
therapy, to be engaged in that.'

The training programme has been kept deliberately small, and
people can apply at any time and join the group of trainees at the
beginning of any term. There are generally no more than fifteen
trainees, and they will all be at different stages of their own personal
training, even though they will all be part of the same seminar
group. The training is thus based on an apprenticeship system.

The introductory year in phenomenology and psychoanalysis is
compulsory before going on to the full training programme. Entry
to this year is preceded by an interview. The curriculum for the full
training programme is set once a year by the Training Committee.
Amongst the texts are the basic psychoanalytic theoreticians:
Freud, Klein, Winnicott, Bion, Laing and Lacan. The philosophers
felt to be relevant to the work of psychotherapy are also studied:
Socrates, Plato, Hegel, Kierkegaard, Nietzsche, Husserl, Heidegger,
Sartre, Levinas and Derrida.

Each trainee has a personal tutor for regular liaison with the
Training Committee and any difficulties that may arise. Once a year
there is also a meeting between the Training Committee and all
trainees.

3. TRAINING STRUCTURE

3.1 *Training Committee*

There are six members of the Training Committee. It is a
subcommittee of the Philadelphia Association Management Committee. The members are all psychoanalytic psychotherapists and
in the main have trained with the PA. Some of these members are
also members of the Management Committee. There is a Director
of Training who is rotated every three years.

The Training Committee meet at the end of each term to discuss
the assessment of trainees and the training for that term. There is a
meeting of the Management Committee which is held every month.
This meeting is for the whole of the PA's business, and may

sometimes include issues of policy concerning the training programme. A separate Committee arranges the introductory year.

3.2 *Selection procedure and admission*

There is one interview for the introductory year. Part of this year is an experiential ongoing group, and personal tutorials for set texts. Trainees wishing to go into the full programme must apply formally. There is an application form and two separate interviews with members of the Training Committee. The applicant must have been in therapy for at least one year before entering the full programme and two references will be taken. There is no formal age limit, but there is a reluctance to take people into the programme who are too young/immature. Academic qualifications are not necessary, but applicants must be able to prove their academic capability.

Normally trainees do not come from other trainings to join the PA's course, but an applicant in this situation may well be accepted as an exceptional case. Between two and five people are accepted each year, out of generally ten or more applicants, and about two graduate each year.

3.3 *Time commitment and length of training*

The personal tutor must be seen at least once a term and more often if required.

The introductory year consists of every Tuesday evening through the term plus the group and meetings with the personal tutor. Trainees following the full programme attend a long evening on Thursdays. Some trainees may be asked to continue to attend the Tuesday meetings when they start the full training.

There are bi-monthly Community Ethos meetings where people working in the communities meet to discuss the work of the communities. This meeting is open to trainees, but is not compulsory. There is great encouragement of trainees to attend all the different lectures that are being held in London, by various organizations. There is a great deal of reading to be done each week on philosophy and psychoanalysis.

Qualification takes from four to six years.

3.4 *Interruptions in training*

Pregnancy is something that is accommodated, but people have
tended not to take much time off. Each case would be assessed
individually.

3.5 *Postgraduate qualification and learned society*

Qualification is not just decided by the Training Committee,
although they do have the final say. A tradition has evolved whereby
trainees must present their case to the whole company of the PA at
a meeting named the Pass. By this time, discussion would have taken
place with fellow trainees about the readiness to qualify, as well as
with supervisors and tutors. The Pass meeting can be very
controversial, and it may well happen that a trainee may not 'pass'
the test. There must be a consensus from the group that the trainee
is indeed ready and worthy to become a psychotherapist.

Once qualified there is automatic associate membership of the
PA. There are monthly meetings for associates and members, for
theoretical and clinical discussions. There are about fifty associates.
Full membership of the PA is not something that is applied for, but
rather something that an associate may be invited to attain.
Associate members of PA who have trained elsewhere are usually
invited, rather than by application, to be full members. There are
eleven full members, two of whom are elected by the Association
to represent them each year.

The PA owns a centre in Hampstead where there is a conference
room, a library, the administrator's office and consulting rooms
which are rented out to trainees and therapists.

4. CLINICAL AND ACADEMIC REQUIREMENTS

4.1 *Personal therapy*

All trainees must be in psychoanalytic therapy with a qualified
therapist or analyst of seven years' experience since qualification
for a period of one year prior to entering training, and, for the
duration of the training, with sessions as many times per week as

are felt necessary, but not less than twice a week. Where a candidate is in therapy with someone of less than seven years' post-qualification experience, this may be allowed subject to interview with the candidate and, where it is felt necessary, with the therapist. The PA believes the therapy and the continuity of the therapy is of such importance that it would not want to interrupt the process of 'gathering the transference' for the sake of an abstract principle without good reason. 'If trainees were themselves to express a wish or the necessity for changing therapist, having outgrown what can be gathered there, of something having gone wrong or become unproductive, that would be discussed with the personal tutor with an in principle openness to a change on the ground that these things happen, and a training has to be sufficiently flexible to accommodate the possibility.'

Whilst the PA places great importance on the reports from supervisors, teachers and tutors, it respects the privacy of the personal therapy and does not ask for reports from the training therapist. Being small by design and operating the principle of apprenticeship, the PA takes responsibility to follow each trainee's personal development.

4.2 *Clinical requirements*

All trainees must have had relevant clinical experience before starting the training, either in their social work setting or equivalent. Consequently from the personal first year onwards, if the Training Committee feel it is right, trainees will be setting up in private practice and having referrals made through the PA.

It is PA policy not to have one or two training patients, but to consider the general experience of working with several patients. By the time of qualification a trainee will have seen at least two long-term patients in twice weekly therapy, as well as a number of other patients, short or long term.

It is expected that trainees will follow a placement in one of the residential communities, but some may not meet that expectation and it is possible to qualify as a PA therapist without ever having anything to do with the therapeutic communities. Due to the special nature of the communities it seems inappropriate to insist on a specific time for such an involvement from a trainee, and a placement often takes place after graduation.

Medical cover is not a requirement, although there are psychiatrists who are part of the PA to whom a trainee may refer if necessary. It is not required of a trainee to write to the GP of a training patient.

4.3 *Supervision*

A root principle of the training method is that of apprenticeship and it is therefore required that either the therapist or one of their two supervisors will be a senior member of the PA. Trainees are in supervision for their clinical work patients, from the beginning. If a trainee is working in one of the teams attached to a community, they will also be getting group supervision as part of the team.

The suitability of supervisors has to be approved by the Training Committee and this is done through personal knowledge, reputation or interview.

4.4 *Papers and written work*

There is no set requirement for written papers except for the final Pass (see 3.5) paper, so that it would be possible to complete the training without having written a paper before then. However, trainees have to present clinical material weekly and theoretical material as required by course teachers.

5. REFERRALS

Training patients get referred through the PA clinic or through personal contacts. The whole range of patients from neurotic to psychotic may be referred to a trainee, depending on the appropriateness of the match. There is no policy for letting a patient know they are seeing a trainee, although often this is obvious because of the low fee.

6. COST OF TRAINING

The introductory year is £120 per term, and the training is £150 per term. There is a £40 application fee to cover the interviews. Therapy may cost from £15 to £30 per session, as with supervision. Thus the most expensive time would be when a trainee is seeing two supervisors, plus therapy and the training seminars.

It is expected that trainees and newly qualified therapists see patients for a low fee. This would be their way of building up a practice. In other words fees are according to experience and qualification, and the ability of the patient to pay. A low fee is around £10. Other referrals from other agencies are permitted, although this is usually discussed with a supervisor.

7. FUTURE EXPECTATIONS/CAREER PROSPECTS

Advice in setting up in practice is something that the trainee is expected to pick up on, throughout the training. It is very difficult to forecast how soon a practice will be viable as it varies from individual to individual. Prospects for teaching and supervision within the PA do exist, but it takes a very long time to move on to this from qualification.

8. TRAINEES' EXPERIENCE

8.1 *Why this course was chosen*

There were four main areas of the PA's training which attracted the present day trainees.

(a) the work and philosophy of R.D. Laing;
(b) the study of the relationship between philosophy and psychoanalysis;
(c) the therapeutic communities;
(d) the apprenticeship system.

The latter was seen as a particular plus because trainees felt they would be treated as adults in training, rather than having to fit into a linear structure as they felt would be required in some of the other analytic trainings.

8.2 *The atmosphere of the course*

However, in practice the apprenticeship system was experienced as sometimes being a problematic area where, because of the feeling of a lack of structure, misunderstandings seemed more likely to take place. There was a sense that 'tyranny could still exist in an apparently equal system, because there is a mystique as to where the power lies'.

On occasions it was felt that information between teachers was inconsistent with information from the Training Committee, which led to confusion and tension. It was acknowledged that having a personal tutor was an essential way of sorting out any difficulties.

The Pass was something experienced as very positive. The writing up of the Pass was the time when trainees felt they had the opportunity of assessing themselves as to how ready they were to become autonomous psychotherapists. That this decision was to be made by the assembled company rather than just the Training Committee was experienced as challenging and right, although in a recent case the Training Committee overruled the trainees' decision, which was experienced by trainees as undermining. However, it was acknowledged that the Training Committee have the constitutional right to make the decisions they deem necessary.

Trainees felt concerned that the requirement to work in the therapeutic communities did not seem to be implemented as it used to be, but they were relieved that there was no requirement to have specific training patients and they experienced the PA's system of building up a practice of more than two patients as much more fluid. The anxiety and tension about keeping a patient becomes irrelevant, and trainees felt they were free to experience a wider patient group, all of whom related to their training as psychotherapists.

The course's aim to relate a study of philosophy to psychoanalytic theory and clinical practice was felt to work very successfully. 'This results in a thoughtful, critical appreciation of psychoanalysis, and an atmosphere of debate and enquiry rather than a dogmatic handing down of received wisdom.' There was a general feeling that the teaching was good and intellectually stimulating, and well rooted in clinical practice.

AUTHOR'S COMMENTS

The Philadelphia Association is an established psychotherapy organization with its roots in the anti-psychiatry movement. Many of the full members are also on the Training Committees of the Guild of Psychotherapists and the Severnside Institute for Psychotherapy.

The course is unusual for the following reasons:

1. There is a deliberate low intake and entry can occur at any time of the year.

2. The apprenticeship system of personal years means that there is no linear curriculum which all trainees follow at the same time.

3. There is great emphasis on integrating philosophy with the practice of analytic therapy.

It is a radical way of training therapists and contains the philosophy of treating trainees as adults who need to go through a personal individualized process in becoming a psychotherapist. It contains the notion of developing at your own pace. The theoretical orientation focuses on psychoanalysis and the theorists of the British Psycho-Analytical Society, plus Lacan. This theory is seen by the PA as needing to be complemented by the study of certain philosophers. Many therapists and analysts would see philosophy as tangential to therapeutic work, and this aspect is very much in the tradition of the work of R.D. Laing, who trained as a psychoanalyst and psychiatrist and used more of a philosophical attitude in his books (*The Divided Self*), particularly the work of J.-P. Sartre and the existential movement.

It seems very clear that a structure is provided by the Training Committee but perhaps striking that some trainees experienced a 'lack of structure'. Questions and reflections on this course would be linked with the coexistence of phenomenology, psychoanalysis, psychotherapy and psychiatry.

SCOTTISH INSTITUTE OF HUMAN RELATIONS (SIHR)

56 Albany Street, Edinburgh EH1 3QR; tel: 031 556 0924.

1. HISTORY

The Scottish Institute of Human Relations was founded in 1969 by Dr John Sutherland. Dr Sutherland had worked for many years at the Tavistock Centre in London and was the Director when he retired in 1968. The SIHR was modelled on that institution and, like the Tavistock, many courses and trainings are offered for professionals working in the field of mental health. In 1973 the training in psychoanalytic psychotherapy was set up by a group of (in the main) psychiatrists initiated by Dr Sutherland. Since that time there have been five intakes who have followed the four-year course and by 1992 the sixth intake of trainees will have completed their training. The possibility of the course running annually would depend on the availability of training analysts.

The major development of the course since its inception is that it has become more intense in the area of supervision. The aims and objectives have not changed and are set out in the brochure thus:

> The course is intended to equip trainees to conduct analytical psychotherapy at a specialist level, to act as trainers within their own professional centres and to stimulate the development through which psychodynamic knowledge can be used more widely in meeting the needs of the community for help with psychological stress.

2. THEORETICAL ORIENTATION AND CURRICULUM

The main theoretical orientation of this course is the Independent tradition within the British Psycho-Analytical Society.

Outline of curriculum

The following is an outline of the theoretical seminars spanning the three years.

The Development of Analytical Psychotherapy (8 seminars)
(a) Dynamic psychiatry in the 19th Century (1)
(b) Overview of the work of Freud (3)
(c) Overview of the work of Klein (1)
(d) Overview of the work of Fairbairn (1)
(e) Overview of the work of Winnicott, Jacobson, Lichtenstein and Kohut (1)
(f) Overview of the work of Mahler, Erikson and Bowlby (1)

Theories of Psychic Development, Psychopathology and their Relationship to Clinical Practice (32 seminars)
(a) The work of Sigmund Freud (13)
(b) The work of Melanie Klein (5)
(c) The work of Ronald Fairbairn and Harry Guntrip (4)
(d) The work of Donald Winnicott (4)
(e) The work of Otto Kernberg and Heinz Kohut (2)
(f) The work of Wilfred Bion (2)
(g) The work of the Independent Group (2)

Theoretical Considerations of Clinical Concepts (12 seminars)
(a) Transference (2)
(b) Countertransference (2)
(c) Interpretation (2)
(d) Therapeutic alliance, acting out, negative therapeutic reaction, resistance to experience in the analytic session (2)
(e) The use of dreams in modern psychoanalytical practice (1)
(f) Projective identification (2)
(g) Termination (1)

Developmental Crises and Responses to Them (6 seminars)
(a) Grief (1)
(b) Depression, normal and pathological responses to mourning (1)
(c) Pathological responses to adolescence (1)
(d) Pathological responses to pregnancy (1)

(e) Pathological responses to ageing and dying (1)
(f) Children's disorders and their treatment (1)

Clinical Syndromes (6 seminars)
(a) Neuroses (1)
(b) Psychosis (1)
(c) Narcissism and borderline states (1)
(d) The schizoid personality (1)
(e) Perversions (1)
(f) Psychosomatic conditions, hypochondriasis and reactions to illness and surgery (1)

Infant Observation seminars are not part of the course.

The forum for trainees' difficulties is a group meeting with the Training Committee at least once a year. The trainee's first supervisor can also act as personal tutor when necessary.

3. TRAINING STRUCTURE

3.1 *Training Committee*

There are nine members of the Training Committee and their trainings and qualifications are mainly in psychiatry and psycho-analysis; five psychoanalysts have returned from membership of the Training Committee and have been replaced by five of the Institute's graduates who started their training in 1973 and 1976, and of the other four, three are psychoanalysts.

There is a Chairman and Honorary Secretary who are voted in, and there is no fixed term of office. The Committee meet between six and nine times a year and conduct the business of the Training Programme at each meeting, which consists of the selection of new trainees, the examination of case reports, the examination of five-monthly case reports, the setting of the curriculum and the upgrading of the curriculum.

3.2 *Selection procedure and admission*

All applicants are required to have held positions of responsibility within the Health Service or privately, so that they are able to recognize psychosis and dementia.

There is no application form. In the first instance the applicant's CV must be sent in for the attention of the Training Committee. This is followed by two separate interviews by members of the Training Committee. There is no age limit.

The applicant and trainee is assessed on the following: professional experience, professional quality, the work record, intellectual level, personality development, the response to personal analysis and after the training. Trainees could join the course at an appropriate stage depending on their previous training. Applicants are generally professionals already working in the NHS, although some do come from education, counselling and other related fields.

3.3 *Time commitment and length of training*

There is one two-hour seminar per week, three terms a year.

Most trainees follow the course whilst in full-time work. The following commitment on a weekly basis has to be taken into consideration: four hours of personal therapy, two hours of supervision, three hours of treatment of the first case, three hours' treatment of the second case. In addition to this there is weekly reading. It generally takes four years to qualify.

3.4 *Interruptions in training*

Interruptions are accommodated, and the limit of the interruption would depend on the individual case.

3.5 *Postgraduate qualification and learned society*

Once a trainee has qualified, application is then made to the Scottish Association of Psychoanalytical Psychotherapists (SAPP) and the year's fee is £20. SAPP is the member of the UKSCP and not SIHR. SAPP holds ten meetings a year where analytical psychotherapy is discussed, and uses the building and library belonging to the SIHR.

Anybody having had an equivalent training elsewhere may apply for membership of SAPP. SAPP does not have an in-house journal and a Code of Ethics is being formulated. There are about forty members of SAPP, and SAPP has an arrangement with the British Psycho-Analytical Society which enables members of SAPP to apply for the membership training of the British Psycho-Analytical Society.

4. CLINICAL AND ACADEMIC REQUIREMENTS

4.1 *Personal therapy*

Each trainee must be in four times weekly analytical psychotherapy throughout the training. Choice of analyst would depend on the vacancy situation of each training analyst. There is no requirement of being in therapy before starting the course.

The criteria for being and becoming a training analyst of SAPP are:

(a) the graduate's personal reputation as an analyst and a professional;

(b) the clinical work carried out by the graduate which must be at a minimum of three cases seen over three years with a minimum frequency of three times a week;

(c) the graduate must submit a clinical study to the Training Committee;

(d) the graduate meets with a small panel of the Training Committee to discuss the clinical study.

There is no consultation with the training analyst during the training.

4.2 *Clinical requirements*

Before seeing a first training patient each trainee must have completed one year of seminars. The first training patient is seen for one year before the second training patient, and this would be in consultation with the first supervisor. The minimum frequency for training patients to be seen is three times weekly. A trainee must have seen the first training patient for two years and the second training patient for one year in order to qualify. Medical cover is not usually required unless there is some concern about the patient.

4.3 *Supervision*

One supervisor is required for each training case, who must be seen once a week throughout the course.

4.4 *Papers and written work*

Five-monthly reports on both training cases must be submitted and final case reports for each case. These reports must demonstrate the trainee's ability to facilitate the patient's psychological process as well as the trainee's increasing understanding of the therapeutic relationship in terms of the transference and countertransference. They give an account of the patient, and of the situation at the start of the treatment, followed by a lengthy narrative of the treatment including graphic interchanges between the two, giving the reader a position of being a close observer within the consulting room. This is followed by summaries of changes in the patient, of the dynamics involved and a prospective view.

5. Referrals

Training cases may be referred to trainees by a variety of routes: the SIHR, the NHS and sometimes the trainee's own place of work. The type of training case is either neurotic or personality disorder. The trainee's supervisor decides on whether or not the training case needs to be seen prior to the trainee starting treatment. The training case would usually know about being in treatment with a trainee.

Trainees may set up in private practice during the training.

6. Cost of Training

This is £105 per term covering the seminars, and supervision and therapy sessions are between £18 and £30; the most expensive time for a trainee would be in the third year. Training cases pay what is commensurate with personal earnings.

There are consulting rooms which may be used by trainees at the

SIHR and for which there is no charge before qualification. The SIHR has no loans or bursaries for this course.

7. Future Expectations/Career Prospects

Practical advice for setting up in practice is talked about with supervisors and all trainees are encouraged to take out malpractice insurance. The majority of graduates in this course, however, tend to stay in their core profession with a small private practice.

The future prospects to teach or supervise depend on the criteria set out for members of SAPP (3.1) to apply to the Training Committee.

8. Trainees' Experience

8.1 *Why this course was chosen*

The majority of trainees who follow this course are from the medical profession – psychiatrists, social workers – although this training is open to people who do not have a core professional background and may come from education or counselling.

All trainees had experienced a need to study psychotherapy in more depth and were attracted to the psychoanalytic aspect of the training. However, it was acknowledged that there was also a dearth of trainings in Scotland and that there was nothing available in between counselling and psychoanalytic psychotherapy.

People felt very clear about the extent of the commitment required of them at the beginning of the course, and agreed that like any course it was not really possible to fully appreciate this commitment until experiencing the course.

The selection procedure was experienced as a good exercise in reviewing and examining personal inner reasons, as well as conscious reasons, for wishing to become a psychotherapist. There was agreement that the interviews were necessarily gruelling. There seemed to be some mystery experienced as to the reasons for refusal and acceptance. However, it had been made clear, at the time of application, that reasons would not be given for refusal or acceptance.

8.2 *The atmosphere of the course*

The Institute is experienced as an organization which really works very efficiently considering how low the resources are in terms of staff, finance and so on, and the experience of the course is that it is of a high quality.

The model of teaching is experienced as successful but very traditional. There is a meeting with the Training Committee once a year for trainees to give feedback on their experience of the course. However, trainees felt this was a difficult and painful procedure and there was a sense that nothing outstanding would change as a consequence of this meeting. It was felt that perhaps there could be more creative ways of providing trainees with more channels to air their views. Not all trainees agreed with this point of view and felt strongly that difficulties needed to be taken back to one's personal analysis. The Training Committee are also the teachers, supervisors and training analysts. Trainees, however, feel that this does not cause problems and that the analytic relationship is kept very separate from the rest of the course.

The areas of confusion tended to be connected with the wealth of theory covered on the training and the problems of application and integration. Trainees had been pleasantly surprised to find a greater sense of freedom, as more theory was learnt, than a more doctrinaire attitude, which had been expected. Theoretical learning, however, was seen as second to personal analysis where confusion of theory needed to be explored. There was a general acknowledgement that not all the complexities could be taken in and that what was studied on the course would be used as a continual source of reference in the future.

The experience of finding training cases was varied and trainees are responsible for finding their own. Most people are working in the NHS and so there are opportunities of finding suitable patients. Another issue is the psychotherapy culture in Edinburgh. Up till now there has not been a strong tradition of psychotherapy in the community, although that is changing, but it creates more problems for finding patients who will commit themselves to four times weekly therapy over a minimum of two years.

Trainees experienced a lack of clarity about the relationship between the Institute of Psycho-Analysis and the Scottish Institute. SAPP members may apply for membership of the British Psycho-Analytical Society once they have qualified, but trainees felt unsure of what that might mean.

There was serious concern for the low resources available to the Institute and people looked forward to contributing to the Scottish Institute in the future as well as to psychotherapy and its future in local communities in Scotland.

AUTHOR'S COMMENTS

As has been mentioned, the SIHR is modelled on the Tavistock, although there are some differences in structure between this training and the training in adult psychotherapy at the Tavistock. Theoretically the Tavistock tends towards Kleinian theory whereas the SIHR leans towards the Independent tradition (see Part One).

Graduates of this course are eligible to apply to the British Psycho-Analytical Society for further training to become Associate Members. This arrangement arose because the British Psycho-Analytical Society wanted to ensure that there were more of their members in the provinces.

The problems of resources are a geographical reality, and the conflicts between psychiatry and psychoanalysis are accentuated in Scotland, where psychotherapy is not as readily accepted in the NHS as it is in London and the South.

SEVERNSIDE INSTITUTE FOR PSYCHOTHERAPY (SIP)

45 Quakers Road, Downend, Bristol BS16 6JF; tel: 0272 562049.

1. HISTORY

The Severnside Institute for Psychotherapy came into being in 1985, when a small number of psychotherapists working independently in the South-west of England and Wales, and often in professionally isolated circumstances, came together as a group. The original intention was to provide mutual support, and to share professional interests. However, it soon became apparent that there was a great hunger for psychotherapeutic knowledge and training within the wider population.

Initially, a one-year Introductory Course in Psychodynamics was offered as part of the extra-mural activities of the University of Bristol (this course is still extant). The response to this was such that within a short time the initial group was embarking upon a psychotherapeutic training in response to local demand.

As potential trainees applied from a widening geographical area, there began a trickle of psychotherapists out of London, settling in or near Bristol. In this way, the supply and demand for training have to date maintained a dynamic balance, and the size of SIP and scale of its activities are slowly but steadily growing.

2. THEORETICAL ORIENTATION AND CURRICULUM

The aim of training is to qualify students to work as analytical psychotherapists. The main theoretical orientation is the broad development of psychoanalysis and analytical psychology from Freud and Jung to the present day. This reflects the background of the Training Committee and founder members which, although diverse, does not include the humanistic therapies.

Since 1986, when the first trainees were accepted, there have been three further intakes. The curriculum has been to some extent determined by the availability of teachers. In recent years, the analytic resources in the South-west have increased quite markedly, and the curriculum has developed and expanded accordingly.

The major theoretical component of the first year is the work of Freud and Jung, and Infant Observation seminars are now compulsory. The second and third years' teaching covers the work of the British Object Relations Group, Klein, Bion, the London Jungian School, as well as the techniques of assessment and treatment.

Each student intake has a Year Tutor who is there to co-ordinate the course and respond to trainees' difficulties. Meetings between trainers and trainees are held each term.

3. TRAINING STRUCTURE

3.1 *Training Committee*

The Training Committee is currently made up of eight members who have been trained at the Tavistock Clinic, the British Association of Psychotherapists, the Guild, the Philadelphia Association and the Institute of Psycho-Analysis. The founder member was trained at the Society of Analytical Psychology.

The Training Committee meet on average once a month. The meetings cover the setting up and monitoring of the training programme and all that that entails. These meetings are necessarily lengthy, in part because of the evolution that SIP, as a new training, is undergoing.

3.2 *Selection procedure and admission*

There is an application form. At present one of the members of the Training Committee is responsible for organizing the selection of suitable trainees. Applicants have two interviews, and the Training Committee discuss each application. Five years of relevant experience are required as well as a professional qualification or degree. However, the emphasis is on personality, and the academic or professional qualification is not essential. There is a lower age limit, but no upper one.

It is not likely that students on another course could enter the training midway. There are between six and nine places for each student intake and a balanced group is what is aimed for, not necessarily of gender but of compatibility. The general background of trainees tends to cover a broad range.

3.3 *Time commitment and length of training*

The personal tutor must be seen at least once a term. Teaching takes place on one evening a week which is divided into two parts: the first devoted to theory, the second a clinical seminar. Since 1991, the evening has begun with an Infant Observation seminar, to be followed by the theoretical and clinical seminars.

The course is designed to be accessible to trainees already in full-time work, although considerable time for reading is expected; photocopying facilities are available.

The formal teaching course takes place over a three-year period. However, it is not expected that students will qualify in less than four years.

3.4 *Interruptions in training*

Accommodation of an interruption would be handled individually, with as much flexibility as possible.

3.5 *Postgraduate qualification and learned society*

Once qualified there is automatic membership of the Severnside Institute for Psychotherapy. Membership is open to qualified therapists from other training organizations, and to date there are some forty members. There are scientific meetings as well as conferences where members meet to discuss their clinical work via the presentation of papers.

SIP does not yet have a building of its own. It has the use of some rooms for meetings and administration, and the library is also housed here. There is an in-house journal and a Code of Ethics.

4. CLINICAL AND ACADEMIC REQUIREMENTS

4.1 *Personal therapy*

The Year Tutor for the relevant year's intake is responsible for ensuring that the trainee will be in therapy with an approved training therapist before the start of the course. The criteria for a training therapist are as follows: a minimum of five years' post-qualification experience, working with patients on a once, twice and three times a week basis; to be practising for at least eighteen hours per week, that practice to include a minimum of three patients in three times a week therapy; to have had a minimum of two years' supervision on those patients; and to have been in therapy oneself on a not less than three times weekly basis. A subcommittee of the SIP Executive Committee is responsible for the approval of training therapists.

Because SIP consists of qualified therapists and analysts from the major training institutions, there is an appreciation of the standards and criteria that are currently accepted in the training of analytical psychotherapists. The requirement is that trainees be in three times weekly therapy at least six months prior to the course, for the duration of the course and until the trainee graduates.

The training therapist would be asked if there are any contra-indications, before the student was given permission to begin work with the first training patient.

4.2 *Clinical requirements*

A trainee may apply to take on a training patient at the end of the first year. Permission is then granted by the Training Committee and it depends on such factors as the experience, level of input into the clinical work discussions and the opinion of the personal tutor.

The requirement is to see the first training patient three times a week for at least two years, and the second patient three times a week for a minimum period of eighteen months. There is an assessment procedure (involving consultation with a psychiatrically qualified psychotherapist) to judge the suitability of a potential training patient before work can begin.

4.3 *Supervision*

Trainees must see an approved supervisor weekly for each training patient. The criteria for supervisors are the same as those for training therapists. Trainees are allowed to choose their own supervisors, after discussion with their personal tutor. There is no group supervision.

4.4 *Papers and written work*

Trainees will give presentations in theoretical seminars and case presentations in the clinical work discussions, both being open to assessment. They also have to produce six-monthly written reports on training patients. Only one paper is required to be written as the qualifying paper; it is not a reading-in paper. It must account for the therapeutic relationship between the trainee and the patient, and involve considerable detail on that relationship as well as a theoretical discussion around the material, preferably in the trainee's own words.

5. REFERRALS

The trainees, in consultation with their supervisor or personal tutor, are responsible for finding their own training patients. The training patient must not be so disturbed as to be a potential management problem for the trainee, but very often may be diagnosed as borderline.

There is no policy on informing the training patient of the therapist's trainee status, although inevitably this can emerge due to the psychiatric assessment and/or the low fee. Trainees tend to use their own discretion in the matter.

6. COST OF TRAINING

The current fees are £200 a term which covers seminars, personal tutor and course tutor provision. Supervision, Infant Observation and therapy are extra. The most expensive time of the course would be during the third year when two supervisors must be paid for as well as the course fees and personal therapy. Fees are currently £15–20, for both therapy and supervision.

A trainee must not charge her training patient more than £12 a session. Consulting rooms are available and trainees are charged a nominal fee.

There is a bursary fund for trainees in financial difficulties.

7. FUTURE EXPECTATIONS/CAREER PROSPECTS

The process of setting up in practice is discussed during the theoretical seminars, although not every trainee intends to work exclusively in private practice.

There is the prospect of future teaching work within SIP. To work as a training therapist or supervisor, graduates would need to meet the requirements as set out (see 4.1).

8. TRAINEES' EXPERIENCE

8.1 *Why this course was chosen*

This is the first analytic training available in the South-west of England, which is the main reason for trainees choosing this course. A large percentage of the 1989 intake say that they chose it because it is eclectic. The selection procedure was experienced as difficult, mainly because of the long wait after the two interviews.

In general people felt clear about the commitment required to follow this course. There are many geographical complications concerning personal therapy, which therapists accommodate as much as possible, such as offering two sessions on the same day.

8.2 *The atmosphere of the course*

The first intake of trainees felt the strain of being the 'guinea pigs'. They experienced difficulties and a feeling of not being looked after – and there were no channels for complaints. The second intake were assigned personal tutors as well as having regular meetings with the Year Tutor. A special day was arranged with a paid facilitator to resolve a group problem at one point.

SIP leases a property and sublets to a counselling organization. Trainees therefore have priority for group rooms and the use of consulting rooms.

Trainees would have liked an opportunity to meet in a less formal setting than the seminars, to find out more about each other as well as to share all the issues involved in undergoing this training. A Student Forum, meeting on a regular basis, has recently been proposed. It was generally agreed that the Training Committee were amenable to suggestions coming from the trainee groups.

Trainees felt they were asked to integrate very different theories and that this caused some confusion as to the meaning of eclecticism (a study weekend in June 1990 was devoted to this subject). Deeper confusion was experienced in work with patients – the experience of another's pain – and it was felt that this had not been talked about enough. Some of the teachers are also training therapists. Trainees with the same therapist tended to avoid discussing this with each other, keeping this area separate from the rest of the training.

Trainees acknowledged that considerable hard work had been put into the setting up of SIP, and there was an excitement about contributing in the future, post-graduation.

AUTHOR'S COMMENTS

This training is very new and has its inevitable teething problems, acutely felt, it seemed, by the first intake of trainees. However, subsequent trainees were satisfied that the training was changing and developing, avoiding the same difficulties being repeated. Fiona Gardner, the first graduate, won first prize for the Student Essay Competition of the *British Journal of Psychotherapy* in 1990 with her paper 'Know what I mean: an exploration into knowing what is meant'.

The Training Committee is made up of graduates who come from a diversity of analytic backgrounds and training, and this could be an enriching contribution to the sort of training SIP offers. However, it could also be one of the main difficulties – that of reconciling conflicting points of view in the same training – and this is something that the trainees were aware of, finding it confusing and difficult. It relates to the debates concerning Freud and Jung, and eclecticism and pluralism (see Introduction to Part Two). How are these conflicts being debated and dealt with in SIP?

Another area pertinent to this training is the issue of a psychotherapy culture. This is something that is not often talked about but Herbert Hahn, one of the founder members of SIP, published a paper in the *British Journal of Psychotherapy* (Vol. 4, No. 3) about the problems of setting up in practice in what he terms an unsophisticated base. There is no doubt that London, in particular North London, is where the majority of analysts and therapists live and work. This has its effect on a patient population who tend to accept the time and financial demands of analytic therapy, perhaps more readily than people who have travel considerations.

Meanwhile, the SIP, with its experienced group of practitioners, is making an important contribution to the world of psychotherapy by pioneering the first analytic training in the South-west of England.

UNIVERSITY OF KENT

Centre for the Study of Psychotherapy, School of Continuing Education, Rutherford College, University of Kent, Canterbury, Kent CT2 7NX; tel: 0227 764000, ext. 3691.

1. HISTORY

This course was developed over several years by a small group of psychotherapists who in 1981 began organizing courses for the University of Kent, for counsellors working with alcoholics. These courses were externally evaluated by the Department of Health. It was largely due to their success that the group, led by Alan Cartwright, was able to create the Centre for the Study of Psychotherapy (in 1985) and start the introductory training in psychotherapy. Since 1991, psychodynamic psychotherapy has become a formal study area within the university, which will in future be awarding Master's Degrees for Research into the area of psychodynamic psychotherapy. Alan Cartwright is employed full-time by the NHS and seconded to the university to take responsibility for the Centre for the Study of Psychotherapy. Patients who are seen by trainees on the courses are considered to be NHS patients.

The first intake of students was in 1984, and the courses in Dynamic Psychotherapy were formalized by 1987. Currently the Centre offers two courses. They are: an Introduction to Dynamic Psychotherapy and the Postgraduate Diploma/Master's Degree in Psychodynamic Psychotherapy. Most trainees expect to undertake the full five-year training programme. The three-year postgraduate diploma is not seen as a full clinical qualification, but may be used by some students to supplement existing professional qualifications. The Centre has links with the Society for Psychotherapy Research and is in the process of developing a project concerned with the practice of psychotherapy. Alan Cartwright's particular interest is concerned with understanding how skills develop and change during training. It is hoped that the university will be able to offer an M.Phil/Ph.D. programme for empirical research in psychodynamic psychotherapy in the next year.

2. THEORETICAL ORIENTATION AND CURRICULUM

The core text of the Centre's philosophy is Luborsky's 'Supportive Expressive Psychotherapy' which is based on research into analytic psychotherapeutic process. The theoretical orientation is psychodynamic and is not wedded to any one theory. The curriculum is as follows:

Introduction to Dynamic Psychotherapy: the academic component of the course will be organized around a series of presentations in which the basic ideas of significant figures in the field of dynamic psychotherapy will be presented and then discussed in groups. The key figures discussed in this course are Sigmund and Anna Freud, Melanie Klein, Donald Winnicott, Heinz Kohut and Carl Jung. Following a lecture, students meet in small discussion groups to discuss their reactions to the lecture material and an experiential group also takes place each week.

Postgraduate Diploma in Psychodynamic Psychotherapy: there are six main courses in the Diploma.

1. Techniques of Clinical Psychotherapy
   This skills-based course seeks to help the student reconceptualize theoretical ideas in practical terms and then act appropriately within the clinical situation. Extensive use is made of tape recordings, transcripts of therapy sessions and dream material to help students develop their listening and conceptual abilities. Role playing is used to help the student develop basic communication skills prior to encountering their first patient.

2. Key Concepts of Analytic Treatment
   This series of seminars focuses on the ways that different
   theorists have used ideas such as transference, defence,
   resistance. It provides a metapsychological approach to
   the issues discussed in the previous course.

3. An Overview of Object Relations Theories
   This course looks at the ways that developmental and
   Object Relations theories have evolved and identifies the
   key concepts and areas of dispute between different
   theorists. Stress is placed on examining the analytic ideas
   in the light of recent advances in empirical studies of child
   development.

4. Applications of Analytic Ideas to a Specific Population
   This is essentially a practical course in which psychotherapists discuss the practice of psychotherapy with different
   groups of patients. The course considers the treatment of
   a wide range of different problems with analytical
   psychotherapy. Particular stress is placed on general
   complaints such as anxiety, depression and addictive
   conditions which are commonly presenting problems for
   patients at the Centre.

5. Psychotherapeutic Assessment
   The basic principles of assessing people for psychotherapy
   and making decisions about long- or short-term forms of
   treatment are considered here. Students are expected to
   understand the basic principles on which assessment is
   based.

6. Psychotherapy in Context
   This is a broad-ranging course which provides a backdrop
   to the practice of analytical psychotherapy. There are
   sections which cover the socio-cultural issues which
   influence the practice of psychotherapy. As well as
   presentations from members of complementary professions, this involves some teaching on alternative forms of
   treatment, i.e. anxiety management and cognitive behavioural therapy.

The Master's Degree in Psychodynamic Psychotherapy: this is an extension of the Postgraduate Diploma, and students who achieve a mark of 50 per cent or greater are allowed to proceed to the Master's Degree. Students embarking on the Master's Degree have to undertake a wide range of different forms of clinical practice. Most will undertake a number of brief psychotherapeutic treatments as well as at least one long-term patient seen twice weekly using the couch. Concurrently the student has to write a clinical dissertation in an area related to the practice of analytical psychotherapy.

Infant Observation is not part of the course as there is simply not enough time and certain topics had to be prioritized. For instance, General Psychiatry is a component that it is felt essential to accommodate in the course because of the links with the NHS.

3. Training Structure

3.1 *Training Committee*

The staff group consists of a senior lecturer and a lecturer who are assisted by two psychotherapists, and they are responsible for planning and conducting the course as a whole. The staff group report to a psychotherapy committee who are responsible for the quality of the training provided. The committee consists of outside representatives and members of the university. This committee is responsible for the appointment of external examiners and any appeals from students. The psychotherapy committee in turn is responsible to the Graduate Studies Committee of the Faculty of Social Sciences.

The staff group maintain close contact with students. Students on the Postgraduate Diploma must have a supervisor who is a member of the staff group and there are regular slots in the timetable for individual tutorials between students and their staff supervisor. Once a term the students and staff meet as a body to evaluate progress of the course and to discuss any complaints or difficulties.

3.2 *Selection procedure and admission*

There are various selection procedures throughout the training programme. Initially there is a selection prior to the introductory year when applicants are seen in a group setting to assess their ability to cope with the experiential aspects of this course.

Selection for the Postgraduate Diploma is through the presentation of a 2,000-word essay on the development of Freud's thought and reports from leaders of the experiential group and the discussion group of the introductory year. The applicant is then called for a series of interviews.

There is ongoing assessment throughout the Postgraduate Diploma. Although most trainees are expected to have a first degree and/or a professional qualification, some suitable candidates are accepted without these. This acceptance is provisional on their achieving a satisfactory academic standard during the early part of the Postgraduate Diploma. A trainee must achieve a mark of at least 50 per cent on both the clinical and academic components of the Postgraduate Diploma before progressing to the Master's Degree.

There is no age limit, but the majority of applicants are in their thirties. Qualities looked for in the suitable candidate are an intellectual ability to conceptualize and think quickly, a capacity to empathize, a personal and intellectual honesty and a lack of defensiveness. The general background of people applying tends to be counselling, nursing, social work and teaching; the majority have first degrees, the most common being psychology. There are between twelve and eighteen places for a biannual intake.

3.3 *Time commitment and length of training*

Formal teaching for the first two years of the Postgraduate Diploma takes place on Thursday afternoons between 3 and 6 p.m. In addition there are the weekly counteractions group, at least two hours a week clinical practice, two hours for supervision, personal therapy and a minimum of six hours for private study.

For those converting to the Master's Degree a minimum of four hours a week clinical practice is required. Those trainees who do not have experience of working within the Health Service also have to undertake at least 200 hours of placements before they complete the Master's Degree. Thus the Diploma takes three years, the Master's Degree two years and including the introductory course it takes at least six years to qualify.

3.4 *Interruptions in training*

This would depend on each individual case.

3.5 *Postgraduate qualification and learned society*

All trainees are students of the university and have access to all facilities including the library where there is a very large section on psychotherapy. There are many opportunities for trainees to attend lectures and conferences organized by the Centre for Psychoanalytic Studies which is part of the Humanities Faculty at the university.

4. CLINICAL AND ACADEMIC REQUIREMENTS

4.1 *Personal therapy*

When prospective trainees indicate that they are interested in applying for the courses and they wish to seek a personal therapist, they are interviewed by a consultant appointed by the staff group who makes recommendations about the most appropriate therapist for them. Because the course has a rule that no trainee may be in therapy with a member of the staff group, there is a shortage of available analytic therapists in the Canterbury area and so students from Canterbury often have to travel considerable distances to find personal therapists. Those travelling to Canterbury for the course are often able to find a therapist nearer London.

The therapist has to be consulted for confirmation of frequency of hours, which are not stipulated by the university examiners other than at least 500 hours of personal therapy. In practice this means that trainees are in a minimum of twice weekly therapy throughout the course of their training. All training therapists must be analytic therapists.

4.2 *Clinical requirements*

Trainees usually start seeing patients during their first year on the Postgraduate Diploma, but all trainees must have completed at least 200 hours of supervised psychotherapy practice before submitting for the Postgraduate Diploma. This latter work should involve at least six different patients, of whom one should have been seen for at least eighteen months. Trainees should have satisfactorily completed at least two psychotherapies before submitting for the Master's Degree; these are usually brief psychotherapies with patients carefully selected for this procedure. However, given the length of training, it is not unusual for patients to have been seen for four years at the time the student submits.

The Centre carries its own professional indemnity insurance for all patients seen by trainees; contact is always maintained with the patient's GP.

4.3 *Supervision*

Each trainee is in supervision with a member of the staff group throughout their training. Supervision tends to take place in small groups of two or occasionally three students. The group lasts approximately forty minutes for each student present. Group supervision is preferred over individual supervision in the early stages of training because there is considerable enhancement of learning from the experience of watching another being supervised.

The counteractions group is also seen as part of the supervision process and trainees are expected to take to this group the problems they encounter with their patients, whether these are countertransference problems or problems associated with role insecurity. Extensive use of tape recordings is made in course supervision.

4.4 *Papers and written work*

Throughout the Postgraduate Diploma trainees are expected to submit six essays on theoretical and applied topics set by the course staff. Essays are expected to be between two and three thousand words in length. A case study supported by audio recordings of the student's work with patients is also required.

For the Master's Degree the students are required to submit a 15,000-word dissertation based on a clinical topic approved by the course staff.

5. REFERRALS

Patients are referred to the Centre from the District Psychotherapy Services, the Psychotherapy Section of Mount Zeehan Alcohol Unit and GPs. The Centre also accepts direct referrals. Patients have to agree to be seen by a trainee and to accept the conditions, which involve the tape recording of all sessions. The psychotherapy provided by the trainees is considered to be part of the NHS services and no charge is made. Patients who agree to these conditions are seen by a staff group member for an assessment which is recorded, and the trainee will listen to this recording before meeting the patient.

Patients who have external management problems are not accepted for work with trainees as the Centre is not able to provide a service outside the immediate clinical context offered by the trainee.

Most psychotherapy takes place on NHS premises.

6. COST OF TRAINING

Fees are at present being revised and are likely to be in the range of £500 for the introductory course, £1,400 per year for the Postgraduate Diploma and £1,000 for the Master's Degree. The cost of the second supervisor is not included in the costs for the Master's Degree. The only additional financial cost is personal therapy and currently sessions are between £25 and £40 each.

7. FUTURE EXPECTATIONS/CAREER PROSPECTS

The course aims to produce a broad-based psychotherapist and trainees are considered to be qualified to work in either NHS or private practice.

8. TRAINEES' EXPERIENCE

8.1 *Why this course was chosen*

Reasons for choosing this course were to do with wanting to practise psychotherapy in more depth. People were aiming to combine working in a voluntary agency or the NHS with a private practice.

The selection procedure was experienced as fairly informal, but trainees were also aware that this had recently been changing and was no longer the case for more recent entrants.

8.2 *The atmosphere of the course*

Some trainees had experienced the experiential group as quite anxiety-provoking as the boundaries of confidentiality were not felt to be clear since the leader was a member of the Training Committee.

There was some concern about taking on NHS patients for long-term work. It was not always clear how long trainees would see some patients, and in some cases trainees had continued seeing patients beyond the NHS placement, for no fee. It was felt that patients could be warned of shorter-term work and that the course should cover brief psychotherapy work.

Confusing issues were associated with applying the theory to the practice, and trainees felt this was something that was inevitable with any training. There was a general feeling that there could be more supervision and some people would have preferred individual supervision. However, the structure of supervision in threes had been experienced as a safe way of exploring clinical work and a very valuable adjunct to personal therapy.

Discussion about the different levels of working with patients took place and there was concern that working analytically could be inappropriate for some patients: that the patient should define the level of work. This was linked with the differences between the Diploma and Advanced part of the course.

For the future, trainees were hoping to develop an association for graduates of the training, where clinical work and other matters concerning working as a psychotherapist could be discussed.

AUTHOR'S COMMENTS

This course is in the unique position of being linked with the NHS as well as a university. Many changes and developments are taking place and, unlike many, this training will lead to an academic qualification. In addition the graduate will be trained towards working as a psychotherapist in the NHS. At present there are very few posts in the NHS for Basic Grade Psychotherapists, and the aspirations of this course, it seems, are to provide a psychotherapy service for the NHS whilst providing trainees with something like an in-service training. It is hoped that this will encourage a working relationship between psychotherapists and the NHS, despite historic and present difficulties.

Working as a psychotherapist under the strictures of the NHS has its own set of problems, two of which were areas of concern for trainees. Firstly, the level of work – patients coming for treatment to the NHS are very often quite disturbed, psychotic or borderline, which means that psychoanalytic psychotherapy could be an inappropriate treatment; and secondly, trainees' placements were short-lived and they found themselves in a position of being trained for long-term work. Both these areas concern the core text of this course which could be seen as linking with the different levels of counselling and psychotherapy. With most of the referrals coming from the NHS, how much experience of analytic therapy can the trainee expect to gain if private practice is the goal?

The theoretical orientation is broad and the mode of teaching uses many of the humanistic methods, such as tape recording sessions and using role play. Many analytic therapists and analysts would be critical of the use of tape recorders, which they would see as interfering with the therapeutic relationship. This course sees it as an invaluable teaching tool and although the analytic literature is part of the course, the sort of psychotherapy taught is skills orientated, which makes the main theoretical thrust of this course nearer what has been described as neo-Freudian than psychoanalytic therapy, where the emphasis is on the political and socio-cultural aspects of an individual's difficulties. To this extent the therapy is more goal orientated (see Kovel, 1976). This sort of emphasis in psychotherapy was pioneered by Adler, one of the first dissenters from Freud, whose dissension was associated with his difference of opinion with Freud about the relationship between psychoanalysis and politics.

This course is contributing to the long struggle of implementing psychotherapy into the NHS, and reaches out to many patients who simply could not afford to see a private psychotherapist.

WESTMINSTER PASTORAL FOUNDATION (WPF)

23 Kensington Square, London W8 5HN; tel: 071 937 6956.

1. HISTORY

The Westminster Pastoral Foundation was founded in 1969 by a Methodist minister, the Reverend Dr William Kyle. Its initial purpose was to provide a resource for counselling and training to the Churches, which were perceived as failing to equip their ministers adequately for the actual pastoral needs of people in the modern world. Bill Kyle's inspiration lay in the American pastoral counselling movement, but he departed from that model from the beginning by accepting lay people 'of all religions and of none' for training. Although the Foundation was first based in Central Hall, Westminster (a huge Methodist church in the centre of London), clients and counsellors alike came to the Foundation without involving themselves with the church. The work was supervised by analysts or psychotherapists, and evolved rapidly in the direction of secular once weekly counselling/therapy.

Several factors contributed to the enormous expansion of WPF. One was the early recognition that there are many highly competent people, keen and well suited to do this work, who are not already members of helping professions. Life experience and personal qualities are the essential prerequisites of training, although in practice a majority of trainees do now come from professional backgrounds. A second factor was the system of payment for counselling. Clients are asked to contribute in accordance with what they can afford – the figure is arrived at following hard discussion, and is not a token. As a result, WPF neither charges the often prohibitive fees of private practitioners, nor does it fall into the financial unreality of attempting to offer an expensive service for nothing. Contributions from clients make up some 25 per cent of the Foundation's budget (which in 1990–91 was about £1m). Most of the remainder comes from training fees (about 34 per cent) and donations. WPF also receives grants from the Department of Health, and the Royal Borough of Kensington and Chelsea. By 1978, WPF had outgrown its premises in Central Hall and it moved to its present setting at 23 Kensington Square. In 1980 Bill Kyle died and his place as Director was taken by Derek Blows, a canon of the Church of England and an analyst trained at the Society of Analytical Psychology. He has recently been replaced by Tim Woolmer, previously head of Continuing Education at Roehampton Institute and a group analyst (Institute of Group Analysis).

In addition to individual long-term once weekly psychotherapy or counselling, the Foundation offers group work and family/marital therapy. An increasing range of specialized services have come into existence: the Young People's Project sees adolescents and young adults on a basis of quicker referral than the main system; the Serious Physical Illness Project offers counselling, including domiciliary visits, to people suffering from a wide range of physical problems including cancer, Aids, multiple sclerosis, cerebral palsy, the after-effects of accidents and so on; Counselling in Companies is a scheme whereby particular firms are able to draw quickly on the Foundation's resources to help employees in emotional difficulties. There is also a programme to develop more short-term, focused methods of counselling. Many community projects in different parts of the country have now begun to set up with a view to providing a similar service. Some fifty centres, in places as far afield as Edinburgh, Southampton, Ipswich and South Wales, make up the national network known as WPF Counselling. In 1990, twenty-two of these had met the standards of training and practice which allow them to be accepted as affiliates of WPF, and another twenty-seven were associates of the programme (implying that they are moving towards affiliation). All these centres retain their own autonomy, but recognize a centrally agreed set of standards and Code of Ethics for training and practice. Four Regional Officers, locally based, oversee different parts of the country.

The Institute of Psychotherapy and Counselling came into being to provide a professional home for graduates of the training. These are all holders of the WPF Diploma in Advanced Psychodynamic Counselling, and Full Members of IPC have in addition done further postgraduate training in psychotherapy. The use of the words counselling and psychotherapy has been a vexed question for a long time at WPF, where much is called counselling which would certainly in many other contexts be called psychotherapy. In 1990, the average weekly attendance of clients at the WPF's two central London premises (in Kensington Square and in King's Road, Chelsea) stood at about 650. Research done in 1987 into the client profile at WPF found no significant generalizable differences between clients attending WPF and patients attending the out-patient psychiatric clinic at Guy's Hospital. The following details cover the Membership Course in Psychotherapy which has been developing at WPF over the past ten years.

2. Theoretical Orientation and Curriculum

WPF trainers aim to 'provide the highest standards of professional practice in counselling and psychotherapy, whilst paying proper attention to the personal search for meanings and values in the pursuit of wholeness'. The main theoretical orientation is psychodynamic, which includes psychoanalysis as well as analytical psychology. The main theoreticians are Freud, Jung, Klein and Winnicott, and the developments of their theories and practice to the present day are also studied.

The Membership Course (hereafter called the Psychotherapy Course) is open to graduates of the WPF Diploma in Advanced Psychodynamic Counselling. This Diploma can be achieved in not less than two years, and often takes four years through a Day Release Course Programme. Only graduates of the Diploma Programme may apply. Clinical seminars within the Diploma Programme and Psychotherapy Course include the following: Developmental Psychology; Psychodynamic Theory; Psychopathology; Social Perspectives; Ontological Issues; Clinical Issues; The Practice of Psychodynamic Counselling; Groupwork; Family and Marital Perspectives.

Within the theoretical and clinical seminars, detailed topics include: Assessing Clients; Management of Regressive States; Narcissistic Disorders; Borderline Personality; Hysteria; Depression; Perversion; Transference and Countertransference; Therapeutic Interventions and Working Through; Resistance; Psychological Defences and Acting In/Out; Working with Dreams; Use of Amplification.

Every trainee has a personal tutor.

3. TRAINING STRUCTURE

3.1 *Training Committee*

WPF has a Training Management Group at its Kensington headquarters, which is responsible for the policy-making of WPF (Kensington) in terms of overall training. This group, together with the Membership subcommittees, assesses trainees, and decides whether or not to award the qualification based upon the Psychotherapy Course. The Training Management Group is made up of eight members and amongst their trainings are: the Society of Analytical Psychology, the Institute of Psychotherapy and Counselling (WPF), the Lincoln Centre for Psychotherapy, the Association of Jungian Analysts and the Institute of Group Analysis.

The Director of Westminster Pastoral Foundation delegates the training authority to the Training Co-ordinator, who is the Chair of the Training Management Group. This group meets fortnightly to discuss a whole range of training issues. The Psychotherapy Course is monitored by a subcommittee of professional staff, teaching and supervising on that programme.

3.2 *Selection procedure and admission*

As indicated previously, the Psychotherapy Course is open only to trainees who have completed the Diploma in Advanced Psychody- namic Counselling. This Diploma has a rigorous selection procedure. Commencing with both an initial appliction and a formal statement of aims for training, the prospective trainee is required to attend an in-depth interview by one of WPF's senior psychotherapy trainers, and participate in two group experiences: the first a case discussion of a counselling relationship and the second an unstructured dynamic experiential group. Of some 150 applicants each year, only twenty-seven are ultimately successful. Application to the Psychotherapy Course can be made during the final year of Diploma training. There is one in-depth clinical interview, as well as a supervisor's report of the trainee's casework within the Diploma Programme. There is no age limit as such, but suitable trainees would be seen as between twenty-five and sixty.

Academic qualifications are not necessary, but the trainee for the Membership Course will have demonstrated an academic and intellectual ability throughout the Diploma Course; two referees are required. A maximum of nine places are available within the Psychotherapy Course and about twice that number apply from the Diploma Programme each year. With help from the Citibank Corporation the WPF is encouraging people from ethnic minority backgrounds to follow the wide range of courses on offer at WPF and the Foundation also wishes to encourage men, who make up a low percentage of their trainees. The general background of people on the Psychotherapy Course is extremely varied.

3.3 *Time commitment and length of training*

As already stated, the Diploma Programme is the prerequisite for entry to the Psychotherapy Course.

Most of the units of training are held during the day, and WPF is aware that this may exclude some people who work full-time. Plans are well advanced to create a parallel programme of psychotherapy training on an evening seminar basis. Time must be arranged within the programme for a fair amount of reading each week. On average three papers are required for discussion purposes weekly. Papers are given to the trainees in advance of the seminars. There are photocopying facilities in the trainees' common room. Personal therapy and work with clients and supervision must also be taken into account.

The Diploma Programme can take between two and four years to complete, depending upon the route undertaken. As the Psychotherapy Course takes at least a further two years, the minimum time to qualify as a psychotherapist at WPF would be four years, but it could take up to six years. A personal tutor is seen twice a term on both the Diploma and Psychotherapy Courses.

3.4 *Interruptions in training*

These can be accommodated, where either pregnancy or illness requires a trainee to take time out from their course; however, in practice this occurs rarely. Each situation is looked at carefully.

3.5 *Postgraduate qualification and learned society*

The Learned Society of WPF is the Institute of Psychotherapy and Counselling, which is a member of the UK Standing Conference in its own right. On qualification from the WPF Psychotherapy Course, the graduate receives automatic membership. The IPC is a separate autonomous body made up of some 300 members, including a large number of Diploma graduates. The fee is £57 a year including subscription and the *British Journal of Psychotherapy*.

There are monthly Scientific Meetings organized by the board of IPC where members present papers or hear lectures by well-known analysts and psychotherapists. Course seminars and scientific meetings are held at the Maria Assumpta Campus where WPF has its headquarters. There is an extensive Counselling Service (650 clients a week) in which trainees do their clinical work. There is also a substantial library and IPC has a quarterly publication which includes features and articles.

The IPC Code of Ethics must be signed by all graduating trainees; membership of IPC is open only to WPF graduates.

4. CLINICAL AND ACADEMIC REQUIREMENTS

4.1 *Personal therapy*

All trainees for the Diploma Course have to be in once weekly analytic therapy and very often choose twice or three times. Trainees wishing to apply for the Psychotherapy Course need to be in three times weekly therapy for at least a year prior to commencement.

Trainees must be in personal therapy with a qualified and experienced member of one of the following organizations, who must have had at least three times weekly therapy themselves: The Association of Jungian Analysts, the British Association of Psychotherapists, the Guild of Psychotherapists, the Institute of Psycho-Analysis, the Lincoln Centre for Psychotherapy, the London Centre for Psychotherapy, the Society of Analytical Psychology and the Tavistock Clinic's Adult Psychotherapy Training. From entry into the Diploma level of training, there is a Therapy Advisory Service to help the prospective trainee commence and continue in appropriate and approved therapy. The therapist or analyst of the trainee is not consulted during training.

4.2 *Clinical requirements*

On the Diploma Programme there is a set requirement for seeing clients which is: at least five clients in the first year rising to six clients in the second year and subsequently.

The requirement on the Psychotherapy Course is that each trainee will have seen at least ten clients throughout their Diploma and Advanced training (with two short-term clients and at least three with more than forty sessions). Two twice weekly clients (the first to be seen for a minimum of eighteen months and the second for a minimum of one year) are required during the Psychotherapy Course. The first client must be seen for at least four months before work with the second can start. There should also be a minimum of three hours' work with other clients per week during the psychotherapy training. Trainees have to attend seminars on Intake and Assessment and subsequently complete a minimum of five satisfactory assessments. The work on all these is individually supervised.

During the Psychotherapy Course trainees must complete a six-month (minimum of half a day per week) psychiatric placement in addition to seeing clients. The WPF's psychiatrist provides medical cover for all trainees.

4.3 *Supervision*

Group supervision is in threes with an experienced therapist or analyst and this is continued throughout training both at Diploma and Psychotherapy level, as supervisors are seen as key trainers in the overall training experience. For the Psychotherapy Course trainees are also required to work with an individual supervisor for twice weekly clients. That supervisor is selected and approved by WPF and submits reports on the trainees' work to the Membership Assessment subcommittee.

4.4 *Papers and written work*

There is written work throughout for the Diploma Programme (four major essays). For the Psychotherapy Course the final written work must be a clinical paper on one of the clients seen on a twice weekly basis, and this will be approximately 10,000 words. The final paper is assessed by two readers and presented to the Membership subcommittee.

5. REFERRALS

Clients are referred to trainees (after assessment) through the WPF Counselling Service. Diploma trainees see their clients at WPF Kensington/Chelsea, whilst Psychotherapy trainees see their twice weekly clients in a private setting.

In the Psychotherapy Programme, there are seminars which focus on moving the client from the institutional location to private practice. The population of clients seen at WPF covers the whole range of diagnosis: neurotic, borderline and psychotic. Current alcoholics and drug abusers are not seen. WPF has a philosophy that clients will not be turned away for financial reasons. Potential clients are apprised of the WPF training function in appropriate literature.

6. Cost of Training

The training fees for the Psychotherapy Course are approximately £250 per term. This would include group supervision, seminars and tutorials, but excludes individual supervision and therapy.

A WPF trainee can set up in private practice only when s/he has satisfactorily completed the Diploma in Advanced Psychodynamic Counselling. Therefore trainees on the Psychotherapy Course may see clients other than their training clients by making their own arrangements and taking referrals from elsewhere, and appropriate fees may be charged accordingly. Training clients for the Psychotherapy Course are allocated from the WPF Counselling Service.

Bursaries and loans from both WPF itself and from the graduate body (IPC) are available, but are limited.

7. Future Expectations/Career Prospects

Psychotherapy graduates can both supervise and/or teach at WPF (Kensington) as vacancies arise. The postgraduate Training-in-Supervision Course, which has been running for eight years, is open also to counsellors and psychotherapists who may have trained elsewhere.

8. Trainees' Experience

8.1 *Why this course was chosen*

Trainees were attracted to the WPF for a variety of reasons:

(a) the training would include the spiritual side of the individual without being religious;

(b) WPF's philosophy of offering low cost counselling to the disadvantaged;

(c) the in-service training;

(d) the WPF's experience and good reputation;

(e) the eminent analysts and psychotherapists connected with the courses.

Most people had started initially to complete the Diploma Course in order to become counsellors. It was during the Diploma that trainees decided to apply for the Psychotherapy Course, because they wanted to work in more depth and privately.

The process of applying to join the Psychotherapy Course from the Diploma Course had been experienced as quite difficult. The main reason for this was the tensions arising in the Diploma training group where not everyone applying for the Psychotherapy Course would be accepted. Trainees had felt quite unhappy about this. The selection procedure had therefore been coloured by the issue of who was going to apply and who was not, and who would be accepted and who would not.

Meanwhile, some trainees had to change therapists, as the criteria for therapists on the Diploma Course are different from those for the Psychotherapy Course. This was experienced as very difficult to begin with; however, it was later on understood as the better action to take. Trainees had experienced other aspects of the selection procedure as thorough and in depth.

8.2 *The atmosphere of the course*

At the beginning of the Psychotherapy Course trainees felt that some aspects of the training had not always been communicated. People realized this was to do with the way in which the training was developing and changing, since it was still quite new. As the course went on difficulties did resolve themselves through channels of communication between the training committee and trainees, via memos, which overall functioned well.

Trainees experienced the teachers as excellent on both the Diploma and Psychotherapy Courses, and the curriculum was also felt to be well organized. The group and family work aspect of the course was experienced as of great value, because although these seminars do not equip trainees to practise, they give a broader base to the training. The knowledge of other fields was felt to help the trainee to be critical of personal methods and ideology, when making thorough assessments, and in communicating constructively with practitioners of psychotherapy in differing fields.

There were many opportunities to talk to fellow trainees, as there is a student room in the Kensington building. This was very much appreciated since people recognized how important it was to share anxieties as well as the positive aspects of training.

Overall trainees were happy with the training they were receiving. There was a concern about the divide between the Diploma graduates and Psychotherapy graduates which trainees felt may never be fully resolved since the IPC was open to members of both courses. Trainees realized this reflected the ongoing debate on the differences between counselling and psychotherapy and the question of status.

AUTHOR'S COMMENTS

WPF has reached large numbers of clients over the years, and continues to offer a much-needed service. Many courses at many levels have been established, providing trainees with an experienced team of analysts and therapists from the longest standing training institutes like the Institute of Psycho-Analysis and the Society of Analytical Psychology.

For many years WPF was seen as more Jungian than Freudian, but this seems to be changing now, with a curriculum which offers an equal amount of the developments of both. For trainees wanting a more focused Jungian training, this change was disappointing. The Psychotherapy Course has been a recent addition, and the route to this is via the counselling trainings. This could imply that WPF's attitude is that a counselling course and being a counsellor is a prerequisite to becoming a psychotherapist. Many counsellors and therapists would agree that there are many overlaps between counselling and psychotherapy, and from studying the WPF's curriculum it is clear that their counsellors will be psychodynamically informed, but they may equally agree that they are methods of working with people that are intrinsically different and require different trainings (see Part One).

The transition between the Diploma and the Psychotherapy Course seems to have caused anxiety and tension in the trainee group. Some were clear quite early on in their training that they wanted to join the Psychotherapy Course, but had to wait until a specific point in the Diploma Course to apply and there were many disappointed trainees who were not accepted for the Psychotherapy Course. Problems of differentiation between counsellor and psychotherapist seem to be exacerbated by this route to becoming a psychotherapist with the WPF. Meanwhile, the WPF maintains that its Diploma Course is more of a psychotherapy training than counselling, if compared with other psychotherapy trainings.

For the person happy with a counselling training and able to wait and see at Diploma level whether or not an application for the Psychotherapy Course was desirable, WPF has proved its success over the years. This may be a desirable route for those applicants who may not be eligible for other psychotherapy courses due to age or qualifications, and who may not feel sure if psychotherapy is what they want to practise. But for the applicants wishing to become psychotherapists, it is a long wait through the various routes to the Diploma to run the risk of an application being turned down.

The in-service training at WPF provides trainees with an experience similar to the Tavistock Adult Psychotherapy Training, in that clients are seen at the WPF rather than privately. This gives trainees a sort of ready-made client group, contributing to an enriching clinical experience. The transition from the institute setting to private practice seems to be reserved for the psychotherapy graduates, creating another dividing line between counselling and psychotherapy. The overlaps between counselling and psychotherapy are probably seen and felt most acutely at the WPF. The debate is likely to continue for some years until perhaps there is a consensus on the distinguishing criteria between the two.

Humanistic and Integrative Psychotherapy Section

ANTIOCH: SCHOOL OF PSYCHOTHERAPY AND COUNSELLING

Antioch University, Psychology Department, Inner Circle, Regent's Park, London NW1 4NS; tel: 071 487 7406.

1. History

This course differs from the majority of organizations included in Part Two, in that it combines an academic degree with a psychotherapy training. The qualification is MA in the Psychology of Therapy and Counselling and this can be achieved by students not wishing to become psychotherapists. Those students wishing to be recognized as psychotherapists by the UK Standing Conference for Psychotherapy must undertake appropriate personal psychotherapy in addition to successfully fulfilling the requirements of the programme. The following brief history has been extracted from the brochure.

Antioch University was set up in America in 1852 by Horace Mann, America's leading educator of the time. His radical ideas of the day in higher learning instigated a tradition of excellence and innovation. It was a hundred years later that Antioch started to establish centres abroad and in 1969 a centre was opened in

London. The MA is awarded by Antioch Education Abroad 'in keeping with its policies of innovative and experiential learning'. In 1977 a group of students interested in humanistic psychology initiated study towards an MA in Humanistic Psychology. In 1982 the psychology programme 'underwent dramatic changes and became the more structured MA in the Psychology of Therapy and Counselling under the Directorship of Emmy van Deurzen-Smith.' The major change was the addition of requirements of a placement and personal therapy for the individual wishing to become a psychotherapist, to the study of 'a thorough academic foundation in the main psychotherapeutic disciplines'.

In 1985 Antioch moved to Regent's College where part of its development has been to offer a student counselling service for students on the Regent's College campus.

2. THEORETICAL ORIENTATION AND CURRICULUM

The primary orientations are existential, psychoanalytic and humanistic but 'at the crux of the teaching is the questioning of assumptions and a look at the philosophical foundations that underlie the different approaches in psychotherapy.' The aim is to produce graduates 'who have really clearly considered the implications and the applications of the therapeutic process'. In terms of the curriculum the intention is 'to acquaint students with the philosophical, historical and theoretical background to the main dynamic approaches'.

> Regent's College see themselves as a non-doctrinaire training and do not expect students to adhere to any particular philosophy or theoretical orientation.
>
> Although they are aware of the hierarchy in the psychotherapy trainings, they feel quite removed from this because of their primary identification with the world of higher education. As an academic department, the Regent's programmes have developed independently of the hierarchically stratified British trainings. What they feel is important is that the course is the only course in Europe which offers this kind of MA and is unique in that it combines the following elements:
>
> 1. The combination of theory and practice.
> 2. A taught MA with a strong emphasis on individual research.

3. Emphasis on qualitative rather than quantitative research.

4. Coverage of a broad spectrum of psychotherapies with a strong focus on existential, psychoanalytic and humanistic approaches.

5. A strong emphasis on underlying philosophical issues and attention to the relationship between psychotherapy and philosophy.

6. A non-doctrinaire programme which does not require trainees to conform to any particular belief system and, indeed, encourages them to criticize existing schools of thought.

The first year academic seminars cover the main dynamic approaches over three terms:

Term One: Existential and Phenomenological Psychotherapy – Husserl, Heidegger, Kierkegaard, Nietzsche, Sartre, Binswanger, Boss, Frankl, May, Rogers, Laing, Kelly and others.

Term Two: Psychoanalysis – Freud, Hartmann, Reich, Klein, Mahler, Kernberg, Kohut, Winnicott, Fairbairn, Langs and others.

Term Three: Humanistic and Integrative – Jung, Perls, Maslow, Assagioli, Berne, Moreno, Adler, Rank, Lewin, Erikson and others.

The experiential seminars are titled the 'training component' and they are weekly group meetings teaching the principles of psychotherapeutic technique experientially using paired and group exercises. These 'training sessions' include self and peer assessment.

In the second year the academic and training seminars continue and students are offered a choice including the following:

Child Development

Cognitive and Behavioural Analysis within a Wholistic Framework

Communicative Psychotherapy

Existential Therapy and Counselling in Practice

Family Therapy

Gestalt in Practice

Human Sexuality

Klein and the Kleinians

Phenomenological Psychology

Philosophy and Practice of Psychotherapy

Psychology of Groups and Social Systems

Psychology of Women

Psychopathology

Therapeutic Approaches to Psychosomatic and Psychiatric Disorders

With sufficient student interest seminars not normally on offer will be specially arranged.

The training seminars of the first year are followed by a psychiatric placement and a supervision group. Each student has a personal tutor, but can also talk to any other member of the faculty over an issue that may arise.

3. TRAINING STRUCTURE

3.1 *Training Committee*

The Training Committee is known as the Core Faculty, who are four practising psychotherapists. Their trainings and qualifications cover clinical psychology, philosophy, psychoanalysis and social work (more details of the Core Faculty and the adjunct faculty can be read in the brochure). The Directorship is a post decided on by Regent's College. Regulation of the course is from the normal university sources and this MA expects to be officially approved by the CNAA within a year.

The Core Faculty meet formally once a month with the Academic Dean, and the running of the programme, relationship with Regent's College and students' progress are among the issues that are discussed at these meetings. In addition to these departmental meetings the programme is monitored by the Academic Board and academic standards committee of Regent's College. Approved training therapists would be those recognized by the UKSCP.

3.2 *Selection procedure and admission*

There are two stages to the admission procedure. There is an informal group meeting where people who are interested can obtain more information about the course. This is to enable people to assess their own suitability. If interested the applicant formally submits an application form and then attends a 45-minute interview with two members of the Core Faculty. Applicants are assessed on the basis of their academic background, their understanding of basic psychotherapeutic theory, their experience of working with people using counselling skills and their personal maturity.

There is no policy on age limit, but there is a caution to applicants who are under twenty-five, since the course requires maturity and life experience among other qualities; there is an attempt to balance men and women in each group. People applying tend to be in their thirties and forties with a first degree (not necessarily in psychology), with a certain amount of previous training in therapy or counselling, and with a fairly substantial experience of working with people therapeutically.

There are sixteen places for each intake and three intakes a year. Because of the selection procedure a high proportion of people who apply are appropriate, but the numbers may often dictate the necessity for waiting lists to join the course.

3.3 *Time commitment and length of training*

For the first year academic and experiential seminars take place one day a week. In the second year the clinical placement would take up a half day a week and often one day a week. Second year seminars require another half day. People in full-time work could follow the course with a regular arrangement for time off, at least one day a week. Writing up of papers and reading must be taken into account as well as personal therapy for those wishing to become involved in the training for psychotherapists.

It takes between two and three years to be awarded the MA and there is the further two-year postgraduate course.

3.4 *Interruptions in training*

Interruptions are accommodated and each case would be dealt with individually. There is usually a limit of two years.

3.5 *Postgraduate qualification and learned society*

Students are encouraged to join societies where they may share their clinical work beyond the MA. There are three learned societies linked with the programme: the Society of Psychoanalytical Psychotherapists, the Society for Existential Analysis and the European Society for Communicative Psychotherapy. Information about these societies would be discussed throughout the course as well as ethical considerations in the practice of psychotherapy. The department also offers a post-qualifying diploma in existential psychotherapy.

The library of Regent's College contains a wide selection of relevant books on psychotherapy. Plans are now under way to establish a library for psychotherapy at Regent's College which will house the libraries of participating institutions, and will be available for the use of visiting scholars. It is hoped that the library will become the most comprehensive resource centre for psychotherapy in the United Kingdom.

4. CLINICAL AND ACADEMIC REQUIREMENTS

4.1 *Personal therapy*

This would be part of the extra requirement for students wishing their qualification to be recognized by HIPS. The Core Faculty are in the process of defining this aspect of the course, but basically students would be required to 'undergo a personal psychotherapy similar in kind, duration, frequency and intensity to that which they intend to practise themselves', as has been stipulated by HIPS.

4.2 *Clinical requirements*

As already stated there is the six-month clinical placement which must be followed in the second year. This placement could be in a private agency or hospital setting. There is no requirement for a student to see training clients since the placement entails seeing people on a one-to-one basis.

4.3 *Supervision*

Each trainee will be in small-group supervision with a member of the faculty, as well as an external supervisor linked with the placement in the second year. Some students already in private practice wish to use their own clients as a placement and they must then seek their own supervisor in addition to attending the weekly supervision groups at college.

4.4 *Papers and written work*

A paper of between 3,000 and 4,000 words must be written for every academic seminar followed. In addition students must produce oral presentations, where they would function as the tutor. The final dissertation must be between 16,000 and 40,000 words. Evaluation is based on looking for a 'logical and informed argument using resources appropriately'. Students are encouraged to demonstrate their understanding of therapy through case study.

5. REFERRALS

Referrals are made during the six-month placement by the agency responsible. The type of patients seen by students will depend on the placement. The department offers a counselling service to students and staff of Regent's College. Students wishing to supplement their placement load may be referred clients through the counselling service.

6. COST OF TRAINING

For students entering the programme in April 1991, the total cost of the course was £5,600. There is a £200 deposit and then six equal payments spread over two years. Personal therapy would be extra and so would supervision for the student in private practice. Consulting rooms would have to be organized by each student.

There is an annual scholarship.

7. Future Expectations/Career Prospects

The setting of the therapeutic relationship is something that is covered in detail throughout the course, as are the practicalities of setting up in practice. The Core Faculty are keen to encourage graduates to return to teach and supervise, but preferably when they have developed their own specializations away from Regent's College.

8. Trainees' Experience

8.1 *Why this course was chosen*

The variety of reasons people were attracted to this course were the following:

    (a) a wish to understand the meaning of eclecticism;

    (b) to gain an overview of the world of psychotherapy;

    (c) for the academic input resulting in the qualification;

    (d) for enjoyment of study and debate.

The selection procedure was experienced as informal and friendly.

8.2 *The atmosphere of the course*

In general students felt very excited by the academic lectures and seminars which they thought were excellent. There were mixed feelings about the experiential part of the course, although students acknowledged that many of them felt very positive about these sessions. The mixed feelings came from a sense of lack of clarity about the purpose of the experiential groups. Some students were confused as to whether the aim was task orientated or to understand the group process. The latter was experienced by some students as being neglected. This was felt to be to do with teachers who may not be trained in group dynamics.

Many students following this MA are already practising psycho-therapists who have trained elsewhere. There was some concern and confusion from them as to whether the Antioch course was a training or an MA because they were aware that some people following this course would feel it enabled them to set up in practice as psychotherapists. Most students felt clear that as a psychotherapy training it was not adequate. There was some agreement that the course could address the aspect of psychother-apy training in the future and that with the extra two-year postgraduate course, depending on the requirements, an adequate psychotherapy training could be established.

There was some discussion regarding the styles of teaching and students were very impressed and happy with the Core Faculty. However, there was some criticism of some members of the adjunct faculty. Although students agreed with the philosophy that they were responsible adults in higher education, it was felt that this could sometimes be used as a reason for a teacher being inadequately prepared. All agreed that, overall, the course had met their expectations as an exciting original MA.

AUTHOR'S COMMENTS

It seemed clear from a student perspective that this course provides an enriching experience. However, there was concern amongst trainees about the MA course being seen as a psychotherapy training. The established analytic trainings would have many criticisms about adding on some requirements to an MA, to create a psychotherapy training. The focus of all long-established therapy trainings is personal therapy, supervision and theory respectively (see Part One), whereas Antioch's focus is naturally the academic theory. On the other hand, academic recognition has been a difficulty with many psychotherapy organizations, some of whom wish to be accredited by the CNAA (which is something that is not often written about). So in many ways Antioch could be seen as initiating and developing a new type of training.

Meanwhile, there is a very broad spectrum of therapies studied, providing a geography of the psychotherapy world. Perhaps a relevant question would be how helpful is it to have this overview to become a psychotherapist? Students who were already therapists agreed that the overview was fascinating and one of the reasons they wanted to follow the course. For the beginner, however, they felt the diversity of therapies could be confusing.

The Core Faculty, Ernesto Spinelli, Emmy van Deurzen-Smith and David Smith, have published many papers and books, some of which will be found in the bibliography. Antioch representatives have been and continue to be active participants at the UKSCP.

BATH CENTRE FOR PSYCHOTHERAPY
AND COUNSELLING (BCPC)

285 Bloomfield Road, Bath BA2 2NU.

1. HISTORY

BCPC was set up in 1984 by Peter Hawkins, who invited Alix Pirani to co-lead a one-year course. This was in response to what Peter Hawkins saw as a growing need for a training in psychotherapy for people in the South-west with a humanistic therapy background. This year's course has now become the present Year 3 of the training.

In 1986 a two-year preparatory course was designed which would lead to the psychotherapy Year 3 and by 1988 a fourth year was added to 'enable experienced practitioners to become accredited psychotherapists'. Each year is a course in itself and there is no automatic progress to the next year, without application.

In 1988 BCPC became a registered limited non-profit-making Educational Company and a member of the UKSCP. Peter Hawkins has been a member of the Council of UKSCP as the representative of the Humanistic and Integrative Psychotherapy Section (HIPS).

The fourth year leads to the Diploma with accreditation in Humanistic and Integrative Psychotherapy, and the first of these were awarded in 1989. In 1991 Stage 3C was added; this leads to a diploma in counselling.

2. THEORETICAL ORIENTATION AND CURRICULUM

The main theoretical orientation is humanistic with a large input from the British School of Object Relations, in particular Winnicott and the post-Winnicottians like Patrick Casement and Christopher Bollas. BCPC would see the latter as the humanistic end of the analytic. They also integrate a transpersonal perspective.

BCPC recognizes two aspects of humanistic psychotherapy which are incorporated into its training. The first is the combination of the humanistic therapies like Gestalt, psychodrama, etc.; trainees are not taught specifically Gestalt or psychodrama, but these models may be used in the experiential groups. The basic counselling which is foundational for all further work is based on Rogers and, to some extent, Egan. The second aspect is that BCPC sees the humanistic therapies as traditionally functioning in a group setting, and as humanistic therapists started to work in a one-to-one framework, so they looked to the analytic tradition.

The training is divided into Stages. These are usually one-year taught courses of one full day a week each, though Stage 4 does not have a taught course and may last two to three years. Stages 1 and 2 are considered foundations for further Stages. At the end of Stage 2, students who are considered suitable are taken on to either Stage 3P (Psychotherapy) or Stage 3C (Counselling). There are therefore two strands – a psychotherapy strand and a counselling strand – both of which offer a diploma.

BCPC feels very strongly that the training should be experience first and theory second, so that in Stage 1 the training day is divided between personal development groups and the theoretical learning of counselling skills. There is a deliberate policy that these two different types of seminar be taught by the same teachers, so that in the experiential group the leader would take on a therapeutic role whereas in the theoretical seminars the role would be more as teacher. Stage 2 continues with the personal development group, and the theoretical seminars concentrate on human growth and development. In addition to this trainees are learning counselling skills in groups of three, and these small groups are working on an adaptation of Egan's Three Stage Model.

Stage 3P seminars are related to three areas: the practicalities of being in private practice; therapeutic skill development; and theory. There is also a group to support the training process. In this Stage trainees work with two or three clients and most of the time is given to detailed supervision of these clients. Stage 3C works towards a counselling diploma and includes further practice of counselling, supervision of two or three clients, and seminars to explore the use of counselling with different client groups (couples, cross-cultural, etc.) and different counselling modes (crisis, etc.). Some of these will form a compulsory part of the course curriculum and some will be voluntary modules. Each student will do at least six of these – the mix to be agreed with their tutor. Students' clients may be seen privately or as part of an agency. There is also a self-development group as part of this Stage. In order to be awarded the diploma students will need to write a case study and a dissertation, and these may be submitted after the end of the year of the taught course.

Suitable students from Stage 3P go on to Stage 4. In this Stage students are not on a taught course, but have a tutor who explores with them their learning needs at this time. Students will be carrying on with a private practice under close supervision, and will usually do a mental health placement during this time and may also attend short courses, lectures, seminars, etc., provided by both BCPC and other bodies. They will also usually be part of a peer group of BCPC students. When they and their tutor think they are ready, they may apply for Stage 5. This usually takes two to five years. Stage 4 is concerned with becoming a psychotherapist and is a consolidation and an 'integration of the skills already learnt'. Each trainee has a personal tutor.

3. TRAINING STRUCTURE

3.1 Training Committee

There are four members of the Training Committee, who are all humanistic psychotherapists in private practice and fully integrative accredited psychotherapists. There is a Chair but no Director of the Training Committee.

The Committee is regulated by an external staff consultant who acts as an external moderator, and there is a Psychiatric Consultant who is also a psychotherapist. The Training Committee meet quarterly and discuss accreditation, examination and training contracts. In addition to these aspects the Training Committee are responsible for looking at the training programme as a whole.

BCPC has some difficulties with finding appropriate therapists for trainees because of the dearth of suitable qualified psychotherapists living and working in the South-west. However, this is changing as more people are moving into the area.

3.2 Selection procedure and admission

As has already been stated, each year has to be applied for, and it is possible to apply for Year 3 or 4 if an applicant can demonstrate relevant previous experience and qualification. Many people who have done a training elsewhere which did not give them an accreditation have joined Year 4 to gain the accreditation of psychotherapist. For new applicants the selection procedure takes the place of a group meeting where a two-way assessment can take place.

There is no age limit, but suitable applicants would be over twenty-eight. Academic qualifications are not necessary. The general background of people applying tends to be the helping professions, although teachers and people from creative professions also apply. There are eighteen places in Stages 1 and 2, ten to twelve in Stages 3C and 3P and ten in Stage 4; there are usually about forty applicants for Stage 1 each year.

3.3 Time commitment and length of training

For Stages 1–3 trainees spend one day per week when the experiential and theoretical groups take place. Stage 4 trainees attend one day a month. In addition to this there is reading, the writing up of notes and papers, personal therapy and training clients (in Stages 3C and 3P).

Trainees could not qualify as psychotherapists in less than five years unless they start after Stage 1.

3.4 *Interruptions in training*

Interruptions are something that BCPC actively encourages for some trainees who it feels need more time between the Stages. It is rare to follow the course without any break between the Stages.

3.5 *Postgraduate qualification and learned society*

In 1989 a student professional body was formed called the BCPC Association. All trainees are part of this Association although there are different types of membership depending on what Stage the trainee has completed.

BCPC acquired its own premises in 1991, but there is no library, and books and papers are obtained from a local bookshop specializing in relevant books. BCPC has a small collection of video tapes for teaching purposes.

There is a Code of Ethics which all trainees will receive as they start the course and BCPC also has a statement of Core Values. The Association publishes a newsletter which includes extracts and abstracts from students' papers.

4. CLINICAL AND ACADEMIC REQUIREMENTS

4.1 *Personal therapy*

BCPC prefers to refer its trainees to appropriate therapists and every trainee must be in a minimum of once weekly therapy. There is a policy that members of staff are not therapists for trainees. The criteria for training therapists are that the therapist is experienced and qualified, and that the focus of the therapy is in the therapeutic relationship. As long as therapists meet this requirement BCPC is not specific about the orientation of the therapists and trainees may often be in analytic therapy. Trainees' therapists are not consulted during the training.

4.2 *Clinical requirements*

Trainees may be seeing clients in their place of work during Stages 1 and 2, but in Stage 3P they are required to see no more than three private clients. They may also see private clients in Stage 3C. These three clients must be in a minimum of once weekly therapy and are expected to be long term (more than one year). Medical cover is advised for a client with a psychiatric history, and this would be negotiated with the client's GP. BCPC has a consultant psychiatrist who is available to give any advice that may be needed.

Each student who has not worked in the mental health professions must complete a mental health placement of about six months of one day a week. These are usually in a psychiatric hospital or a day hospital. Students must show that they understand the workings of the Health Service, can relate to other professionals and can work with severely disturbed patients.

4.3 *Supervision*

Supervision is not given in Stages 1 and 2, but is given considerable emphasis in Stages 3 and 4. There is both group supervision and individual supervision with members of BCPC staff. In Stage 4 trainees may also have individual supervision with approved external supervisors.

4.4 *Papers and written work*

There is at least one paper to be written for each training year, and a longer in-depth case study to be written towards the completion of Year 4.

5. REFERRALS

Training clients must be found by each trainee, although BCPC gives trainees advice on contact with different agencies and often makes referrals. The whole range of client groups may be seen, and there is a strict policy of letting training clients know they are seeing a trainee who is in supervision.

6. COST OF TRAINING

Training stages vary in cost. Individual supervision would be extra, as would personal therapy: these sessions tend to range from £18 to £25. Trainees are given guidelines as to what they may charge a training client and this would usually range from £10 to £15. Consulting rooms are expected to be arranged by each trainee.

There are no bursaries or loans at the moment, but the BCPC Association can give advice on this issue.

7. FUTURE EXPECTATIONS/CAREER PROSPECTS

There is a lot of practical advice on setting up in practice. However, trainees are advised not to expect to replace a full-time job with a psychotherapy practice. Most people can expect a practice of between ten and fifteen clients who are not usually in more than once weekly therapy.

There are many opportunities for graduates to teach and supervise with BCPC, which has already invited four of its graduates on to the staff group.

8. TRAINEES' EXPERIENCE

8.1 *Why this course was chosen*

It was mainly the spiritual and intuitive aspects of the course which attracted people to this training, as well as the breadth of the course in counselling and psychotherapy.

The selection procedure was a positive experience for trainees in terms of it being a day spent in a group, discovering if this was the way in which they wanted to work and train. It was also a useful way of acquiring information about the course – requirements, commitment, etc.

8.2 *The atmosphere of the course*

The experiential groupwork and emphasis on personal process are experienced as vital to this training as an important contribution to the process of becoming a psychotherapist. A very different energy was experienced in the experiential sessions from the theoretical seminars. There was some concern that the issue of psychotherapy and counselling was fudged. Trainees sensed that there was a current issue associated with the completion of two years without a counselling accreditation. This was in the process of being addressed, but there was a general feeling that BCPC ought to be clearer about the distinction between counselling and psychotherapy. Since this was talked about (summer 1990), BCPC has implemented changes by creating the parallel courses as outlined in 1–7 above.

People were agreed that reapplying for each Stage was a good idea. It was experienced as a continual struggle but in a positive, challenging way. Trainees had not found many aspects of the training confusing. Occasionally, the experiential component during co-counselling sessions had caused confusion, but in general people felt they were getting the training they had hoped for and beyond.

AUTHOR'S COMMENTS

BCPC's theoretical orientation is a combination of different types of humanistic therapies (Gestalt, psychodrama, etc.) as well as psychoanalysis and analytical psychology. The issue of combining many different and sometimes conflicting theories is relevant to this training (see Introduction to Part Two).

The debate concerning counselling and psychotherapy is also relevant. BCPC sees a difference between counselling and psychotherapy and therefore presumably the trainees would separate after Stage 2 into two groups – potential counsellors from potential psychotherapists. This is a recent change and has addressed the feeling in the trainee group that the issue of counselling and psychotherapy was being 'fudged'. However, the relevant questions here would be linked with the inevitable tensions arising in the group at Stage 2 as to why some people could go on to Stage 3P and others to Stage 3C. How does BCPC distinguish between counselling and psychotherapy within its humanistic framework? What would its criteria be for separating the trainee group?

BCPC has been and continues to be an active member of the Humanistic and Integrative Practitioners Section (HIPS) of UKSCP. BCPC is one of the more recent training organizations in the

South-west, which is still developing and evolving its own style of working and training.

CHIRON CENTRE FOR HOLISTIC PSYCHOTHERAPY

26 Eaton Rise, Ealing, London W5 2ER; tel: 081 997 5219.

1. HISTORY

Chiron was set up in 1983 by a founding party of six, out of which the three current directors are Bernd Eiden, Jochen Lude and Rainer Pervoltz. They have a long-standing background in humanistic psychology, mainly biodynamic and Reichian body psychotherapy, Gestalt and transpersonal psychology. They had been teachers and trainers at the Gerda Boyesen Institute before they founded Chiron.

2. THEORETICAL ORIENTATION AND CURRICULUM

The main theoretical orientation is a combination of body concepts as taught in different Neo-Reichian schools and Gestalt philosophy. One cornerstone is the biodynamic principle of 'learning to trust your inner impulses; the belief that there is an inherent healing power in the body and that the more it is acknowledged, the more it can unfold in a self-regulating way.' Gestalt philosophy is based on the understanding that inner growth takes place most effectively at the 'contact boundary', which means in relation to other people. Therefore Chiron attempts 'a form of bodywork which takes place in relationship'. Goal of the therapy is to set free the inner 'charge', which is the 'unhindered tingling or streaming of energy that occurs when two people meet without the restrictions of the past'. The state of the body changes during the therapeutic process from being 'a restrictive, often tense and painful carrier of inner unfinished business to a finer instrument with a lighter energetic frequency, which can promote a relative effortlessness to live your life and open the contact with the Higher Being within yourself.'

Trainee therapists, therefore, learn to develop a capacity to use themselves as a 'body of resonance' and to follow their own inner impulses within the therapeutic work. Chiron acknowledges some similarity between this emphasis and that of the analytic transference/countertransference, but the Chiron-trained therapists would see themselves as being more active and use the body as a fundamental instrument for 'healing the wounds of old relationships'.

The first year course is mostly experiential and there are training groups in body-centred psychotherapy. There is also biodynamic massage and anatomy. The second year covers Advanced Massage Training, Advanced Body Psychotherapy Training and the first year Gestalt Training. During the third year, training continues in Advanced Massage and in Charge Therapy, a specific form of Gestalt Bodywork. At this final stage, trainees also have to show their learned therapeutic abilities and skills in small weekly groups of three, with a supervisor present (they take it in turns to be client, therapist and observer). There is also a weekly seminar on humanistic and traditional therapeutic theories, as well as character structures.

Main topics of the training are as follows in brief (more details can be obtained in Chiron's brochure):

Circulation of energy and its blocks in different personality types

The formation of muscular, tissue and psychological armour (including Reichian segments)

The breathing rhythm/wave and its dysfunction; its meaning

Work with regression and the Inner Child

Exploring the different layers of the personality (primary impulses and secondary defences)

Learning to trust and foster inner impulses

Learning energetic self-regulation

Evoking and exploring inner images

Dialogues

Rigid, too loose and flexible boundaries

Correspondence between inner and outer relationships (vertical and horizontal connections)

Transference and countertransference/the therapeutic relationship

Exploring relationships (lovers, parents, friends, colleagues)

Sexuality and sexual development

Ways of helping to open the spiritual path

There is a recommended reading list; main theorists are: Wilhelm Reich, Gerda Boyesen, Jack Lee Rosenberg, David Boadella, John Pierrakos, Alexander Lowen and Fritz Perls.

3. TRAINING STRUCTURE

3.1 *Training Committee*

There are at present six members of the Training Committee, and in future one member from the Chiron Association will join. The Chiron organization is currently a partnership with two directors. There is no student representative.

The Committee meet monthly, when issues to do with the training are discussed. A working party of the Training Committee meet weekly. There is an External Moderator who advises the Training Committee.

There is a Code of Ethics including a complaints procedure.

3.2 *Selection procedure and admission*

There is an application form, followed by two interviews with members of the Training Committee.

Clinical experience is not necessary for the basic training. During the postgraduate phase mental health assignments are required. Experience of individual and group therapy is looked for and an ability to relate to people. Academic qualifications are not necessary.

As a rule applicants are requested to enrol for the full training, but in exceptional cases training can be joined for selected courses. There is a lower age limit of twenty-five, but no upper age limit.

There is no policy for balancing groups with men and women, but at this stage more women seem to apply and more of a balance is hoped for; the general background of people applying is middle class. There are twelve places for each training group and in general there are about forty applicants per year.

3.3 Time commitment and length of training

There is a personal tutor who may be seen as many times as is wanted.

During the three-year basic training there are approximately ten hours of training weekly, plus one hour individual psychotherapy. The basic training extends over three years and leads to the Certificate which entitles the graduate to start practising as a Holistic Psychotherapist under supervision. The training can easily be stretched over a longer period of time.

The supervised period (postgraduate level) is necessary for a minimum of two years (can also be stretched) and leads to accreditation as a qualified Chiron Psychotherapist (Diploma).

3.4 Interruptions in training

Interruptions may occur through life crisis (during which the trainee is encouraged to do more personal work on themselves), through childbirth, and through difficult work situations. They are, as a rule, welcomed, and a slowing down of the training process is sometimes even encouraged.

3.5 Postgraduate qualification and learned society

Chiron is in the process of creating an association to act as a forum for postgraduate education and research; it will also monitor standards of practice according to the Association's Code of Ethics. Qualified therapists would have to apply as there is no automatic membership.

A library is being formed.

4. CLINICAL AND ACADEMIC REQUIREMENTS

4.1 *Personal therapy*

Trainees are required in addition to undergo at least a one-year psychotherapy group experience while in training and to be in once weekly therapy. The Training Committee are responsible for referring trainees to therapists and Chiron would like trainees (at least for a certain period of time) to be in therapy with a Chiron trained therapist. Existing therapeutic relationships are, however, respected. There is no consultation with a trainee's individual therapist as Chiron sees this relationship as a 'sacred space' for the trainee.

4.2 *Clinical requirements*

Trainees are in an ongoing assessment process during the training. In the postgraduate phase each trainee must see at least two clients over a period of eighteen months, and they are expected to see other clients concurrently. Medical cover is not required.

4.3 *Supervision*

There is a minimum of two years' regular supervision with a Chiron approved supervisor (in a weekly group for two years; or individually, fortnightly for one year plus in a weekly group for a further year). Two case histories of 5,000 words each must be presented to complete the supervised phase.

4.4 *Papers and written work*

At the end of each year one paper must be submitted: 1,500 words for the first year, 2,500 words for the second year and 4,000 words for the third year. These papers are to demonstrate the trainee's individual process, relationship with training clients and an elaboration of one of the basic theories of Holistic Psychotherapy. Further course papers must be written at various stages.

5. Referrals

All referrals are made by the senior trainers of Chiron. The client's background is discussed at a staff meeting and an appropriate therapist is allocated. Chiron believes there is always a meaning and mutual learning when two people – in this case therapist and client – happen to meet and work together.

6. Cost of Training

Training costs are approximately £2,000 per year. Students can choose to spread the training over a longer period of time and therefore annual costs could be lower. Supervision and therapy are extra and cost between £20 and £26.

Trainees can charge training clients between £18 and £22 (sliding scale) and mostly work at Chiron. Chiron encourages them to build up their own practice. Their private consulting rooms must be of professional standard. There are as a rule no loans or bursaries.

7. Future Expectations/Career Prospects

Advice is given on the practicalities of setting up in practice. In general enough clients are seeking therapy for qualified trainees to be supported in building their own practice. There are prospects to supervise and teach in the future with Chiron, but it is being done gradually and selectively.

8. Trainees' Experience

8.1 *Why this course was chosen*

Chiron's brochure had impressed trainees and the general feeling was that it would be a training where they would be respected as individuals by trainers who had their feet on the ground. The expectation therefore was that each individual would be encouraged to grow in their own way and would not be pressured or dictated to by orthodox theory. At the same time, it was felt that a rigorous professional attitude would be maintained. The other aspects of the training that people were attracted to were:

(a) the emphasis on bodywork;

(b) that the therapist's approach was active.

Some people were very clear that the course was a way of becoming a psychotherapist, whilst others came to partake in the courses for personal therapy. Trainees felt that at some point in the training people have to acknowledge whether or not they want to go on to train as therapists. However, trainees felt that this was never a pressure from the trainers and that this was a reflection of how flexible Chiron was in allowing people to use the training in the way that was best for them.

Individual therapy was seen as very different for each individual depending on their needs, so that sometimes a lot of bodywork was the mode of therapy whilst at other times more dialogue may be appropriate. Trainees felt that their individual therapists allowed them to choose what they needed at a given time and they all experienced a great sense of flexibility and freedom in this approach.

8.2 *The atmosphere of the course*

The training groups could be taken up with one or two trainees' personal problems. The approach that included personal therapy as part of the training groups was experienced by trainees as something that was very caring on the part of the trainers, who acknowledged that sometimes it was more important to offer individuals the space in which to work out their own problems rather than stick to the curriculum. It sometimes happened that trainees were in a group whose leader was their individual therapist and some other members of the group were also in therapy with the leader. This was not experienced as a problem but rather something that could be worked with.

Holistic was understood very much as the therapist not ignoring what the body was saying. Trainees felt that the body never lies and that the unconscious was the body. They also felt there was a real openness about feedback to trainers and that criticisms were heard and taken on board; people saw that things were changed as a consequence. However, it was also felt that there should be more of a structure for feedback – a proper channel, which to date there was not. Trainees acknowledged that some complaints were very much linked with individuals' process and their transference to Chiron. The experience was that Chiron was aware of this and really helped each trainee to understand the difficulty from all levels.

A difficulty arising was the issue of post-qualification. Trainees, who were sometimes also clients, were then joining the association and becoming colleagues of their therapists. It was experienced as a tricky area because of unresolved transference issues which had to be lived with. Trainees all experienced permission to air critical feelings about the course and that criticisms were listened to. This had sometimes been anxiety-provoking but because the trainers had not penalized people for their opinions trainees felt relieved and reassured that they could express, sometimes very difficult, emotions.

There was a feeling that the academic side of the course was not rigorous enough, but others disagreed with this opinion, saying that they liked the way the academic was woven in with the experiential part of the training. People had experienced going through disturbing times during the course of the training, and the holding provided had been experienced as incredibly flexible and supportive.

Trainees were aware of other humanistic trainings, but had a very strong sense that Chiron was the best for them and they were all very glad to be training there: initial expectations had been more than fulfilled.

AUTHOR'S COMMENTS

What Chiron is naming holistic therapy is its own combination of body-centred Neo- or post-Reichian therapy and Gestalt philosophy and therapy. The emphasis and use of the therapist's inner impulses and body as the fundamental instrument in the therapeutic relationship, with the incorporation of massage techniques, makes

Chiron an unusual training amongst the humanistic trainings which are members of the UKSCP. The sort of therapy and training on offer at Chiron would link with what Joel Kovel has described as the Mysticotranscendent approach (Kovel, 1976).

Some therapists may say that Chiron's therapeutic stance implies that a therapy which does not include 'bodywork' is not whole or complete; that something important (the body) is excluded. Most therapists, analytic and humanistic, would not deny the importance of the body as a vessel of unconscious communication. However, that is a different issue to using the body in the therapeutic relationship. In the analytic attitude, touching a client is something that Freud decided, before the turn of the century (from his own experience), interfered with the therapeutic relationship and this is something that is adhered to by analytic therapists and the analytic trainings (see Part One).

There tended to be a consensus from trainees that analytic therapy was 'in the head', which is why they had chosen a body-centred therapy. An analytic criticism of bodywork therapy would be that it denies the importance of the intellect and denigrates the capacity to think, which could lead to a division of mind and body, rather than an integration (see Part One – The Humanistic Attitude). These issues are very pertinent to the arguments for and against, between analytic and humanistic therapies; debates which in one form or another have long been in discussion since Freud's first dissenters. Does Chiron see the roots of its therapy as an important component in its course?

GESTALT CENTRE

64 Warwick Road, St Albans, Herts AL1 4DL; tel: 0727 64806.

1. HISTORY

The Gestalt Centre evolved into a training from the demand of individuals coming together for Gestalt therapy. By 1980 the training had become formalized, starting out as a four phase modular training now in transition to become a two-year fixed Basic Training and a three phase modular Advanced Training. The Basic Training is primarily aimed at personal development and use of Gestalt in work context, and the Advanced Phase is for trainees wishing to become Gestalt psychotherapists. The aims of the Centre are:

1. To increase awareness and creative use of personal power.

2. To encourage individuals to recognize their responsibility for their lives, their society and their world.

3. To further the use of Gestalt in relevant fields, i.e. the helping professions: education, management, etc.

2. THEORETICAL ORIENTATION AND CURRICULUM

The aim of the programme is to train people to use Gestalt in their work or to become both group and individual Gestalt psychotherapists. Gestalt is the main theoretical orientation, as initiated by Fritz and Laura Perls and Paul Goodman.

The two-year Basic Training concentrates on personal development. 'The ongoing group is the forum in which we focus on styles of interaction, develop skilful communication and experiment with changing outdated patterns of behaviour. It also includes fundamental Gestalt theory, skills development and discussion of clinical practice.' This Basic Training programme may be for people who do not wish to become psychotherapists, but who will be training to incorporate the Gestalt attitude into their life and work.

The Advanced Training leads to a Diploma in Gestalt Psychotherapy and this is the part of the training followed by those trainees wishing to become psychotherapists. The work of the Basic Training is taken to a more advanced level plus a comparative study of the major psychotherapeutic models, and trainee therapists also begin working with individuals and groups under supervision. There is ongoing staff, peer and self-assessment on all aspects of study and practice, culminating in a thesis to demonstrate understanding of Gestalt theory and its application. Supervision and group meetings provide support and a base for study and exploration.

Trainees during the Advanced Training will become 'apprentices' assisting a member of staff facilitating a group from one of the groups on the Basic Training, which is a requirement of the training. The emphasis of the training is on the individual in relation to the group/community. The annual five-day Easter Residential for the whole centre is an opportunity to experience large-group processes and participate in developing the Centre as a working community.

Infant Observation and analytic therapy are not studied because of the lack of time. However, trainees are encouraged to follow external courses on occasions and to read as widely as possible as well as being required to undertake an external course in background psychology if not covered before.

3. TRAINING STRUCTURE

3.1 *Training Committee*

There are three Directors who function as the Training Committee, and a faculty of six, with visiting trainers invited regularly. Directors meet once weekly to discuss individual trainees, management, the direction of the training, the curriculum, administration. Twice termly meetings with the faculty are held to discuss the monitoring of trainees. There is an external moderator.

3.2 *Selection procedure and admission*

Selection for the Basic Training is made on the basis of an in-depth application form and attendance at Centre-led groups. The Basic Training will then be an opportunity for trainers to assess the suitability of trainees to continue to the Advanced Phase. Academic qualifications are not necessary for the Basic Training, but a counselling skills course or similar work experience will be expected. A basic course in abnormal psychology is required for the Advanced Phase.

There is a lower age limit of twenty-five, and qualities looked for in the applicant are a willingness to be introspective, a natural freedom and creativity and an ability to express. The general background of trainees tends to be 60 per cent core professions and 30 per cent from the management field, whilst 10 per cent are seeking a career change. There are about thirty-five applicants for twenty places.

3.3 *Time commitment and length of training*

Each term of the Basic and Advanced Training comprises ten evening groups, one leaderless evening group, two residential weekends, one lecture/discussion day. There is a five-day Residential at Easter (see section 2). It generally takes between four and six years to fully qualify.

3.4 *Interruptions in training*

These are accommodated in the Basic Phase and sometimes recommended in between Basic and Advanced Training, but discouraged in the Advanced Training.

3.5 *Postgraduate qualification and learned society*

The Gestalt Centre Associates is the group which graduates of the Gestalt Centre have set up. It is a recently formed group (1988) and is in the process of developing autonomously whilst still being linked to the Gestalt Centre. After two years members may apply to become members of the Association of Humanistic Psychology Practitioners. There is a small library of papers and books related to Gestalt therapy.

The Code of Ethics is that of the Association of Humanistic Practitioners.

4. CLINICAL AND ACADEMIC REQUIREMENTS

4.1 *Personal therapy*

Directors and members of faculty will refer trainees to an individual therapist if the trainee is not already in therapy. The criteria for training therapists are that they are Gestalt therapists and members of the Association of Humanistic Psychology Practitioners. Directors or members of the faculty may be training therapists. However, sometimes, for geographical reasons, a trainee may be seeing a therapist who is not trained in Gestalt and this could include analytic therapists. The frequency requirement is a minimum of once weekly, and the therapist may be consulted during the training.

4.2 *Clinical requirements*

A minimum of three clients are expected to be seen over a period of one and a half years, in order to qualify. Medical cover is not a requirement, but all trainees are expected to make arrangements for personal indemnity insurance.

4.3 *Supervision*

Supervision is held in groups for training clients on a fortnightly basis, and fortnightly or weekly individual supervision depending on the caseload.

4.4 *Papers and written work*

There is a final thesis in the Advanced Year on Gestalt theory and application, and regular assignments throughout the training.

5. REFERRALS

Training clients are seen by Directors or members of Faculty to assess suitability. Psychotic clients or people with a medical history are not seen as suitable. Trainees may accept clients from other referral sources in consultation with supervisors.

6. COST OF TRAINING

The training costs £450 a term. Additional costs include individual psychotherapy, individual supervision, apprenticeship and residential weekends. Sessions for therapy and supervision are usually between £25 and £30. Trainees are expected to see clients for a low fee of between £12 and £15, and make their own arrangements for consulting rooms.

There are some concessionary rates for the training.

7. FUTURE EXPECTATIONS/CAREER PROSPECTS

Practical advice on setting up in practice is relevant only to the Advanced Phase. Referral networks are expected to be created by trainees depending on their work situation.

Prospects to supervise and teach within the Gestalt Centre Training Programme are at present highly unlikely, although there are possibilities for representing the Centre at conferences, external consultancies and workshops.

8. TRAINEES' EXPERIENCE

8.1 *Why this course was chosen*

Gestalt, geography and good reputation are the main reasons for people being attracted to this course.

The selection procedure was experienced as challenging because of having to write about very fundamental reasons for wishing to join the Basic Training. There was a sense of being taken care of in the selection interview and there is no wait to hear of acceptability. The commitment in terms of time and finance was clear from the beginning and as changes came about trainees were promptly informed.

8.2 *The atmosphere of the course*

The Basic Training was felt to be a very good way of discovering personal experience of learning how it was to be in a group. The focus was more on each individual's personal process; this has recently changed by combining more theory with the therapeutic aspect. The Gestalt Centre was experienced as learning through doing, which was the aspect of training found to be the most valuable.

The differences in teachers were experienced as stimulating as they brought a diversity of styles which encouraged individual style rather than cloning. Professional development is linked with understanding personal readiness to move on to the next phase, and this was an aspect of the training which sometimes felt confusing but challenging. Many people do stop after the Basic Training and there is a subsequent written application for those wishing to carry on to the Advanced Training.

It was felt that there is not enough input on the course to help trainees beyond graduation, but this is something that is at present being addressed. The Gestalt Centre Associates is something for graduates to look forward to beyond qualification as well as joining the Association of Humanistic Psychology Practitioners.

AUTHOR'S COMMENTS

Gestalt therapy nowadays has developed from its original roots and there are many different Gestalt training organizations in the UK. Not all have joined the UKSCP. Do they represent different strands of Gestalt? Where does the Gestalt Centre belong amongst the differences?

According to this training they see no difference in philosophy and theory or practice of Gestalt between themselves and the Gestalt Psychotherapy Training Institute (GPTI). The differences are in the structure of training: GPTI keeps training and therapy strictly separate whereas the Gestalt Centre keeps therapy and training together. This difference relates to the issues of boundaries between trainers and trainees as discussed in Part One (The Humanistic Attitude). Analytic therapists would be critical of this way of training therapists and there are now many humanistic trainings which see the importance of keeping a distinction between personal therapy and training.

However, it would appear that the majority of people joining this course are more interested in self-development and the application of Gestalt in their place of work than in training to become a psychotherapist, and the Advanced Training is something that few people commit themselves to.

GESTALT PSYCHOTHERAPY TRAINING INSTITUTE IN THE UNITED KINGDOM (GPTI)

P.O. Box 620, Bristol BS9 7DL; tel: 0272 744389.

1. HISTORY

GPTI was set up in 1985 after a meeting Malcolm Parlett had with Petruska Clarkson (of Metanoia). They were concerned that Gestalt psychotherapy did not play a significant role in the National Health Service, and felt there was a need for a training in Gestalt psychotherapy for people already professionally qualified. A board of teaching members was created who were the founder members and are still the board responsible for the Diploma qualification at GPTI.

There is no such thing, however, as a GPTI course. GPTI provides 'a framework of training and accreditation for Gestalt psychotherapists in the making, so that the Institute itself doesn't train . . . the training is done by other organizations such as Metanoia, the Sherwood Psychotherapy Centre, Manchester Gestalt Centre and Gestalt South West.' Effectively speaking, GPTI is a federation of Gestalt trainers in the United Kingdom. 'Our intention is, that progressively, there will become more trainings allied to this institute so that hopefully we can provide a national framework.'

The courses chosen by trainees will depend on where they live. There is a system of allowing credit training hours from different training centres and trainers to combine towards the Diploma in Gestalt Psychotherapy offered by the GPTI. On completion of the requirements and examinations for the Diploma, trainees automatically become accredited members of GPTI.

2. THEORETICAL ORIENTATION AND CURRICULUM

There is a core curriculum of GPTI which 'governs our teaching, and which gives a very thorough grounding indeed . . . We're particularly keen to get away from the idea that Gestalt is a bundle of techniques.' GPTI feels that there tends to be a misperception of Gestalt therapy: that Gestalt is synonymous with Fritz Perls and that in fact there were many different forms of Gestalt evolving and developing at the same time as Perls was still developing, notably the work of his wife Laura Perls in New York as well as the work of the Polsters and others at the Cleveland Institute. The leading figures in Gestalt today are working in very different ways to that of Fritz Perls.

The main theoretical orientation of GPTI is, of course, Gestalt philosophy, theory and methodology, based on phenomenological enquiry, existentialism, and psychophysical field theory. Some of the main theorists in the USA are: Isadore From, Erving and Miriam Polster, Gary Yontef, Ed Nevis, George Brown, Joseph Zinker, Robert Resnick. The following members of the GPTI have recently published material on Gestalt therapy: Petruska Clarkson, Peter Philippson, Malcolm Parlett.

The first year, for most trainees, involves a basic grounding in Gestalt theory, philosophy and methodology. From the outset, there are several components: personal development, skill training and conceptual development: 'So that what we have is a tripartite development going on – . . . the ideas, and how the trainees apply the ideas in work with clients, as well as how they apply them to themselves.'

The exact course of preparation for trainees will depend on the training course which is being undertaken. Each trainee has a training consultant who is seen on a six-monthly basis. It will very much depend on the trainees' development in the three areas already mentioned, as to how long it takes them to qualify.

The following is GPTI's core curriculum:

1. History of Gestalt; 'Perlsism' and Gestalt; intellectual and philosophical roots of Gestalt psychotherapy theory; the historical and contemporary relationship with psychoanalysis.

2. Basic concepts of Gestalt psychology, figure and ground, the field theory perspective, holism, systems theory.

3. Organismic self-regulation, homeostasis, needs and wants.

4. The nature of awareness, present-centredness, therapy as phenomenological enquiry, bracketing, tracking.

5. The contact boundary, contact, Buber and I–thou/I–it; dialogic therapy (inclusion, presence, non-exploitation, living the relationship).

6. The experience cycle and its interruptions, Gestalt formation and destruction, the awareness continuum.

7. Interruptions to organism/environment transactions: main emphasis on introjection, projection, retroflection, confluence; also – egotism, proflection, deflection, desensitization, reaction formation.

8. 'Resistance' and working with and against resistance.

9. Support – environmental and self-support.

10. Responsibility, existential thinking, language changes.

11. The paradoxical theory of change, theories of development, stages of developing awareness, polarities, multilarities.

12. Themes and theme development, experimentation, grading and design of experiments.

13. Bodywork in Gestalt, similarities to and differences from Reichian approaches; patterns of emotional expression.

14. Dreamwork, use of fantasy, metaphor, stories, and artwork; left and right brain functioning.

15. Gestalt and its relation to formal diagnostic systems (like the DSM-III and ICD-10); working with particular client-types: e.g. borderline, adult victims of child abuse, anorexics.

16. Group process, Gestalt in groups, developmental stages of groups.

17. Introduction to Gestalt in systems.

18. Gestalt work with couples and families.

19. Gestalt work with sexuality and gender issues.

20. Gestalt and development: child and adult stages; patterns of changes in the course of therapy.

21. Initial interviews and the Gestalt approach to treatment design.

22. Ethical issues in Gestalt psychotherapy; professional practice guidelines; management of a therapy practice.

23. Gestalt as a personal discipline; its relation to spiritual development; Gestalt and Jungian ideas; Gestalt, Zen and the Tao.

There is no Infant Observation.

The Training Consultant is the personal tutor who will be the same tutor throughout the course and will be there to follow the trainee's choices, as well as give advice where necessary. This would also be the channel for the trainee's difficulties.

3. TRAINING STRUCTURE

3.1 *Training Committee*

The Training Committee is known as the Board of Teaching Members. There is no Director or student representative. The board's training is in Gestalt, transactional analysis and clinical psychology. There is an external moderator who is used as the regulator of training issues.

3.2 *Selection procedure and admission*

Trainees make their own application to the affiliated organizations and, to be accepted, will have already gained a professional qualification in counselling, psychotherapy or one of the other helping professions.

Most trainees wishing to work towards the Diploma in Gestalt Psychotherapy will have begun their training in the Gestalt approach. Each trainee is asked to sign a contract with GPTI if the Training Consultant and Board of Teaching Members feel that the trainee has a good chance of attaining the Diploma, and this makes the trainee a student member of GPTI (more details are described in the Training Handbook).

There is no age limit, but GPTI would like to encourage more people from a wider social class range and ethnic origin range, and are exploring the area of equal opportunities.

3.3 *Time commitment and length of training*

This of course is very much an individual issue and would depend on the trainee's choice of courses and the structure of training which exists in the particular training centre where the individual is studying. With more money and time, more modules or years of study could be covered, but this would not necessarily mean that the trainee was ready to qualify.

The minimum time to achieve the Diploma is three years, but it tends on average to take five years. A trainee with a lot of experience and previous training in Gestalt in another reputable training organization can achieve Diploma standard in two years under a special arrangement.

3.4 *Interruptions in training*

This is always possible with GPTI and indeed an interruption may often be advised. There is no limitation to interruptions because GPTI believes that the individual would probably return as a more enriched individual, which would be seen as an enhancement of maturity and thus an advantage to the Gestalt training.

3.5 *Postgraduate qualification and learned society*

As has already been stated, signing of the contract makes the trainee a student member of GPTI. Accredited members of the Institute comprise the teaching staff and former trainees who have gained the Diploma, who are full members. The annual membership fee is £60. Registration fee once the contract has been signed is £40, and is renewable annually. To date there are sixty-one student members, four members, four Associate Teaching Members and seven Teaching Members.

GPTI is very new and still developing itself. What has been agreed is that in 1992 there is going to be a Peer Competence Review Seminar Conference. This will be for members to present their recent work and ideas in order to maintain accreditation, and this is planned to occur every three years. A journal has been initiated by GPTI called *British Gestalt Journal* and Malcolm Parlett is the editor.

There are occasional meetings where Gestalt psychotherapists meet to discuss clinical work, but these are not under the aegis of GPTI. There is no building, as it is not required, but the administration office is in Bristol and can be reached through the above address. There is no formal library as such, though collections of books and papers are available at the participating centres.

There is a Code of Ethics and Professional Practice Guidelines which student members agree to abide by when they sign a training contract.

4. CLINICAL AND ACADEMIC REQUIREMENTS

4.1 *Personal therapy*

The ideal is that all trainees will be in personal Gestalt therapy for the duration of their training up to qualification. However, this can sometimes be very difficult to arrange, depending on where the trainee lives. GPTI stipulates that each trainee must have had at least a year in individual Gestalt therapy before completing the Diploma. Meanwhile, a therapist with a different orientation would be acceptable from the following schools: psychosynthesis, bioenergetics, transactional analysis or integrative. Psychoanalytic therapy and rational emotive therapy are less appropriate.

In the main, GPTI training consultants trust their trainees to ascertain how they felt about their own therapy: 'If they felt it was being of great benefit to them, and if they seemed to be maturing and developing and becoming, and having a higher phenomenological sensitivity and greater ability to support themselves; to cope with a whole variety of different environmental situations . . . then [we] probably wouldn't question the therapy they were getting, even if it wasn't Gestalt.'

The Gestalt model is once weekly, but again this can vary, depending on the geography of trainee and therapist, and longer sessions are sometimes possible and even desirable. A session is usually sixty minutes.

If a trainee was clearly having difficulties during the training, and teachers were concerned, the therapist would be consulted, but only with the permission of the trainee.

4.2 *Clinical requirements*

The minimal clinical requirement is that a trainee will have had 600 hours of seeing clients, 300 of which should be using the Gestalt approach. Trainees who have not had relevant experience must undergo a psychiatric placement. The trainee is responsible for arranging such a placement.

Malpractice insurance must be taken out, but not medical cover. If it is felt necessary, the client's GP may be contacted.

4.3 *Supervision*

Trainees normally experience both individual and group supervision; the latter is favoured, again because of geography and also the limited numbers of sufficiently experienced Gestalt supervisors. Very often group supervision will involve six trainees spending six hours (an hour each) on their clinical work with clients.

4.4 *Papers and written work*

A case study of 5,000–9,000 words, including a theoretical discussion from a Gestalt therapy perspective, must be presented towards the Diploma. This is examined by two teaching members and an independent, non-Gestalt senior psychotherapist or psychiatrist. There is also an examination of two hours where the trainee presents recordings and transcripts of work with clients, which is then a basis for discussion.

5. REFERRALS

There is an informal network. Referrals are often done over the phone, where as much information as possible is gathered: where people live, how much they can afford, how old they are, and so on; they would then often be referred to an advanced trainee. On occasions, if felt necessary, the client will be offered a consultation, but there are too many people enquiring for this to be offered all the time. Metanoia has a formal referral system for clients seeking Gestalt psychotherapy.

Clients range across the psychiatric diagnosis spectrum. Gestalt is very much an alternative epistemological attitude and approach to psychotherapy, rather than a fixed technique or methodology, and therefore a Gestalt therapist may work in a very different way with a psychotic client from that with a client who may be borderline or neurotic. There is a policy of letting clients know that they are seeing a trainee.

6. COST OF TRAINING

This would also depend on where the module is taken, but it would cost between £1,000 and £1,500 a year, which would include everything except supervision and personal therapy.

Trainees charge fees that are appropriate to their level of training and experience. Fees are set in consultation with a Gestalt supervisor. Consulting rooms must be provided by each trainee.

There are no bursaries or loans available from GPTI at the moment, although this is being looked into by the various training bodies, who may have their own bursary or loan systems.

7. FUTURE EXPECTATIONS/CAREER PROSPECTS

Practical advice for setting up in practice is something that is discussed with the Training Consultant and in special workshops on psychotherapy practice. Many people do not intend to go into private practice, but would use their training to complement the work they already do as social workers, doctors or clinical psychologists. There would be prospects to supervise and teach, at the minimum of a year beyond achieving the Diploma, but only when an individual has been accepted as an Associate Teaching Member of GPTI.

Over the last ten years, it is felt, a lot has been done by the members of the Board of GPTI to correct the misconceptions of the definition of Gestalt therapy. GPTI feels this has been achieved and continues to be achieved, through the publication of books and articles and the start of the new journal in Gestalt Psychotherapy (mentioned above), as well as the increasing interest in Gestalt therapy from professionals working within the National Health Service. With more and more trainees already working in the Health Service, Gestalt therapy and its application with clients is not only becoming better known but also gaining a new and different reputation from that of the 1960s. Petruska Clarkson and Malcolm Parlett have published papers and books which will be found in the bibliography.

8. TRAINEES' EXPERIENCE

8.1 *Why this course was chosen*

Trainees were attracted to GPTI because it offered a flexible framework for people thinking of training as Gestalt therapists, wishing to become therapists or using Gestalt therapy as an adjunct to their work situation.

Information on each stage of the training was as clear as it could be, but trainees acknowledged that to some extent they were guinea pigs and that requirements were changing in parallel with the developments at UKSCP. Some communications about certain requirements came a bit late and there was a general dissatisfaction with this, even though it was being addressed and trainees were aware it was part of the teething process of a new organization.

8.2 *The atmosphere of the course*

The roles of teachers, trainers and therapists often overlap and trainees felt the advantages of this way of training outweighed the disadvantages. However, for some trainees, the merging of these roles initially instigated confusion.

Integrating what is learnt in personal therapy and supervision and then applying this to work with clients was a general area of difficulty. This was helped when a client prepared to work with a trainee in front of a group joined the trainee group, thus trainees could then have the opportunity of seeing a demonstration of how the process works. Using each other as clients in a training group was another advantage towards understanding the application of theory to practice. A discussion arose concerning the type of client who will most benefit from Gestalt. This issue is being publicly debated now and concerns the different types of Gestalt to be used depending on the level of disturbance of the client.

It was felt that Gestalt had come a long way from the Gestalt of the 1960s and that there was now an acknowledgement of its psychoanalytic roots. There was particular interest in the British Object Relations School of the psychoanalytic world and an interest in Freud's writings which made trainees aware that there was not such a gulf between psychoanalysis and Gestalt therapy.

Generally people felt challenged by the future of GPTI within the world of psychotherapy and how different organizations were beginning to communicate through the UKSCP. Trainees looked forward to being part of these new developments.

AUTHOR'S COMMENTS

Still a new organization, GPTI, like the Institute of Transactional Analysis (ITA), is providing a federal structure that makes training more widely available geographically, giving trainees choice and flexibility.

It seems quite significant that GPTI does not see psychoanalytic therapy as a compatible therapy for trainees, and yet trainees demonstrated an enthusiastic interest in the psychoanalytic roots of Gestalt therapy, in particular the development of psychoanalysis as seen in the work of the Independent Group of the British Psycho-Analytical Society. Trainees were aware that some of the problems they had experienced during training were related to the difficulties arising in any new organization at the beginning. GPTI has been and continues to be active in its participation in the UKSCP.

INSTITUTE OF PSYCHOSYNTHESIS

The Barn, Nan Clark's Lane, London NW7 4HH; tel: 081 959 1935.

1. History

During the early 1970s Joan and Roger Evans worked in Italy with R.A. Assagioli, who was the originator of psychosynthesis. At that time psychosynthesis was being practised mostly in Italy and San Francisco, and it was in California that Roberto Assagioli advised Joan and Roger Evans to gain their training. By 1973 the Institute of Psychosynthesis had been set up under the directorship of Joan Evans and in the early years the founder members would commute between London and San Francisco, where the training in psychosynthesis was being most developed.

The Institute started much more as a place for facilitating a journey of self-exploration for people. The changes and developments that have occurred over the years have been in response to the market-place, and by 1980 the Institute offered a training in psychosynthesis for professionals wishing to become therapists. The Institute of Psychosynthesis is well aware of the discussions concerning counselling and psychotherapy (psychosynthesis therapists are normally called 'guides'). In 1987 the Institute made the decision to speak to that distinction and to focus its training only on psychotherapy – rather than the two, which had been the case since 1978. Another development is the inclusion of psychodynamic theory and psychoanalysis in the curriculum, which now constitutes 10 per cent of the training.

2. Theoretical Orientation and Curriculum

The main theoretical orientation is psychosynthesis, and the following has been taken from the prospectus.

Year 1 focuses on the basic models of psychosynthesis. Students also undertake their own psychotherapy from a guide selected from the Institute's list of recommended therapists. Topics covered are:

Psychosynthesis Models of the Personality; Right Relations Skills; Will and Motivation; Creative Thinking; Meditation; Self Realization and Psychological Disturbances.

Year 2 focuses mainly on the acquiring of basic therapy and guiding skills and, when appropriate, ensures that the trainee begins to build their own clinical practice. Topics covered are: Psychosynthesis Therapy Skills; Context and the Guiding Relationship; Right Relations Skills; The Individual and the Group; Ego Development and the Core Personality; The Imagination; Dreamwork; Crisis of Meaning; The Will and the Process of Manifestation.

Year 3: now that a basic understanding of psychosynthesis and its integrative perspective has been established, the year involves working in both the depths and heights of the psyche. This is done by using the expertise from a number of different disciplines. In addition to continuing to build a practice under supervision, students are expected to write up at least two comprehensive case studies on clients with whom they work during the year. These will be presented to the training board on completion of the year. Topics covered are: Introduction to Psychoanalytic Psychotherapy; Right Relations Skills; Strategies and the Process of Change; Family Therapy; Group Work and Group Dynamics; Family and Couple Therapy; The Chakras; The Creative Process.

Year 4: this final stage of training focuses on the use of psychosynthesis as a psychotherapeutic method, working with the unconscious and understanding relationships between classical psychopathology and the realms of spiritual awakening. Both theory and practical courses during this final part of study help the trainees develop their own understanding of their life journey and the deeper unconscious process as that conditions their life. Topics covered are: The Art of Therapy; Psychospiritual Pathology; Chakras Applications; Psychology of Groups; Wisdom and Synthetic Thinking; Transpersonal Psychotherapy and Spiritual Praxis.

Infant Observation is not part of a psychosynthesis training although the individual's early personal development is seen as an important aspect of the overall training. All training takes place within the group and group therapy is also part of the course. Once qualified, graduates are able to practise psychosynthesis in groups as well as individually.

3. TRAINING STRUCTURE

3.1 *Training Committee*

There are six members of the core faculty group and nine junior staff members who are personal tutors. They are all trained in psychosynthesis in addition to core professional and educational qualifications.

There are meetings twice monthly for discussing all matters relating to training and students. Joan Evans is the present Director of Training.

3.2 *Selection procedure and admission*

There is an application form for the Fundamentals to Psychosynthesis Course. This is an intensive week-long course. The Fundamentals is used by applicants and trainers to assess suitability for joining the full programme. The Institute looks for qualities of self-reflection and exploration in the suitable candidate.

To continue, another application must be made, followed by one interview with two members of staff and the Director. Trainees are never taken on for the four years: the contract is made for a year at a time.

There is no formal age limit, although in practice an applicant under thirty is unlikely to be seen as ready to train. Life experience is seen as more important than academic qualifications.

Trainees may, and sometimes do, join the Institute's training from another course if it is seen as compatible with the Institute's training. There is an upper limit of forty places for the first year. Generally trainees stop after two years and by this time they will have had sufficient training to apply for accreditation by the British Association of Counsellors. By the third and fourth years the groups usually number about 15.

3.3 *Time commitment and length of training*

Personal tutors are seen on a monthly basis and more if required by trainee or tutor.

Training takes place over nine weekends a year, plus one week of Summer School. In addition to these weekends, there are at least two days per month inter-weekends needed to cover all course requirements, increasing to a day a week in the third year. Personal therapy, supervision, reading and written work must also be taken into account.

3.4 *Interruptions in training*

Sometimes trainees are advised to interrupt their training, if it is felt they need more therapy or life experience. There is flexibility and trainees could return after three or four years and hook back into the training.

3.5 *Postgraduate qualification and learned society*

The Association of Psychosynthesis Practitioners has been set up by graduates of the Institute, as a place to continue to share clinical work and practice. The Institute acts as an accrediting body for graduates of psychosynthesis and there are plans to extend this body to include graduates of the Psychosynthesis and Education Trust, and possibly others within HIPS who share similar aims. There are about sixty psychotherapy graduates of the Institute and a further 150 trainees who have completed the first two years.

The Institute has clinic and group rooms in the Finchley Road and runs weekend training at a centre in Mill Hill, and there is an administration office at the above address. There is a library of psychosynthesis publications, and there used to be an in-house journal which is planned to be restarted in the near future. There is a Code of Ethics.

4. CLINICAL AND ACADEMIC REQUIREMENTS

4.1 *Personal therapy*

Through the Fundamentals course trainers have a sense of who would be an appropriate guide for a new trainee. Trainees must be in therapy at least once a fortnight with graduates of psychosynthesis psychotherapy.

Psychoanalytic psychotherapy is seen as valuable for certain trainees at a certain point later in training – for instance when it is clear that a trainee's childhood is being stirred up as a consequence of the training, there may often be a recommendation to see a psychoanalyst. Psychoanalysis is acknowledged by the Institute of Psychosynthesis as part of its roots: dealing with childhood and the lower unconscious. Transpersonal therapies, also part of its roots, serve a forward direction.

4.2 *Clinical requirements*

In general trainees start seeing clients in the second year. Two clients must be seen on a long-term basis (at least a year) and by the third year more clients would be seen, culminating in a practice of about twelve clients by the fourth year.

4.3 *Supervision*

There are 60 three-hour supervision groups throughout the four-year training.

4.4 *Papers and written work*

There is a requirement of at least twenty-five written assignments throughout the course, and two case studies at the end of the third year plus the final thesis.

5. REFERRALS

The Institute is moving towards creating a service where a member of the counselling service will see clients before referring them on to a trainee. At present trainees find their own training clients in consultation with their supervisor.

Fourth year students are capable of working with borderline clients, and the psychosynthesis context which reframes psychosis within the framework of psychospiritual disturbances often provides a valuable context for these clients. All trainees must inform their clients that they are trainees in supervision.

6. Cost of Training

The first year is £1,700, second year £2,000, third year £2,000 and the fourth year £2,500. This covers everything except extra curricula and individual therapy.

Trainees must charge individual clients between £10 and £15 rising to £20 in their final years. The Institute is responsible for trainees' clients until qualification, as long as the client has been declared and brought to supervision.

There are no bursaries but extended payments can be arranged.

Consulting rooms can be hired, although many trainees come from all over Britain and sometimes from abroad.

7. Future Expectations/Career Prospects

Setting up in practice is an ongoing part of the course and there are plenty of opportunities for postgraduate work.

8. Trainees' Experience

8.1 *Why this course was chosen*

Trainees had chosen this training for the following reasons:

1. They felt that psychosynthesis was respectful of where the individual was at a given time.
2. Roberto Assagioli's book *Psychosynthesis* had provided meaning that trainees had found useful.
3. Psychosynthesis combines the past with the present.
4. Psychosynthesis incorporates an interest in religion and philosophy.

The Fundamentals course left people with time to reflect and to think about the choice to carry on or not.

The selection procedure was experienced in a variety of ways. One trainee had remembered that there was a considerable amount of writing to do as part of this process, others had not remembered that there was so much writing to do. The common experience was the insecurity about whether or not each trainee would be accepted. Present day advanced trainees were aware that the selection procedure had recently changed. There was a general welcome that a re-evaluation came at the end of each year in order to go on to the next.

There was concern that some trainees were rejected at any given stage, although, at the same time, trainees felt reassured that the organization did not just accept anyone. Once accepted, trainees felt that information about the various stages of the course was very clearly set out. Everybody experienced a trust in the system.

8.2 *The atmosphere of the course*

Trainees enjoyed the experiential learning on the course and felt it evoked wisdom through the experience of watching others in the group sessions. The emphasis on individual process within the group and in individual therapy was felt to be very helpful. Criticisms here were linked with a sense that there could be more experiential groupwork and that there was not enough work on examining the group process – that personal stuff was sometimes left behind.

Some confusion and difficulties were associated with the 'transpersonal – spiritual disorder' and 'higher self' was not clearly understood. It was clear that trainers understood and that was reassuring. Trainees felt their difficulty in understanding some of these concepts was all par for the course and it was perhaps a matter of waiting for some things to become clearer as their training continued.

The increase of a psychoanalytic input was seen to be a reflection of the Institute's membership of the UKSCP. Trainees enjoyed this input and sometimes found it more understandable theoretically than psychosynthesis. Most people experienced a personal struggle in marrying the two approaches, psychosynthesis and psychoanalysis, together. Here there was some discussion between trainees where some felt that the two could not be married and some felt that the meaning of synthesis was to integrate the differences. One trainee felt that this struggle made her look for her own answers which was felt to be the positive aspect of the difficulties.

Some trainees were not comfortable about the position of psychosynthesis and the Institute's role in relation to the world of psychotherapy and the UKSCP. One trainee looked forward to contributing to this in the future and to redress a balance even if it meant following an analytic training. However, there are trainees who greatly appreciate how the Institute addresses the marketplace, thus contributing to psychosynthesis psychotherapy being taken seriously. All experienced the people who organized the training as very open and available.

AUTHOR'S COMMENTS

One of the debates relevant to both trainings in psychosynthesis presented in this book is the differentiation between psychotherapy and counselling. According to Joan Evans the psychosynthesis taught and practised at the Institute of Psychosynthesis is the same as the psychosynthesis taught and practised at the Psychosynthesis and Education Trust. However, the Trust has defined its training as 'counselling' whilst the Institute has recently (1987) defined its training as 'psychotherapy'. A pertinent question would therefore be how do these two trainings distinguish between psychosynthesis counselling and psychosynthesis psychotherapy?

It is apparent that the two different organizations represent different developments of psychosynthesis, depending on the choice of topics that are seen to be compatible with a psychosynthesis approach. For example, psychoanalysis has recently been added to this course as a study of the 'roots' of psychosynthesis. This has been an addition which trainees see as a response to the developments at the UKSCP.

Psychosynthesis has always claimed that it is a therapy aimed at treating the healthy neurotic. The Institute's recent change is that their fourth year graduates are capable of working with borderline clients. It is perhaps worth wondering why these differences have come about at this time in the history of the Institute. Has psychosynthesis been adapted to meet the requirements of the clients who need help, or are the changes reflecting the pressures of the requirements of the UKSCP, which are being felt by every member of the UKSCP? According to the Institute, it continues to adapt and deepen its understanding of psychosynthesis and membership of the UKSCP is part of that process.

It is quite striking that psychoanalytic therapy is seen as valuable for trainees at a particular time in their training, if the trainee's childhood is being stirred up. What does this indicate about psychosynthesis therapy? According to Joan Evans 'psychosynthesis psychotherapy addresses the clients' crises of meaning in relation to the wider, interpersonal context in which they are living', and psychosynthesis and psychoanalytic therapy are wholly compatible. 'The hallmark of a successful outcome of psychosynthesis psychotherapy is the resolution of the client's narcissistic conflict.'

The Institute trains large numbers of trainees a year, some of whom travel great distances, including from the continent, to follow the course.

INSTITUTE OF TRANSACTIONAL ANALYSIS (ITA)

B.M. Box 4101, London WC1 3XX; tel: 071 404 5011.

1. HISTORY

Eric Berne (1910–70) began developing TA during the 1960s in his work as a psychotherapist. Since that time its applications have extended far beyond the realm of therapy and today TA is used in a wide variety of ways including management training, the training of trainers, school teaching and counselling.

TA started in England in 1973 when several individuals practising TA in their place of work independently of each other came together to form the Institute of Transactional Analysis.

International context

The professional association for TA practitioners is the International Transactional Analysis Association based in San Francisco. The UK

TA Association, the ITA, is affiliated to the European Association for Transactional Analysis (EATA) which in turn is affiliated to the ITAA. ITAA is an international organization, but professional training is the responsibility of the independent Training and Certification Council and at present there are two broad models in existence. In Europe, EATA handles all training and certification issues under the auspices of the Training and Certification Council (ITAA/COC). A similar scheme is operated all over the world, and the TA qualification is regarded as an international qualification.

National context

In the UK, the Institute of Transactional Analysis is the responsible body which performs the following tasks:

(a) to promote the constructive and creative use of TA;

(b) to set and safeguard the standards of professional TA trainers and practitioners;

(c) to keep a register of approved professional TA trainers and practitioners;

(d) to provide a liaison service for the members of the Institute and the public;

(e) to provide information about professional training.

The ITA is a federal structure, therefore, and people wishing to train to become a transactional analyst choose a trainer from the ITA or ITAA register. Each trainer will have his or her own individual training programme, which will conform with the training qualifications laid down by the ITAA. The primary object of the ITA is 'to advance the education of the public generally with regard to the study of theory and practice of transactional analysis and its application in accordance with the recognized standards of professional competence in the practice of transactional analysis in the United Kingdom of Great Britain and Northern Ireland.'

2. THEORETICAL ORIENTATION AND CURRICULUM

An individual wishing to become a psychotherapist who uses the structure of Transactional Analysis would usually choose an accredited trainer as a sponsor. The trainer's aim would be to teach, supervise and monitor the overall progress of the trainee.

The main theoretical orientation is Transactional Analysis, which covers the theory instigated by Eric Berne, now known as the Classical School. Other developments in theory are drawn from the Eric Berne Memorial Prize winners and the students of the Re-Decision, Schiffian and Levin Schools. The main theorists studied are Berne, Steiner, Dusay, James, Erskine, Freud and Jung.

Each trainer devises his or her own programme based on a core curriculum. The following is a course outline:

I. *Statement of the Purpose of the TA Course*

II. *Definition and Philosophy of TA and its Areas of Application*
    A. Definition of TA
    B. Philosophical assumptions
    C. Contractual method
    D. Areas of application – Differences in process
        1. Clinical
        2. Educational
        3. Organizational
        4. Other

III. *Brief Overview of the Development of TA*
    A. Eric Berne
        1. Who was Eric Berne?
        2. Development of ideas
        3. Books written by him
    B. Growth of TA
        1. San Francisco Social Psychiatry Seminar
        2. International Transactional Analysis Association (ITAA)
        3. Regional and national TA associations

IV. *Structural Analysis*
    A. Definition of ego states
    B. Recognition and diagnosis of ego states
    C. Behavioural descriptions (i.e. critical parent, nurturing

parent, adult, free child, adapted child)
  D. Contamination and Exclusion
V.   *Transactional Analysis Proper*
  A. Transactions
    1. Definition of a transaction
    2. Types of transactions
    3. Rules of communication
  B. Strokes
    1. Definition of strokes
    2. Stimulus and recognition hunger
    3. Types of strokes
  C. Discounts
    1. Definitions of discounts (behaviour or internal process)
    2. Levels of discounts
    3. Reasons for discounting
  D. Social Time Structuring
    1. Structure hunger
    2. Six ways of structuring time

VI. *Game Analysis*
  A. Definition of games
  B. Reasons for playing games
  C. Advantages of games
  D. Examples of games
  E. Degrees of games
  F. Ways of diagramming games
    1. Transactional diagram
    2. Formula G
    3. Drama triangle

VII. *Racket Analysis*
  A. Significance of internal/intrapsychic processes
  B. Definitions of rackets and trading stamps
  C. Relationship of rackets to transactions, games and script

VIII. *Script Analysis*
  A. Life positions
    1. Definition of life positions
    2. The four life positions

    3. Relationship of life positions to games and scripts

B. Script
1. Definitions of script
2. Origin of script in child's experiences
3. Process of script development (e.g. injunctions, programme, counterinjunctions, early decision, attributions)
4. Changing scripts

C. Autonomy
1. Awareness
2. Spontaneity
3. Capacity for intimacy

The above is the required theory towards the exam. The aim over the years is to facilitate the trainee's experience of being a therapist, which is practised in the training groups, along with supervision of people's work. The theory is applied in a practical experience and through personal supervision. By the time a trainee reaches exam level, familiarity with psychiatric diagnosis and some experience of working in the NHS or a supervised placement have been achieved. Infant Observation is not part of the course, but child development is an integral part of the training. A comparison of analytic therapies as well as the other humanistic therapies is an additional part of the course.

3. TRAINING STRUCTURE

3.1 *Training Committee*

The Training and Standards Committee is a subcommittee of the ITA Council and has close contact with the relevant European and international committees. The Training and Standards Committee meet once every two months to discuss matters concerning training. Responsibility for a group of trainees rests with each individual trainer who may call on the Institute and other trainers for support, sharing of ideas and monitoring. This committee also organizes regular meetings for the trainers.

3.2 *Selection procedure and admission*

The following applies to the majority of trainers but some may vary slightly in ways of selecting.

A letter and CV are required before an interview. Many applicants are already academically and professionally qualified and wish to use TA in an existing work situation. However, some applicants may have the necessary qualities and life experience but no formal qualifications, and in these cases selection is determined by the trainer. Progress would be carefully monitored throughout the introductory year and formal contracts are not usually exchanged until after the second year. By agreement with the trainers, suitable applicants may join the training programmes at any level. There is no age limit, and size of training groups is varied but is unlikely to exceed twenty. Qualities looked for in the suitable applicant would be an ability to attach, congruency of behaviour, a good sense of humour, intelligence, the ability to conceptualize and self-care.

3.3 *Time commitment and length of training*

Six hundred hours' Advanced training in clinical work of which 350 may be course work from a relevant degree or equivalent training; 250 must be TA work, of which 50 must be course work and 50 may be therapy knowledge of drug treatments; knowledge of developmental psychology and psychopathology.

Supervision: 150 hours, of which 75 must be in TA; 40 hours of this must be with one trainer over a minimum of one year. Normally it takes three to four years to acquire that amount of hours; many trainers are able to offer training and supervision on weekends.

3.4 *Interruptions in training*

Sometimes interruptions are recommended and they can always be accommodated.

3.5 *Postgraduate qualification and learned society*

The following are the membership categories:

Founder Member

Affiliate Member
Open to all persons interested in Transactional Analysis.

Regular Member
Open to those satisfying the following criteria: successful completion of a recognized Introductory Course or associated open-book examination. Application forms available from ITA, to be submitted with appropriate certificate.

Trainee Member
Open to all persons in contractual training for professional accreditation.

Professional Member
Open to all ITA-recognized Accredited Practitioners, including:

Certified Transactional Analysts (CTA): Those certified to this level under the ITAA training scheme previously explained in Section 3.

Provisional Teaching and Supervising TA (PTSTA)

Teaching and Supervising TA

These members are qualified Professional Members who additionally are endorsed to train other practitioners. Each Teaching Member will have a speciality, e.g. Clinical, Educational, Organizational or Counselling, and will take trainees who wish to apply TA in their own professional field within one of these broad categories. These specialities are normally indicated in parentheses after the designation, e.g. CTA (C) is a Certified Transactional Analyst with a Clinical Speciality.

Rights and responsibilities of membership: all categories of membership except Affiliate confer voting rights in the ITA. All members are invited to the annual conference, and all members can subscribe to a quarterly publication with academic articles and news.

4. Clinical and Academic Requirements

4.1 *Personal therapy*

Trainees often find a therapist in consultation with the sponsor.
These therapists may be trained in TA, but other approaches may
be acceptable. It is expected that this therapy will be as intensive
in terms of frequency, type and duration as the form of
psychotherapy normally to be practised after qualification.

4.2 *Clinical requirements*

Trainees take on clients when they and their trainer feel they are
ready. The minimum of clinical hours with clients required is 1,500,
which must include at least 500 hours' application of TA in the field
of specialization. A minimum of 120 hours in a psychiatric
placement is also required.

4.3 *Supervision*

One hundred and fifty hours of supervision of the trainee's
application of TA in the field of specialization is required as well as
supervision with a TA therapist other than the sponsor.

4.4 *Papers and written work*

In the foundation year the written work is voluntary. Beyond this
the amount of written work is decided on in consultation with the
trainer. For qualification there is a written exam, a presentation of
work with a selected tape and a case study.

5. Referrals

Training clients are usually refered via GPs, psychiatrists, social
workers and members of the caring professions. Psychotics,
alcoholics and clients with a long psychiatric history are generally
felt to be unsuitable for trainee therapists. Trainees inform their
training clients that they are in training.

6. Cost of Training

Costs vary with each trainer but generally the trainee must expect to pay between £30 and £40 per day. Supervision is £30 a session, but trainees may see a supervisor together. Personal therapy sessions are from £20, and trainees usually charge a low fee to training clients, from £10.

Bursaries and loans are available from the International organizations.

7. Future Expectations/Career Prospects

Practical advice on setting up in practice is talked about from the first year, and most trainees may expect to be working in private practice within four years. Prospects to supervise and teach beyond qualification (level 1) are in the form of further training to become a trainer.

Some posts currently held by TA practitioners are:

(a) psychotherapists in local NHS surgeries;

(b) counsellors for alcoholic units;

(c) therapists working in private adolescent homes;

(d) career counsellors;

(e) therapists in communities for people suffering from psychotic illness.

8. Trainees' Experience

8.1 *Why this course was chosen*

People had come to TA via various routes such as education, social work and counselling. The aspects of TA which most attracted trainees were:

(a) the clarity of the techniques;

(b) TA is clear to explain to clients;

(c) the results are noticeable;

(d) TA is very positive;

(e) TA empowers the client.

Trainees felt that the way in which most psychoanalysts worked implied that they had the knowledge and the patient did not – that the analyst had the truth and therefore the power. This model of working, trainees believed, disempowered the patient. TA, it was felt, was a very clear tool aimed at empowering clients to solve problems and effect a change in their life themselves.

Trainees had enjoyed their personal experience of TA and felt that it had many advantages over other therapies they had experienced. One of the most beneficial features of TA that impressed trainees was the emphasis on change.

The selection procedure had been experienced as much more of a two-way assessment between trainer and trainee over several months. Trainees felt this was a much better system because it gave them the freedom to choose in an informed way about the kind of commitment that was required when making a contractual agreement with a sponsor (trainer). Trainees had experiences of different trainers which had been encouraged as part of the ITA's principles of training. There was general agreement that the cross-fertilization of ideas and input was invaluable to the process of becoming a TA therapist.

8.2 *The atmosphere of the course*

Trainees felt well informed about the stages of the training at the beginning. The various requirements are set out in the contract and agreed on between trainer and trainee at the appropriate time. Other information is published in the TA newsletter which is sent to all members three times a year.

Confusing aspects of this training for one trainee were linked with the differences between counselling and psychotherapy and what label to use – counsellor, therapist or transactional analyst. Trainees agreed that this was unimportant in relation to clients and relevant only to other professionals. This led into a discussion of the different labels and their meanings in different contexts. People agreed that each description they would use tended to depend on the professional context.

The different schools of thought in TA were sometimes confusing since they represented opposing views but trainees felt that these differences were important and could be used in different circumstances with different clients. Not all trainees experienced confusion.

The experience of supervision was very positive because of how clear and observable TA concepts were made. There was some concern that TA did not address the spiritual side of the individual. However, it was felt that this would be dealt with through the ITA in the future.

In general it was felt that the ITA was a positive and progressive organization despite the occasional hiccup. There was some concern that it should beware of being too complacent and that there was a need to promote broader issues such as social awareness and the application of TA in education.

AUTHOR'S COMMENTS

Training in TA, through the ITA, will introduce people to a network of TA therapists rather than one training establishment. The ITA is the federal organization, like GPTI, bringing the network of practitioners together. In addition it is the accrediting professional body, responsible for setting standards, ethical and professional.

Eric Berne was a Freudian psychoanalyst who created TA using the theory of psychoanalysis. In the 1960s it was a very popular form of therapy, particularly in America (Kovel, 1976). The emphasis is on conscious behaviour and the conscious attempt to change unwished for feelings and behaviour. Clearly there is very much in TA that is taken from psychoanalysis, but how is the unconscious addressed in TA? Some therapists would say TA oversimplifies complex mental structures formulated by Freud. TA sees its system as a way for relatively healthy people to gain quick access to the cause of their difficulties.

It seems that most trainees use TA as an adjunct to skills and techniques they have already acquired, like counselling or Gestalt. This perhaps begs the question: are the theory and practice of TA enough to practise as a psychotherapist? According to the ITA it is

acceptable that all psychotherapists use a variety of models in their
work and they see TA therapists as no exception.

KARUNA INSTITUTE

Foxhole, Dartington, Totnes, Devon; tel: 0803 867940.

1. HISTORY

Karuna was set up in 1979 by Maura and Franklyn Sills, who are
now co-directors. Their backgrounds have shaped the course in
Core Process Psychotherapy, and the following biographies have
been extracted from the Karuna brochure.

Maura Sills was District Head Occupational Therapist at
Middlesex Hospital and Senior Lecturer in Psychology and Group
Dynamics at the London School of Occupational Therapy. She was
also a Buddhist nun and trained with Dr Rina Sirca in Buddhist
studies. Her background includes trainings in Reichian and Gestalt
therapies and an intensive training at the Esalen Institute in
California. Franklyn Sills is Consultative Director of the Polarity
Therapy Educational Trust. He has studied Ayurvedic medicine and
polarity therapy as well as learning craniosacral therapy. He was a
Buddhist monk, studied for a doctorate in Buddhist psychology and
has written a textbook on polarity therapy.

Courses started off as introductory and gradually became longer,
till in 1985 a three-year model was established. In this year Karuna
also became a member of the UK Standing Conference for
Psychotherapy and had to start adhering to the criteria of the
Humanistic and Integrative Section. Karuna's brochure states: 'Aims
are to offer a professional training in psychotherapy based on
Awareness Practice and to create a milieu for that inner training.'

2. THEORETICAL ORIENTATION AND CURRICULUM

In the view of Maura Sills: 'Trainers hope to support the inner,
self-reflective practice of the student, to cultivate mindfulness,
equanimity and the ability to separate experience from reaction,

developing our ability to concentrate the mind at will, and to enable expansive awareness of both client and therapist within the moment of arising experience. This practice is then extended to form the basic structure of the therapeutic encounter.'

The main theoretical orientation is Buddhistic based on the Theravardin Buddhist Psychology. The psychotherapy training is in Core Process Psychotherapy, which is a Buddhist-orientated psychotherapeutic practice. Infant Observation is not included in Karuna's training. Originally the course was based on Neo-Reichian Gestalt, but it has moved away from these techniques. The curriculum is theoretical and experiential.

The first two years are described in the brochure:

> . . . seven themes of core process work are revised and deepened. The core model of personality and personal process is reviewed. Awareness of our body, feelings and mental states is developed and students learn to use this process as a transformative tool. The therapist's attitude towards the client is stressed. Basic attitudes of acceptance, non-judgement, tolerance, support, congruency and empathy are explored. The difference between resonance and reaction is experienced and the skilful use of reflection as therapeutic intervention is developed. The inner process of both therapist and client is stressed and the work is perceived as a joint practice. In the second year interpersonal work and group process is explored. Paradigms of group process are investigated in relationship to core work. Western and Eastern models of personality are presented and the understanding of transference, countertransference and projection are explored in relationship to the core process model.

> Throughout the first two years breathwork, imagery, focusing work, core somatic bodywork, movement, regressive work and interpersonal work are used to help the trainee gain access in mental, emotional and physical aspects of personal process. In the third year this work is integrated with an understanding of professional practice. Supervision, ethics, self-regulation, confidentiality, case history and record keeping are topics which are treated as an integral part of the growth process.

The channel for trainees' difficulties is 'direct access to staff members outside of sessions'. There is also an external moderator to mediate between trainers and trainees if necessary.

3. Training Structure

3.1 *Training Committee*

There are five members of the Training Committee, two senior staff and three others. They are all Karuna graduates with additional professional qualifications. There is no student representative on the Training Committee, but trainees are involved in course assessment biannually. The Director is self-elected and not rotated. Meetings are 'as required', but at least biannually there is a meeting for staff and non-committee members.

3.2 *Selection procedure and admission*

The six-month foundation course is a prerequisite to joining the three-year course. There is an application form, and one interview with a member of the Karuna staff. Academic qualifications are not essential, but a trainee must be able to work at a postgraduate level. There is no upper age limit, but there is a lower one of twenty-seven.

There are a maximum of twenty-four applicants accepted each year, and they are divided into two groups of twelve. There are on average forty applicants a year for the foundation course and between eighteen and thirty for Year 1. It is not possible to join the course halfway through because of its specialization.

There is no general background of the sort of people who apply, but 'most have some meditation or contemplative experience'.

3.3 *Time commitment and length of training*

This course may be followed by someone in full-time employment.

A personal tutor is seen monthly. There is a Friday evening seminar and weekend workshops once a month. There is, in addition, a five-day residential, and trainees would be expected to use their annual leave for this.

Reading time is between six and ten hours per week, and there are also ten hours of peer exchanges per month, peer support groups, individual therapy and supervision.

In general it would take between three and four years to qualify.

3.4 *Interruptions in training*

Interruptions are accommodated, but there would be a limitation of one year.

3.5 *Postgraduate qualification and learned society*

If trainees meet the requirements for the course, they are eligible to join the association and there is a £15 membership fee. The number of meetings per year depends on the interest shown by members; they can be accommodated at Dartington, but are usually rotated in people's homes. At Dartington there is a small video, audio and book library, and there is a newsletter two to four times annually.

A Code of Ethics is given to all graduates.

4. CLINICAL AND ACADEMIC REQUIREMENTS

4.1 *Personal therapy*

The criteria for a training therapist are: four to five years' postgraduate experience and training in advanced supervision and private practice. The orientation of the training therapist is not stipulated, and could be humanistic or analytic. A Core Process graduate or other integrative therapist is most appropriate as a training therapist, however. Frequency is a minimum of once weekly. The training therapist is not consulted during training unless it is agreed with the client/trainee.

4.2 *Clinical requirements*

Trainees are encouraged to accept training clients during Year 2. Maura Sills states: 'Occasionally if [they have] prior experience of client work, some students may have training clients near the end of Year 1. Students must maintain 2–4 training clients for a minimum of 6 months, 4 clients for a minimum of 12 months, 2 clients for a minimum of 18 months. Students must declare their trainee role to clients. All sessions must be recorded and available to staff. During

Year 3 students must have a caseload of 6–8 clients. This client requirement is a prerequisite to completion of training.' At present this caseload is under review.

Malpractice insurance is recommended, but there is no policy about medical cover.

4.3 *Supervision*

There is ongoing course supervision in years 2 and 3, and individual supervision is requested. The supervisor must be integrative or Karuna approved.

4.4 *Papers and written work*

Year One:
three short essays of 2,000–3,000 words
summer essay – 5,000 words;
self-evaluations – at 6 months and end of the year;
two peer evaluations at the end of the year.

Year Two:
two short essays – 2,000–3,000 words;
one case presentation;
summer essay – 5,000 words;
self-evaluation – at 6 months and end of the year;
two peer evaluations at the end of the year.

Year Three:
thesis – 7,000–10,000 words;
two case presentations;
self-assessment;
client records and reports;
two peer evaluations at the end of the year.

Maura Sills states the procedure of assessment: 'The papers are read by two staff, and feedback is given; assessment is based on the depth of grasp, an ability to extrapolate and an ability to communicate in writing.'

5. REFERRALS

Training clients are referred by word of mouth and by training staff. Psychotic clients are usually not referred to a trainee unless the trainee has had previous experience. People in 'spiritual crisis' could be seen.

6. COST OF TRAINING

For Year 1 the cost is £1,600 for the full residential course: for local trainees £950 including lunches; Year 2 costs £1,600. The six-month introductory course in London is £585. If a trainee chose to follow that course in Devon residentially, it would cost £820. Supervision and therapy are extra, and the most expensive time would be towards the end of training.

The trainee may charge two-thirds of the full fee to clients, depending on the geographical area in which the client is being seen (cost of therapy and supervision tends to be marginally less outside London). Trainees must make their own arrangements for consulting rooms.

There are some bursaries available.

7. FUTURE EXPECTATIONS/CAREER PROSPECTS

In the third year there is intensive support in setting up in practice, but there can be no forecast on what the trainee may expect in terms of career prospects since it depends on each individual.

8. TRAINEES' EXPERIENCE

8.1 *Why this course was chosen*

Trainees heard about Karuna and its training through colleagues and friends. The reason that they all felt they wanted to know more about Core Process Therapy was because of the trust they felt in the people they met associated with Karuna and Core Process Therapy.

The aspects attracting trainees were the integration of Buddhistic psychology with Western psychotherapy. Trainees also felt that on the introductory course Core Process Therapy and the meditation involved really helped them to find their feelings in a way they had not experienced before. It felt important to trainees that Core Process Therapy was based on meditative practice which enabled them to go deeper than previous therapies they had experienced.

8.2 *The atmosphere of the course*

The selection procedure beyond the introductory course was experienced as quite demanding. An essay with specific questions must be produced, about the trainees' reflections on their individual process, the effects of Core Process Therapy and why they wanted to become psychotherapists. Interviews were not always necessary because the six-month introductory course had been used as a way of assessing the suitability of trainees (this is no longer the case as there are now interviews for all).

Trainees felt that confusion about becoming a psychotherapist gradually faded as the course progressed. All felt there was a great deal of theoretical input about the different schools of psychotherapy as well as the Buddhistic tradition.

Throughout the course there is an emphasis on the practicalities of setting up in practice as well as the practice of psychotherapy. It was felt to be really important to practise being a psychotherapist with fellow trainees. These are known as 'peer exchanges' which are an integral part of the training, and something that each trainee felt was an invaluable experience.

People felt that they were well informed about the different stages of the course as well as the aims of the course. However, recently goal-posts had been changed and this was experienced as confusing. Learning theoretical concepts in the context of Core Process Therapy was also experienced as sometimes being confusing.

Some trainees were using the course to become psychotherapists in private practice and others were hoping to complement their work within the NHS with skills they were learning as individual psychotherapists. Trainees very much appreciated the method of teaching, which incorporated theory with experiential groups.

There were some frustrations about finding a Core Process Therapist and supervisor because there are so few at this moment. Trainees felt, however, that although it was preferable to be in therapy with a Core Process Therapist, it was important to be in therapy and analytic therapy was not seen as incompatible.

AUTHOR'S COMMENTS

Core Process Therapy has been created by Maura Sills and is described thus: 'It brings together Eastern and Western under-standings of the process of consciousness and its interactions in the world. Its initial focus is on inner process and how personal inner process manifests as our relationships and as the things of our life. Its foundations are found in the work of Freud, Reich, Lowen, Perls and others within the greater context of Buddhist psychology and practice. The work between client and therapist is experienced as a joint awareness practice where both must be aware of their inner process in the present and its manifestations in the therapeutic relationship.'

It is clearly a very new therapy and training, and the Buddhistic/Transcendent component makes it what Kovel would describe as the Mysticotranscendent approach (Kovel, 1976), although this is a description that Maura Sills sees as 'inappropriate as it does not include the wholism of the approach and also misinterprets Awareness Practice'. Some trainees are practising Buddhists, but not all, and it was made clear that it was not a necessary requirement for following the course in Core Process Therapy.

This training has very recently joined with the two trainings in psychosynthesis to form a postgraduate professional body to act as an Accrediting Society. The emphasis on the transcendent, spiritual and transpersonal are shared aspects of the three trainings.

METANOIA PSYCHOTHERAPY TRAINING INSTITUTE

13 North Common Road, London W5 2QB; tel: 081 579 2505.

1. HISTORY

The following are excerpts from a more complete history of Metanoia entitled *Metanoia Means Change in the Service of Physis*. It has been written by several individual members and can be obtained on request from the above address.

> Metanoia Psychotherapy Training Institute has evolved from a core of four individuals – two clinical psychologists, one psychiatrist and one educational specialist who have been in some form of collaborative learning and practice community since the late 1960s. In addition to each one's individual academic training, all four professionals garnered substantial national and international training in psychotherapy, both during their professional training and subsequently. All share a thorough grounding in academic psychology or psychiatry as well as many years' learning in psychoanalytic and psychodynamic approaches. In addition they have sought high-quality training in several humanistic and existential approaches.
>
> In 1977 Petruska Clarkson, Brian Dobson and Sue Fish established The British Institute of Systemic Therapy. Although the Institute had practically existed since 1981 when the first training courses had commenced, it was on the 4th of May 1985 that Petruska Clarkson formally christened their centre, their dream-made-reality – Metanoia, an ancient Greek word for CHANGE. The symbol for Metanioa is an equilateral triangle, the Greek letter meaning change. Metanoia, dialectical rationality, a praxis of reconciliation and dynamic unity, is an enterprise of continual and continuing reappraisal and renewal, constantly bringing forth new experience with deepening understanding and wholeness.
>
> At Christmas 1985 Maria Gilbert, eventually to become Director of Clinical Training, joined Metanoia.
>
> The Metanoia training philosophy has always been to encourage freedom of thought, excitement of exploration, emphasis on individuality and a reluctance to accept a single doctrine as an ultimate truth. At

the heart of this orientation is the concept of individual responsibility for individual behaviour (whether conscious or unconscious) as well as responsibility towards others. So while we seek excellence of individual development, we attempt to encourage this within a framework of respect for the person and our shared common humanity.

In the training of psychotherapists the person needs to be suitable and their perfomance needs to meet certain standards. Throughout the history of our work we have contributed to or led in setting standards and developing an impetus for excellence in the field of work in which we were engaged. At the same time we have tried to balance this with the professional demands of the time, comparability with other organizations of a similar nature and the inherent fallibility of human achievement against the perfectionistic ideal.

. . . We believe that humanistic and existential approaches to psychotherapy on their own, as well as integrated with psychodynamic and cognitive behavioural approaches, can make a genuine and alternative contribution to alleviating human distress in the private and the public sector as well as promoting growth, development and education in healthy and exceptional individuals and societies.

Our educational philosophy works towards a high distillation of experiential learning with syllabus-based work on the best theoretical literature available at the time. The learning community and the educational dialogue is valued as much as the content. Individual learning styles are honoured in so far as they can interact productively with the common goals of personal development, theoretical understanding, clinical competence and professional responsibility. We expect that people who train with us will influence our structures as long as their integrity can be maintained. We respect the choices of individuals to train elsewhere if their values are more compatible with other approaches.

2. THEORETICAL ORIENTATION AND CURRICULUM

Trainers have basically two aims: to be as flexible as possible for their trainees by tailoring the course to the needs of the trainee, and to focus on high standards and excellence while individual therapists grow in realizing their potential. Although Metanoia offers courses in several approaches to psychotherapy (Transactional Analysis, Gestalt Person-centred and Integrative), the main theoretical orientation is Integrative, incorporating Humanistic/ Existential, Behavioural/Cognitive and Psychoanalytical approaches.

In the first year of any of the psychotherapy training courses the trainee will be taught the basic principles of Transactional Analysis, Gestalt or Integrative psychotherapy, their theory and practice. The aim is to create a learning environment for people to grow in their own way. The Code of Ethics and Professional Practice would also be part of the ongoing input that Metanoia would see as a crucial part of the preparation of becoming a psychotherapist.

Systemic Integrative Training

The Systemic Integrative Psychotherapy Training is a post-qualification training which is open to people who have a qualification in one approach to psychotherapy and substantial experience of at least one other approach. The two years of the Systemic Integrative Training cover advanced clinical training in the major diagnostic categories: neuroses, borderline and narcissistic, and other personality disorders. Theories studied are: Bioenergetics; Principles of Psychosynthesis; Jungian Archetypal Psychology; Organ Language; Transactional Analysis; Gestalt Therapy; Cognitive Behavioural Therapy; Systemic Family Therapy; Transpersonal Psychology. Theoreticians studied are: Freud, Federn, Fairbairn, Jung, Kohut, Masterson, Laing and Kernberg amongst others. The essence of Systemic Integrative Psychotherapy is personal integration within which style is linked to syllabus and philosophy. Trainers encourage each individual to conceptualize what integration means and to create models. Different types of integrative models are studied in the course of the two years and trainees are invited to use these, others or to create their own.

Transactional Analysis

This training takes at a minimum three years and the following is the first year Syllabus Outline: Theory and Supervised Application; Contracts and Case Studies; Structural Analysis of Ego States; Transactional Analysis; Games Analysis; Racket Analysis; Script

Analysis; Group Dynamics; Child Development; the Fundamentals of Psychopathology; Self and Peer Assessment.

The second year: Supervised Concepts and Techniques – Supervision and Treatment Planning; Structural Analysis of Ego States; Transactional Analysis Proper; Games Analysis; Racket Analysis; Script Analysis; Group Treatment; Human Development; Advanced Psychopathology; Self and Peer Assessment.

The third year: Comparative Theory and Exam-Focused Supervision – Contracting and Case Study Review; The Cathexis School; The Cathexis School Practical Application; Redecision Therapy; The Classical School; Transference and Countertransference; Integrated Psychotherapy and Personal Style; Comparative Group Psychotherapy; Ethics and Professional Responsibility Review; Examination Preparation and Peer Assessment. This is frequently followed by Clinical Specialization training groups as well as a Case Study Supervision Group and an Examination Preparation Supervision Group.

Gestalt

There is a one-year foundation course consisting of ten weekends. This may be taken in conjunction with a selection of advanced training workshops.

During the course of the self-directed Gestalt clinical training, there are workshops comprising the core curriculum which has to be completed for qualification. The core curriculum workshops are as follows: Interruptions to Contact; Experiment and Enactment; Field Theory; Gestalt as Existential Psychotherapy; The Shadow Archetype in Gestalt; Principles of Psychotherapeutic Practice; Gestalt Bodywork. Other workshops available are: Dreams; Intimacy; Group Process; Retroflection Intensive; Projection Intensive; Introjection Intensive; Deflection Intensive; Confluence Intensive; Couples and Families; Systems and Organizations; Large Group Process; The Initial Interview; Personal Psychotherapeutic Style; Consultancy; Aggression; Training and Educational Design; Working with Resistance in Psychotherapy and Organizations; Psychopathology and Psychodiagnosis; Bereavement and Loss;

Celebration of Creativity; Gestalt and Jungian Psychology; Burn-out – Prevention and Management; Strategic Leadership.

Trainees' developmental needs and curriculum planning are dealt with through a personal tutor. Since the training is run on a modular basis, individual trainees complete this training at their own pace, usually taking from four to five years to meet the requirements for the Gestalt psychotherapy examination.

3. TRAINING STRUCTURE

3.1 *Training Committee*

There is a core group of five specialist directors who monitor what is happening in the four different trainings. Their trainings are in Clinical Psychology, Psychoanalysis, Transactional Analysis, Gestalt and Psychodrama, and they are all practising psychotherapists, supervisors and consultants. There are, in addition, three medical Directors, one of whom is a Consultant Psychotherapist to the NHS and another an Adult Psychiatrist. Regulation of the Training Committee is worked on a formal 'feedback system'. Meetings are regular and, because the Directors are in frequent contact with each other, issues are discussed on a regular and informal level as well as at formal meetings, where the whole community comes together.

3.2 *Selection procedure and admission*

For the basic psychotherapy trainings, a letter of application and a CV are required. This is usually followed by a two-day introductory course, and dependent on the outcome of such a mutual assessment period an assessment day and/or further interviews. For the Systemic Integrative course a very detailed application form must be completed which must show extensive experience/training in at least two approaches to psychotherapy. Most applicants to the basic qualifying courses are required to have a professional qualification in psychology, social work or the equivalent, such as a counselling diploma; there is no age limit, and Metanoia is open to trainees coming from other psychotherapy trainings with accreditation if these organizations are nationally or internationally recognized.

On average there are 16–20 trainees in each group. Between six and eight applicants may be turned away on the recommendation that they have more therapy and/or training before reapplying. Metanoia's policy is to try and accommodate on its courses suitable applicants by inclusion on existing courses or by creating additional courses or learning facilities. The balance of men and women on most training groups reflects the statistical distribution of men and women in the helping professions. An affirmative action policy is operated to enhance opportunities for mobilizing trainee differences (in terms of race, age, sexual orientation, etc.). The usual applicants are individuals with appropriate academic degrees such as psychology or psychiatry, and others from the professionally qualified helping professions.

3.3 *Time commitment and length of training*

The personal tutor, known as the Training Consultant, is seen as often as is thought necessary, either by consultant or trainee.

There are three- or five-day training blocks and both weekend and weekday workshops, so that someone working full-time would usually need to organize study or annual leave. There is also a regular amount of reading to be done.

All trainee psychotherapists are required to complete a psychiatric placement in the course of their training of at least one to three months' duration, unless they (as frequently happens) already have substantial psychiatric experience. The purpose of such a placement is to familiarize the trainee with psychiatric procedures, emergency measures and psychiatric diagnoses and generally to enable trainees to converse with their professional colleagues. Although the basic psychotherapy training course usually covers three years, most people take between four and five years to qualify as psychotherapists.

3.4 *Interruptions in training*

Interruptions are accommodated as much as possible, but generally trainees limit time out from the ongoing programme to a year. At present Metanoia runs an informal crèche for trainees with young babies and/or children.

3.5 *Postgraduate qualification and learned society*

On qualification trainees become graduate members of Metanoia, as well as members of the TA Institute or the Gestalt Psychotherapy Training Institute, depending on the course they have followed. There is a two-year Systemic Integrative Training at a post-qualification level for trainees who have already completed two or more trainings in psychotherapy.

There is a re-accreditation programme which has been formalized. Graduate members will share clinical work through the presentation of case studies, theoretical contributions and practice training audits at a re-accreditation meeting. Psychotherapists from other trainings can join Metanoia only by applying to take the Systemic Integrative postgraduate course.

Metanoia owns a Victorian house where the workshops and courses are run, as well as renting premises such as Regent's College on an occasional basis and other premises on an annual basis. There is a substantial library, resourcing in-house researchers and tutees, and a smaller one for trainees in the Metanoia annexe. There is an in-house journal – *Metanoia News*.

The Code of Ethics and Professional Practice is presented to each trainee at the start of their training and serious consideration is given to how they incorporate this in their psychotherapy practice throughout their professional life, with several modules devoted solely to exploring these issues.

4. CLINICAL AND ACADEMIC REQUIREMENTS

4.1 *Personal therapy*

All trainees need to be in ongoing individual and/or group psychotherapy. Through the Metanoia assessment referral service, trainees can be referred to suitable psychotherapists. In each individual case it is attempted to match the training therapist of whatever orientation to the personal and professional needs of the individual trainee psychotherapist. Metanoia has a wide resource network of psychotherapists of a variety of orientations in the UK and accepts as training therapists or training analysts a variety of compatible approaches, for example the Association of Jungian Analysts.

4.2 *Clinical requirements*

Many trainees are already seeing clients within their own work context when they start training because they are already practising mental health professionals. The clinical requirement is client contact hours including the necessity of seeing one client for a length of time. All trainees must have from 400 to 500 client contact hours in their particular approach to psychotherapy. These contact hours would include groups as well as short- and long-term work with a client (long term would be more than two years). Many trainees will already have hundreds of client contact hours to their credit in the context of their respective helping professions.

Medical advice/cover is available through the psychiatrists already working within Metanoia. Letters to GPs are not essential, unless there is cause for concern.

4.3 *Supervision*

There is ongoing group supervision as well as individual supervision. Trainees are given a choice of their individual supervisor, but will have experience of a number of different supervisors in the course of their training. Supervisors have to be accredited from the relevant organization: Transactional Analysis, Person-centred, Gestalt or the British Institute for Integrative Psychotherapy.

4.4 *Papers and written work*

Written clinical presentations are expected of the trainee at least four times a year. A dissertation is also to be handed in at the end of the course, and there are externally moderated oral exams. The oral exam would consist of the trainee bringing in tape recordings of sessions with clients. This would be the basis of an exam with an exam board excluding the primary trainer and supervisor, and comprising four experts in the field of which at least three out of the four are external to the training institute. The oral examination is a competency-based examination: the criteria, for example of the TA examination, are internationally recognized and applied to TA psychotherapists worldwide. Similar criteria have been adopted for both the Gestalt and the Systemic Integrative Psychotherapy examinations. There is ongoing research in this area to establish the reliability and validity of these oral examination criteria. In the course of the examination, candidates are required to discuss interventions they have made and the relationship of these to overall aspects of psychotherapy planning and process.

5. Referrals

Metanoia has a referral service staffed by a senior psychotherapist and several assessing psychotherapists. Clients come from the whole range of psychiatric diagnosis, borderline, psychotic or neurotic. Suitability of clients referred to a particular trainee will be assessed on the basis of the trainee's previous experience and/or present work situation.

All clients will know that their therapist is a trainee in supervision, and will be asked permission to tape sessions for training/supervisory use. Referrals are also frequently made to Metanoia's accredited graduate members.

6. Cost of Training

Each training year will cost between £750 and £1,000. In addition there will be individual therapy, group therapy and supervision (individual and group). Individual supervision rates are between £25 and £46, depending on the seniority of the supervisor. This would be the same for group supervision except the cost would be shared with the trainees in the group. Group therapy costs between £15 and £24 for one session per week, and individual therapy would cost anything from £20 to £46. The most expensive time would probably be when a trainee is preparing for the exam, but by this time many trainees will have a full-time practice. Referrals from other agencies have to be discussed in supervision; consulting rooms are available at a negotiated fee.

There is a bursary system where fees are waived for some trainees, and a barter or loan system. Metanoia is a registered charity now and has helped trainees with financial difficulties since its inception.

7. FUTURE EXPECTATIONS/CAREER PROSPECTS

Trainees starting a course at Metanoia get plenty of opportunity to meet with trainees who have nearly qualified or have qualified, and they are encouraged to discuss setting up in private practice. This is done in supervision and by means of special training events or workshops. All the trainees near completion have very successful work practices in the public and private sectors.

Not all trainees want to go into full-time private practice and they remain in the public sector, e.g. probation, social services, NHS. The people who do make the change to private practice generally take four to five years to make the transition from social work or clinical psychology into private practice. Full-time work would be between 30 and 35 hours a week.

All trainees must take out malpractice insurance as soon as they start working with clients.

8. TRAINEES' EXPERIENCE

8.1 *Why this course was chosen*

Many trainees are already practising psychotherapists when they come to the course, and all will have a core professional background which is one of the entry requirements.

Trainees were attracted to Metanoia's trainings for the study of the group process as well as the offering of TA Gestalt. Selection procedure was experienced as an in-depth process of reflecting on the reasons for becoming a psychotherapist.

8.2 *The atmosphere of the course*

The learning environment was experienced as extremely liberating in terms of offering people the choice of how they wanted to learn, with the emphasis on individuals developing at their own pace. Trainees felt enriched by the wealth of experience the trainers bring to their teaching, which means they are able to offer a variety of approaches which are shared in an integrative way. In general Metanoia is experienced as a very generous organization.

Information was communicated in a precise and clear way and the experiential aspect of the training was felt to be a very thorough way of learning theoretical principles and concepts. Moreover, the latter are contextualized, so that, say, for instance Freud's theories are looked at in the context of the era in which they were written as well as how they may apply to today. The experiential aspect of the training is not seen as therapy although there are inevitable overlaps, but there is a complementary academic input. There are plenty of opportunities for sharing information and concerns about setting up in practice with fellow trainees as well as trainers and teachers.

Problems and confusions were not seen as a problem because of the open system that is practised within Metanoia. Trainees experienced an atmosphere which encouraged the discussion of problems and difficulties.

Trainees felt that post-qualification there was an enormous amount that Metanoia offered regarding postgraduate exchanges and courses as well as opportunities to teach and supervise.

AUTHOR'S COMMENTS

The trainings offered at Metanoia are for professionals already working in the field of mental health, and applicants not working in this field would have to demonstrate an equivalent experience. Although Metanoia offers three trainings with its own theoretical orientations, the main theoretical orientation is 'Integrative' which incorporates Humanistic/Existential, Behavioural/Cognitive and

Psychodynamic (Psychoanalysis and Analytical Psychology). This bringing together of different theories has been pioneered by Petruska Clarkson, who has devised what are referred to as 'meta models' (see Clarkson, 1990). There may be many therapists who would see this combination of such different theories as a simplification or watering down. However, trainees did not experience this and found the meta models clear and accessible.

Reflections and questions on these trainings would be linked with the history of enmity between the different schools (particularly psychoanalysis and behaviour therapy), and how the reconciliation of such differences is demonstrated in the meta models.

MINSTER CENTRE

57 Minster Road, London NW2 3SH: tel: 071 435 9200.

1. HISTORY

Helen Davies set up this training in 1978. Coming from a humanistic and Reichian background, as well as having undergone a personal Jungian analysis, she found that there was no training already in existence which incorporated both humanistic and psychoanalytic orientations. Thus the aims and objectives of such a training were to 'integrate' humanistic and analytic therapy. Teachers from different backgrounds came together and gradually a core group evolved. Helen Davies, John Gravelle, Elizabeth Abrahams and Lavinia Gomez are the present training Directors.

2. THEORETICAL ORIENTATION AND CURRICULUM

The trainers' aim is to give their trainees a number of philosophies and therapeutic tools. The main assumption is that people will find their own way of coping with all the contradictions of the world of psychotherapy. They come out of the training equipped to use multiple methods and techniques. They often specialize in specific techniques which they feel suit their own personal development.

The Ground Year contains four modules. Module 1 contains Styles of Facilitation based on the use of psychotherapy and counselling tools from different forms of therapy. The second module is a theoretical module where the first term is devoted to Freud and the Post-Freudians. The second term covers Jung and Transpersonal work and the third term is Reich and Humanistic Psychology. In this module access to all the language used in the main body of the training is made available. The third module is a therapy group. The fourth module is three weekend workshops in the year.

Appropriate students continue on to follow the first year of training. However, there are an additional six weekend workshops that are largely experiential. These include birth work, sexuality, the family, death and bereavement and transpersonal work. The theoretical work to back up the workshops is incorporated.

In the second and third years of the main body of training, students continue in weekly therapy groups, small supervision groups and two two-hour theoretical/experiential seminars per week. In the second year the theoretical areas covered are Humanistic Psychology in theory and practice in one module and all aspects of Bodywork, Reichian and otherwise, in the other module.

In the third year the theoretical modules include Object Relations – theory and practice – and another module of the theoretical work of Jung and Freud. All modules in the second and third years are two hours apiece, weekly for the academic year.

In the second and third years all students are required to do four further weekend workshops. The students follow weekend workshops in specific areas: Psychodrama, Object Relations, Politics and Therapy, Transactional Analysis, Cognitive Therapy, Bodywork, Group Dynamics, The Family, Gestalt, Phenomenology and Jung – Imaging, Dreams and Fantasies. The intention of the structure of the course is for the students to be able to handle and relate directly to their own physical and emotional states before moving into psychodynamic work, which is the analysis of those states.

3. Training Structure

3.1 *Training Committee*

There are four Directors who do not refer to themselves as the Training Committee as such, but function as one. There is no formal procedure for them to meet because they feel they see each other frequently enough to deal with anything as it may arise. The trainings of the other Directors are in group analysis and humanistic therapy.

There is a therapist who is not part of the Minster Centre, who is required to act as an ombudsman, and this is one of the ways in which the course is regulated. However, to date he has not been used as such. He also does a one-day consultancy with all the staff at the end of each year.

There are meetings twice a year of the entire student body, where any difficulties students may be having can be discussed. These meetings also enable trainees to say what they would like in terms of changes or additions to the curriculum. Each year has student representatives who negotiate with directors and staff.

3.2 *Selection procedure and admission*

There is no application form, but a CV, a short biography, a history of therapeutic experience and reasons for doing the course are requested in writing from each applicant, and there is one interview with two staff members. The Ground Year is also used to assess people's suitability for going on to the full programme, and in most cases this is obligatory although it is sometimes waived for trainees with relevant experience. Relevant experience would mean having done a counselling course or equivalent elsewhere for at least two years, or the ground year of another psychotherapy training course. There is no age limit, but those over twenty-five are preferred. No referees are required and no academic qualifications are necessary, but suitable life experience and academic ability are preferred.

The Ground Year has groups of ten to twelve students. It has about 28 students, split into two groups for theory, and four groups for Styles of Facilitation. Therapy groups vary between eight and twelve participants depending on philosophy and kind of group. Supervision groups include between three and six members per group.

There tend to be three types of people who apply and follow the course. The first are people who are perhaps working in the helping professions or education and who do not intend to become psychotherapists, but come mainly for self-exploration. Then there is the group who become qualified as counsellors, and thirdly the group who go on to qualify as psychotherapists. The majority of applicants come from the helping professions along with teachers and people with an Arts background.

3.3 *Time commitment and length of training*

Trainees would have to attend for one half day a week. The rest of the course can be covered in evening seminars and weekends. In the Ground Year there are three weekend workshops; in the first year, six to seven weekend workshops; second year, four weekend workshops; third year, four weekend workshops. Ground Year and first year have one evening seminar a week and the second and third years have two evening seminars a week. Reading is required throughout the course, particularly in the second and third years. To follow the course which leads to the qualification of psychotherapist takes four to five years, but may take longer for some people.

3.4 *Interruptions in training*

All interruptions are accommodated. Sometimes it may be felt that an interruption needs to be encouraged when a trainee may not be ready to carry on without more therapy and/or life experience.

3.5 *Postgraduate qualification and learned society*

The Institute of Traditional and Humanistic Psychotherapy was set up for graduates of the Minster Centre, and there are associate members and a small group of members. Day workshops are organized on various topical themes. A therapist must have been working for at least two years before applying for full membership.

There is no library yet. Seminars take place in two Victorian houses which have been renovated into one. There are group rooms, seminar rooms and a communal kitchen where people can make tea and coffee and meet in between groups.

There is a Code of Ethics which is taught on the course and applies to the Institute of Traditional and Humanistic Psychotherapy. The Minster Centre has formally taken on the current (1990) Code of Ethics evolved by the BAC.

4. CLINICAL AND ACADEMIC REQUIREMENTS

4.1 *Personal therapy*

All trainees must be in once weekly psychotherapy and in general people find their own therapists. The Minster Centre's policy is that trainees should be in therapy with someone outside the Minster Centre teaching staff. The therapist is usually contacted initially, so that Minster Centre knows their training and the way in which they work. It is felt important not to interfere with the therapeutic relationship and the therapist is never consulted during training: 'Whether the therapy is effective or not is always fairly obvious from the teacher's point of view.'

4.2 *Clinical requirements*

Trainees who have no clinical background in psychiatry must involve themselves on a psychiatric team in their last year. For trainees already working in the field, this is not necessary. One training client must be seen for at least forty hours, as well as a further forty hours of seeing clients who may or may not stay longer than a few sessions.

Medical cover is not something that is compulsory, but if the referring therapist is concerned about a client the trainee is encouraged to be in contact with the client's doctor. There is a psychiatrist on the teaching team of the Minster Centre who can also be consulted. The students and staff are fully insured for training clients and work done on the premises.

4.3 *Supervision*

Supervision takes place in groups throughout the course, and is essential to qualify. Later on, individual supervision may be taken up, especially if the trainee has several clients, but extra supervision is not essential to qualify. It is assumed that all practising therapists continue in supervision after qualification and it is maintained in order to gain continued accreditation. External supervisors have to be approved of in the same way as a training therapist.

4.4 *Papers and written work*

In the Ground Year, one short paper is to be written for each term. For the first year, after the Ground Year, a longer paper is required. The second and third years complete four papers a year, finishing with a dissertation on a relevant subject negotiated with a tutor. There are also written case studies to be presented.

5. REFERRALS

Clients coming to the Minster Centre for therapy are seen by a member of the staff who then refers them on to the appropriate trainee. All types of clients may be referred to trainees, and there is a policy of letting clients know their therapist is a trainee in supervision.

6. COST OF TRAINING

The cost for training for the Ground Year is £1,500. Each year will then be charged according to the hours of work. Personal therapy and individual supervision would be extra.

Training clients negotiate a fee with trainees per session and pay the trainee directly, but the money then goes to the Minster Centre. There are consulting rooms available for trainees.

There are no bursaries or loans at the moment, but it is hoped that there will be in the future.

7. FUTURE EXPECTATIONS/CAREER PROSPECTS

Trainees start setting up in practice in their second year of training and get as much practical advice as needed. It is difficult to forecast how well people will do: 'If they're good, word gets round and they do well; others may struggle for years and perhaps should not be psychotherapists.'

Minster Centre has just set up a programme for training trainers and so there are lots of possibilities for people to supervise and/or teach beyond qualification.

8. TRAINEES' EXPERIENCE

8.1 *Why this course was chosen*

People were very attracted to this course because it offered a combination of traditional and humanistic methods of working with clients. Trainees also felt that there was great emphasis on their own personal growth and process and that throughout the training they were working out what was their personal 'style' in terms of working with clients.

Trainees really enjoyed the experiential side of the course and felt they were not really taught, in the way that most people think of being taught. Seminars are conducted by introducing theories, mixed in with an experiential group. This is what people felt was the main attraction of the course and the most satisfying, in terms of learning the meaning of the theory. The anticipated training was fulfilled and sometimes exceeded expectation.

8.2 *The atmosphere of the course*

Communication was not always as clear as trainees would have liked it to be; however, people felt that issues could always be addressed directly with the teacher(s) concerned. Sometimes information from a teacher was inconsistent with that of a Director, but mostly this was satisfactorily resolved.

Because of the nature of the course and the environment, the house and kitchen, people felt they all really got to know each other in a very intense way. There were plenty of opportunities to relate to people, from one year to the next. The hierarchy of the course was felt more by people in the Ground Year, who do not work with any of the Directors.

People who were finishing their training felt that it was difficult to know how they would describe themselves. Psychotherapist with traditional and humanistic approaches, or psychotherapist with an integrated approach? Most people agreed that although the training concentrated on each person acquiring his or her own 'style', at the end of the day there really was inevitably a Minster Centre 'style', because of the choice and mix of humanistic and psychoanalytic schools that are studied.

AUTHOR'S COMMENTS

The combination of psychoanalytic therapy and humanistic therapy causes theoretical and technical conflicts because of the very different starting points: analytic is non-directive and humanistic directive. The analytic therapist would never touch the patient while the humanistic therapist uses touch, massage and bodywork as part of the therapy. It is therefore difficult to know exactly how combining approaches would work in practice.

All therapists, whether analytic or humanistic, aim to work towards the integration of the unconscious for all their patients/clients, but the two approaches have different methods of achieving this (see Part One). How is a Minster Centre therapist to know which approach is most valuable and most helpful to their client at a particular time? Is it possible to use the very direct techniques of bodywork 'combined' with psychoanalytic interpretation with the same client in the same session? Yes, it is possible, according to Helen Davies. This combination may well be criticized by humanistic and analytic practitioners alike, who may argue that using such different approaches makes it confusing for trainees and in turn their clients; that in 'combining' so many therapies with such fundamental philosophical and technical differences, nothing can be learnt in any depth and therefore has no chance of really being 'integrated'. On the other hand, there may equally be a number of therapists who would say that the Minster Centre's course challenges the trainee to make a choice by not restricting the type of therapy to be taught. Perhaps what needs to be asked is: what is the meaning of 'integration' and 'style' in this training? Many people join the course seeking self-development and fewer people continue through to the psychotherapy training.

PSYCHOSYNTHESIS AND EDUCATION TRUST

48 Guildford Road, Stockwell, London SW8 2BU; tel: 081 622 8295.

1. HISTORY

The Psychosynthesis and Education Trust was founded in 1965 under the guidance of Dr Roberto Assagioli, who became its first president. Other founding members were Sir George Trevelyn, Dr Martin Israel and Geoffrey Leytham.

The Trust was established with the objective of fostering psychological research into the various elements of human nature and disseminating its findings to the public through educational, therapeutic, scientific and charitable activities. These aims and objectives have persisted throughout the years to the present time. In 1980 Diana Whitmore, who had previously worked in psychosynthesis for ten years, was invited to carry on the work of the Trust and to incorporate her existing programme into the framework of the Trust. The Trust currently offers a variety of activities, educational courses and lectures for the general public, postgraduate training for professionals, a counselling service and an international youth project. Eighty per cent of the Trust's work is comprised by its Professional Training Course in Counselling and Psychotherapy.

2. THEORETICAL ORIENTATION AND CURRICULUM

The Professional Training Programme prepares students to become competent and effective therapists using the psychosynthesis model of individual therapy work. It is also postgraduate professional training for those already in the helping professions who wish to enhance their therapeutic skills: doctors, nurses, social workers, established psychotherapists and pastoral care workers. The course is also applicable to people in fields such as business, sport, art and law who want to enrich their work and the quality of their professional contact with others.

The core theoretical model of the training is psychosynthesis. Psychosynthesis is a psychology which offers a broad perspective of human life and development, with a special focus on the evocation of an individual's potential. As a transpersonal psychology, psychosynthesis recognizes and emphasizes the essential transpersonal nature of the human being (the Self or Soul); places high value on the realms of intuition, inspiration and creative insight, and the discovery and cultivation of the will as a central psychospiritual function.

Personal psychosynthesis aims to foster the development of a well-integrated personality. This work involves addressing the pain and neurosis in the personality, while transpersonal psychosynthesis offers the possibility of realizing one's deeper nature and purpose in life. Psychosynthesis integrates principles and techniques drawn from many classical and contemporary approaches of both Eastern and Western psychology, as well as contributing various psychological and spiritual models and methods of its own. It can be applied to the personal, interpersonal, professional and social aspects of life.

The curriculum of the training provides a blend and a balance between two primary thematic elements: the basic principles and methods of counselling and psychotherapy, including specific techniques and related therapies which are integrated within the psychosynthesis model; and the basic principles and methods of psychosynthesis, with an in-depth emphasis on their relationship and application to therapy.

Year One:

Group therapy: trainees participate in small (12–14) ongoing therapy groups to further and deepen their work on their own growth and on their interpersonal relationships within the dynamics of the group. This occurs in weekly sessions of three hours, for forty weeks. (In the second and third years, trainees attend group therapy sessions quarterly.) The curriculum includes:

> The Integration of subpersonalities I and II
>
> The 'I' and identity
>
> Childhood and the Lower Unconscious
>
> The Discovery and Cultivation of the Will I and II
>
> Psychosynthesis and the Body I
>
> Psychosynthesis and Sexuality
>
> Basic Counselling Skills
>
> Gestalt Therapy I
>
> The Practice of Psychosynthesis Therapy I

All curriculum courses draw upon relevant theories in psychology throughout. Additional theoretical models integrated are: Psychoanalysis (Freud, Erikson, Klein, A. Miller, Adler, Angyal); Analytical Psychology (Jung); Humanistic Psychology (Maslow, Janov, Perls, R. May); Existential Psychology (Wilbur, S. Grof, C. Narango, F. Vaughn); Main Theories of Mysticism (Buber, Keyserling, E. Underhill, R. Boecke, W. James).

Year Two includes:

> The Creative Use of Pain, Crisis and Failure
>
> Interpersonal Psychosynthesis I and II
>
> Psychosynthesis and the Body II
>
> Sexuality II
>
> Self Realization and Psychological Disturbances I and II
>
> Creativity and Mind Development I
>
> Gestalt II

Psychopathology

The Practice of Psychosynthesis Therapy I

Supervision: 20 weeks of two hours

Year Three includes:

Creativity and Mind Development I

Transpersonal Realization and the Psychosynthesis Typology

Theories of Human Nature

Gestalt III

The Practice of Psychosynthesis III

The Individual and Society

Transpersonal Psychosynthesis and Daily Life

Year Four includes:

Seventeen days of advanced course work

Course curriculum:

The Therapeutic Relationship

Psychopathology

Depth Work and the Unconscious

Existential Themes in Psychotherapy

Working with the Transpersonal in Psychotherapy

The Trust's Professional Course takes a pragmatic and experiential approach to learning. All courses have a blend of experiential and theoretical learning with components of practicum work for the student to practise what is being learned.

Training modalities:

Seminar and discussion

Individual and small-group work

Critique, feedback and reflection

Demonstration and observation

Audio and video recording

Written assignments

Reading assignments

Lectures by visiting mental health professionals

3. TRAINING STRUCTURE

3.1 *Training Committee*

The training is organized and developed by a Training Committee of three senior trainers (who meet every two months) and the everyday running of the training is overseen by the Core Training Staff of six senior trainers (who meet fortnightly). Each training group has a student representative (who meets with the Core Training Staff once a term). There are two Co-Directors of Training who are also Co-Directors of the Trust and its most senior practitioners of psychosynthesis (who meet weekly). The third member of the Training Committee is a rotating position. Additionally there is a Training Co-ordinator responsible for the organizational side of the training (who meets with the Co-Directors of training whenever needed).

All staff meetings cover the following areas: organizational issues around the training; discussion of each training group and its well-being; relevant feedback from both trainees and the student reps; policy and decision-making; team building and group process; discussion of new projects and developments.

3.2 *Selection procedure and admission*

Prospective students for Professional Training first enrol in the introductory programme, the 'Essentials of Psychosynthesis', which surveys the fundamental principles and methods of psychosynthesis. This programme offers thematic seminars, study groups, reading and written assignments, a personal therapy session for each student, and observations of other individual therapy sessions with fellow students as clients. Upon successful completion of this programme, prospective students make written application to enter the training, following a detailed questionnaire provided by the Trust, requiring references from individuals who are familiar with the applicant and his or her work.

Following application, each applicant attends a personal interview with two members of the Course Training Staff. Selection criteria and issues for exploration during the interview are: previous professional training and experience; motivations, needs, personal and professional goals; intended field of application; potential ability to form a helping relationship; capacity to deal effectively with the psychological and cognitive demands of the course; ability to be self-critical, introspective and discriminating; ability to make use of and reflect on life experience; commitment to one's own individual growth and development; ability to function co-operatively in a group with awareness and sensitivity. These criteria are applied to the applicant and assessment made by four staff members: the two interviewing staff and the applicant's two 'Essentials' trainers.

There are no rigid age limits, but people under twenty-eight are seldom accepted. There is no upper age limit. Both academic qualifications and previous clinical experience are highly valued but not mandatory to be accepted on to the course. Each year twenty-five students are accepted (one new training group – as one graduates). There are usually about 100 applicants.

3.3 *Time commitment and length of training*

The training is four years part-time. Upon successful completion of the first three years trainees receive a 'Counsellor's Diploma', recognized by the British Association of Counselling. Students must then reapply for the fourth year for the 'Advanced Psychosynthesis Therapy' Diploma.

Each year of the training requires students to be at the Trust twice during the week (usually evenings) and one weekend a month; additionally there are four five-day courses (one per year). Approximately eight hours per week of additional home study is required. The total number of training hours is approximately 1,500.

3.4 *Interruptions in training*

Students are encouraged to take a break from training if their life circumstances make it appropriate. The break may be anywhere from one term to one year.

3.5 *Postgraduate qualification and learned society*

There is automatic Graduate membership for which there is no fee at the moment, and postgraduate courses are offered. The Trust has a building and a library open to all students and graduates; there is no in-house journal.

The Trust has a Code of Ethics and a complaints procedure.

4. CLINICAL AND ACADEMIC REQUIREMENTS

4.1 *Personal therapy*

At the beginning of professional training students select a psychosynthesis therapist from a list of staff therapists provided by the Trust. The individual therapy occurs weekly, later becoming fortnightly throughout the duration of the course. Trainees must have a minimum of 82 one-to-one sessions with their therapist. In the fourth year trainees are encouraged to work with a therapist from a different discipline of their choice. The only therapy incongruent with psychosynthesis would be behaviour therapy. The trainee's therapist is never consulted during training. The therapeutic relationship is kept strictly confidential.

4.2 *Clinical requirements*

The requirements prior to taking on practice clients using psychosynthesis are as follows:

1(a) Before starting with practice clients Counselling Skills I and II and the Practice of Psychosynthesis Therapy I and II must be completed, unless the trainee has previous experience and training in counselling and psychotherapy.

(b) The trainee must have completed a minimum of thirty individual sessions.

(c) The trainee is required to subscribe to a 'Treatment Risk

Scheme'. Some may already be doing so through a professional organization, but those who do not hold such a policy must arrange insurance before applying for permission for his or her practice client.

(d) The trainee consults his or her first year supervisor and one trainer to receive a written affirmative recommendation to begin with practice clients. This is then sent to the Training Director who files it in the trainee's administrative file.

2. To begin with, the trainee should take on only two practice clients. The first practice clients must not be clients with severe pathology of any kind, as it is not appropriate to work with individuals who are medicated, actively suicidal or have had recent psychiatric help (within the past five years). Ideally practice clients should be 'healthy neurotics'. The work should be contracted in six session series, with the clear understanding that the trainee is under supervision.

3. Practice clients should begin therapy at a fee of £5 a session.

4. The trainee must submit 'Six-monthly Reports' to his or her current supervisor and a 'Final Report' before graduation on therapeutic work with all practice clients.

5. The trainee must have read and agreed to abide by the Trust's Code of Ethics and Practice.

All trainee practice clients are first interviewed by a member of the Trust's Counselling Service for assessment to ascertain if they are a suitable practice client for the trainee. Trainees must be supervised on each practice client, and in some cases additional individual supervision is required.

Accurate and detailed records of work with all clients are kept by beginning students, which are reviewed regularly by course supervision staff. By qualification students must have had 500 client contact hours.

4.3 *Supervision*

Year Two: two terms of 10 weeks of two-hour supervision groups (groups of six students).

Year Three: continuous weekly supervision of two hours for 35 weeks (groups of six students).

Year Four: fortnightly group supervision of four students for three hours; monthly individual supervision; one term of fortnightly peer supervision.

All supervisors are recognized psychosynthesis supervisors.

4.4 Papers and written work

Year One: an autobiographical paper (3,000 words or more) applying the learning of the year to the trainee's own life history and existential situation.

Year Two: trainees are required to keep detailed written accounts of their work with practice clients and of how they are using psychosynthesis in practice.

Year Three: a theoretical paper (3,000 words or more) relating psychosynthesis to other theories and systems of psychology; an extensive case history (5,000 words or more) of work with a client the trainee has seen for extensive therapy.

Year Four: another extensive case history ´3,000 words or more) and a supervision project of the student's choice.

5. REFERRALS

Trainees are referred low cost clients from the Trust's Counselling Service, but they also may bring practice clients found elsewhere through the Trust's referral system. In addition, there is a small number of placements in GPs' practices and additional referrals of clients from the Royal College of Art. For the type of practice clients recommended, see section 4.2. All practice clients are screened by the Trust's Counselling Service through an 'Intake Interview'. Where there is any doubt as to suitability of the client, a psychiatric assessment is encouraged, with one of the Trust's staff psychiatrists.

Upon completion of training, graduates are invited to apply to join the Trust's Counselling Service. Otherwise there is no system for providing future clients for graduates.

6. Cost of Training

The four years of training cost £160 per month which covers all training, except individual sessions and individual supervision. Individual sessions are usually by sliding scale fees, but the average is £25 a session and likewise for individual supervision.

The policy for trainees' fees for practice clients is £5 a session, unless the trainee is already a practising therapist. Consulting rooms are available to be rented from the Trust.

The Trust has scholarship funds available for students. However, no bursaries are given in the first year of training, but interest-free loans have been awarded in the past.

7. Future Expectations/Career Prospects

Practical advice on setting up a practice is given in the supervision groups, and a graduate course on 'Setting Up a Private Practice' is offered periodically. Advice is given on setting up referral networks among students and graduates. The general experience has been that it takes anywhere from six months to a year to set up a viable practice.

Every two years the Trust offers a 'Training of Teachers of Psychosynthesis' programme which is a two-year programme leading to a certificate as a teacher of psychosynthesis.

8. Trainees' Experience

8.1 *Why this course was chosen*

This course was chosen by trainees for the following reasons:

1. Psychosynthesis is seen as a transpersonal psychology, i.e. it recognizes the existence of the spiritual dimension and seeks to address meaning and purpose in life. It is a holistic psychology in that it addresses and explores the relationship between body, feelings, mind and spirit.

2. The experience of the Essentials course was positive.

3. The training was seen to provide much opportunity for

personal development because of its experiential component.

4. Contact with the Trust, as client or Short Course participant,
had engendered a sense of trust in the organization.

5. The positive experience of a psychosynthesis therapy.

6. The Trust does not have an upper age limit for admission.

The selection procedure was experienced as searching and very
in-depth in terms of the nature of the application form and the style
of the interview. Trainees felt they had as much information as they
needed at the beginning of the course.

8.2 *The atmosphere of the course*

There was overall satisfaction about the way in which topics were
taught and particular value was placed on the way in which theory
is interwoven with experiential work and on the way in which
trainees are given the opportunity to do practicums on each other.
There was an appreciation of the style and teaching methods of the
trainers and of the fact that they responded well to criticism and
questions and allowed open discussion. However, discussion was
limited at times either because of the constraints of the teaching
schedule or differences which could not be resolved. Some trainees
felt dissatisfied with the level or the content of theoretical input.

Confusion and frustration were associated with the language that
is used in psychosynthesis, which was experienced as conflicting
with a politically aware equal opportunities attitude. Bringing up
some of these issues was sometimes felt to be avoided and brushed
aside by teachers who tended to take the attitude that it was a
demonstration of a sub-personality. It was felt that the psychology
of race, gender, class, sexual orientation were not adequately
addressed in either the theory or practice of the training.

Most of the aspects of psychosynthesis theory were covered
well, but some trainees were left wanting more input in some areas,
e.g. bodywork, sexuality and sexual behaviours, the various
neuroses. There was an awareness that this is a training in individual
psychosynthesis psychotherapy with adults and that though there

is a substantial amount of time spent in groupwork, both therapy group and large-group learning and process, there are trainees who would like to see the Trust offer further training in groupwork and also in work with children and couples/partners.

Trainees saw the Trust as a new and expanding organization which is undergoing changes, both structurally and professionally. Trainees have experienced changing course requirements as the Trust has become accredited by the British Association of Counsellors (BAC) and as a result of its participation in the HIPS group of the UKSCP. Trainees have been informed of these changes and each training year group is represented at regular meetings about the professional training.

Trainees were pleased that the Trust has a postgraduate training programme and supervision system and that there are opportunities to get involved in the Trust's Counselling Service and other activities. The Trust has contact with psychosynthesis organizations in other countries and there are regular international conferences which trainees are looking forward to participating in.

Trainees experienced the training as an extremely supportive one in relation to their professional learning and their own development.

AUTHOR's COMMENTS

The Trust's three-year course leads to a Diploma in Psychosynthesis Counselling, and has only just recently included a fourth year which will provide the graduate with the 'psychotherapist' qualification. This recent addition brings into focus the debate concerning the differences between psychotherapy and counselling, amongst the humanistic and analytic trainings. According to Diana Whitmore, the fourth year has been added because 'we wanted to have a more substantial training than current standards even though the three-year training has been assessed and approved by the Humanistic and Integrative Psychology Section [HIPS] and the 1,700 hours of training is above the norm for the HIPS criteria for membership.' It remains, however, that the three-year course qualifies 'counsellors' and the fourth year creates the qualification 'psychotherapist'. Is a year enough to make the transition from counsellor to psychotherapist?

Unlike the Institute of Psychosynthesis, the Trust retains the view that psychosynthesis is aimed at treating healthy neurotics. Many therapists would take the point of view that a healthy neurotic in the patient population is very hard to find and assess, and that even the most experienced practitioners are capable of making an incorrect diagnosis in one interview. How does the psychosynthesis therapist assess the 'healthy neurotic'? According to Diana Whitmore and the Trust, their use of the label 'healthy neurotic' refers to the relatively stable person as opposed to the chronically mentally ill person. This is something that is stressed to trainees: that the training is not one to address working with chronically severely disturbed individuals. 'This is not to say that clients do not, at times, have psychotic episodes or severe crisis moments – which our practitioners do indeed handle. For this purpose the Trust employs a psychiatrist as consultant who works for us half a day a week to support and supervise such moments.' Many analytic therapists may take the view that stable people are not necessarily 'healthy neurotics' and indeed may be extremely disturbed. Assessment and diagnosis is an area of great controversy and debate, perhaps particularly between humanistic and analytic therapists.

This course reflects a different development of psychosynthesis therapy from the psychosynthesis developing at the Institute of Psychosynthesis. The differences seemed to be based on the different emphasis and style of the leaders and the eclectic combination of what are seen as the complementary therapies to psychosynthesis.

BIBLIOGRAPHY

Place of publication is London unless otherwise indicated. *SE* denotes James Strachey, ed., *The Standard Edition of the Complete Psychological Works of Sigmund Freud*, 24 vols, Hogarth, 1953–73.

Assagioli, R. (1975) *Psychosynthesis*. Turnstone.

Aveline, Mark (1990) 'The training and supervision of individual therapists', in Dryden (1990), pp. 313–39.

Balint, M. (1953) 'Analytic training and training analysis', in Balint, ed. *Primary Love and Psychoanalytic Technique*. Tavistock (1965 edn).

Bannister, K. *et al.* (1955) *Social Casework in Marital Problems*. Tavistock.

Benvenuto, B. and Kennedy, R. (1986) *The Works of Jacques Lacan, An Introduction*. Free Association Books.

Berke, J. (1977) *I Haven't Had To Go Mad Here*. Pelican.

—— (1989) *The Tyranny of Malice*. Simon & Schuster.

Berke, J. and Barnes, M. (1971) *Mary Barnes: Two Accounts of a Journey Through Madness*. Free Association Books 1991.

Berne, E. (1964) *Games People Play*. Penguin.

Bollas, C. (1987) *The Shadow of the Object: Psychoanalysis of the Unthought Known*. Free Association Books.

—— (1989) *Forces of Destiny*. Free Association Books.

Bosanquet, C. (1988) 'The confusion of tongues and the Rugby Conference', *Br. J. Psychother*. 5: 228–40.

Breuer, J. and Freud, S. (1893–95) 'Studies on hysteria, Case 1: Fraulein Anna O', *SE* 2, pp. 21–48; paperback edn: The Pelican Freud Library 3, pp. 73–102.

Brown, D. and Pedder, J. (1979) *Introduction to Psychotherapy*. Tavistock.

Clarkson, P. (1989) *Gestalt Counselling in Action*. Sage.

—— (1990) 'A multiplicity of psychotherapeutic relationships', *Br. J. Psychother*. 7: 148–63.

Cremerius, J. (1990) 'Training analysis and power', *Free Associations* 20: 114–38.

Dicks, H. (1970) *Fifty Years at the Tavistock Clinic*. Routledge & Kegan Paul.

Dryden, W., ed. (1990) *Individual Therapy: A Handbook*. Open University Press.

Dyne, D. (1988) 'Whither Rugby? Towards a profession of psychotherapy', *Br. J. Psychother.* 4: 148–55.

—— (1985) 'Questions of training', *Free Associations* 3: 92–147.

Dyne, D. and Figlio, K. (1989) 'A response to J. Pedder's "Courses in psychotherapy"', *Br. J. Psychother.* 6: 222–6.

Ellenberger, H.F. (1970) *The Discovery of the Unconscious*. Allen Lane.

Ellis, M. (1992) 'Lesbians, gay men and psychoanalytic training' (unpublished).

Ernst, S. and Goodison, L. (1981) *In Our Own Hands*. The Women's Press.

Foster, Sir J. (1971) *Enquiry into the Practice and Effects of Scientology*. HMSO.

Foulkes, S.H. and Anthony, E.J. (1957) *Group Psychotherapy – The Psychoanalytical Approach*. Karnac.

Freud, A. (1955) *The Psycho-Analytical Treatment of Children*. Hogarth Press.

Freud, S. (1905) 'Three Essays on the Theory of Sexuality'. *SE* 7, pp. 135–243; paperpack edn: The Pelican Freud Library 7, pp. 45–169.

—— (1926) 'The Question of Lay Analysis'. *SE* 20, pp. 183–258.

—— (1940) 'An Outline of Psycho-Analysis'. *SE* 23, pp. 141–207. Hogarth Press and Institute of Psycho-Analysis.

Gay, P. (1988) *Freud: A Life For Our Time*. Dent.

Fenichel, O. (1946) *Psychoanalytic Theory of Neurosis*. Routledge & Kegan Paul.

Fordham, F. (1953) *An Introduction to Jung's Psychology*. Penguin.

Gardner, F. (1990) 'Know what I mean: an exploration into knowing what is meant', *Br. J. Psychother.* 6: 440–7.

Hahn, H. (1988) 'On establishing the psychotherapeutic alliance in an unsophisticated environment', *Br. J. Psychother.* 4: 253–62.

Hart, M. (1989) 'The arrival of the bee box: poetry and mental mechanism', *Br. J. Psychother.* 5: 564 –73.

Herman, N. (1989) 'Ilse Seglow in her time: reflections on her life and work', *Br. J. Psychother.* 5: 431–41.

Hinshelwood, R.D. (1985) 'Questions of training', *Free Associations* 2: 7–18.

—— (1986) 'Eclecticism: the impossible project – a response to Deryck Dyne', *Free Associations* 5: 23–7.

—— (1989) *A Dictionary of Kleinian Thought*. Free Association Books.

Hinshelwood, R.D. and Rowan, J. (1988) 'Is psychoanalysis humanistic? A correspondence between John Rowan and Bob Hinshelwood', *Br. J. Psychother.* 4: 142–7.

Illich, I. (1971) *Celebration of Awareness*. Penguin.

Jones, E. (1957) *Sigmund Freud: Life and Work*. Penguin.

Klein, M. (1932) *The Psycho-Analysis of Children*. Hogarth Press and Institute of Psycho-Analysis.

King, P. and Steiner, R. (1991) *The Freud–Klein Controversies 1941–45*. Routledge.

Knight, L. (1986) *Talking to a Stranger: A Consumer's Guide to Therapy*. Fontana.

Kohon, G. (1986) *The British School of Psychoanalysis: The Independent Tradition*. Free Association Books.

Kovel, J. (1976) *A Complete Guide to Therapy*. Pelican.

Laing, R.D. (1972) *Laing and Anti-Psychiatry*. Penguin.

Laplanche, J. and Pontalis, J.-B. (1983) *The Language of Psycho-Analysis*. Hogarth Press and Institute of Psycho-Analysis.

Lomas, P. (1973) *True and False Experience*. Allen Lane.

—— (1990) 'On setting up a psychotherapy training', *Free Associations* 20: 139–49.

Malcolm, J. (1982) *Psychoanalysis: The Impossible Profession*. Karnac.

Martindale, B. (1990) 'Comments on the Conference: "The Future Career of the Adult Psychoanalytic Psychotherapist in the NHS: The Ways Ahead"', *Newsletter of the Association for Psychoanalytic Psychotherapy in the National Health Service* 7: 9–10.

Milner, M. (1932) *A Life of One's Own*. Virago, 1986.

McGuire, W. (1979) *The Freud/Jung Letters*. Picador.

Obholzer, A. (1988) 'Fostering a climate for growth', *Br. J. Psychother.* 5: 186–91.

Parlett, M. and Page, F. (1990) 'Gestalt therapy', in Dryden (1990), pp. 175–98.

Pedder, J. (1989) 'Courses in psychotherapy: evolution and current trends', *Br. J. Psychother.* 6: 203–21.

Perls, F. (1969) *Gestalt Therapy Verbatim*. Real People Press.

Pokorny, M. (1985, 1987, 1988, 1989, 1990, 1991) 'Reports from the Chairman of the Working Party of the Rugby Conference', *Br. J. Psychother.* 1: 230–2, 3: 391–2, 4: 447–9, 5: 463–4, 574–6, 7: 206–7, 303–6.

Réguis, M.C. (1988) 'A tale of two chairs', *Br. J. Psychother.* 4: 282–93.

Ruszczynski, S. (1992) 'Some notes towards a psychoanalytic understanding of the couple relationship', *Psychoanalytic Psychotherapy* 6, 1.

—— (1992) *Psychotherapy with Couples: Collected Papers from the Tavistock Institute of Marital Studies*. Tavistock.

Rycroft, C. (1968) *A Critical Dictionary of Psychoanalysis*. Pelican.

Samuels, A. (1985) *Jung and the Post Jungians*. Routledge.

—— (1989) *The Plural Psyche*. Routledge.

Samuels, A., Shorter, B. and Plaut, F. (1986) *A Critical Dictionary of Jungian Analysis*. Routledge & Kegan Paul.

Sandler, J. (1988) 'Psychoanalysis and psychoanalytic psychotherapy: problems of differentiation', *Br. J. Psychother.* 5: 172–7.

Scarlett, J. (1991) 'Getting established: initiatives in psychotherapy training since World War Two', *Br. J. Psychother.* 7: 260–7.

Schafer, R. (1983) *The Analytic Attitude*. Hogarth Press and Institute of Psycho-Analysis.

Segal, H. (1979) *Klein*. Fontana.

—— (1973) *Introduction to the Work of Melanie Klein*. Hogarth Press and Institute of Psycho-Analysis.

Smith, D. (1990) 'Psychodynamic theory: the Freudian approach', in Dryden (1990), pp. 18–38.

Spinelli, E. (1989) *The Interpreted World: An Introduction to Phenomenological Psychology*. Sage.

Steiner, J. (1985) 'The training of psychotherapists', *Psychoanalytic Psychotherapy* 1: 55–63.

Stanton, M. (1990) 'Psychoanalysis in British universities: the Kent Case', *Free Associations* 20: 104–13.

van Deurzen-Smith, E. (1988) *Existential Counselling in Practice*. Sage.

—— (1990) 'Existential psychotherapy', in Dryden (1990), pp. 149–74.

Waddell, M. (1988) 'Modes of thought in psychoanalytic psychotherapy', *Br. J. Psychother.* 5: 192–9.

Wolff, H. (1988) 'The relationship between psychoanalytic psychotherapy and psychoanalysis: attitudes and aims', *Br. J. Psychother.* 5: 178–85.

Wallerstein, R.S. (1989) 'Psychoanalysis and psychotherapy', *Int. J. Psycho-Anal.* 70: 563–91.

Woodhouse, D. (1990) 'The Tavistock Institute of Marital Studies: evolution of a marital agency', in C. Clulow, ed. *Marriage: Disillusion and Hope.* Karnac.

INDEX

This first edition of
Individual Psychotherapy Trainings: A Guide
was finished in June 1992

The book was commissioned by Robert M. Young,
edited by Robert M. Young, Selina O'Grady and Ann Scott,
copy-edited by Vivienne Robertson,
proofread by Gillian Beaumont,
indexed by Linda English,
and produced by Ann Scott
for Free Association Books